Money, Trust, and Banking

Other titles by the Author:

REGULATION AND STABILITY IN THE BANKING INDUSTRY

Money, Trust, and Banking

An Integrated Approach to Monetary Theory and Banking Theory

By Guido K. Schaefer
Vienna University of Economics and Business Administration

palgrave
macmillan

First published 2005 by
PALGRAVE MACMILLAN
Houndmills, Basingstoke, Hampshire RG21 6XS and
175 Fifth Avenue, New York, N. Y. 10010
Companies and representatives throughout the world

PALGRAVE MACMILLAN is the global academic imprint of the Palgrave Macmillan division of St. Martin's Press, LLC and of Palgrave Macmillan Ltd. Macmillan® is a registered trademark in the United States, United Kingdom and other countries. Palgrave is a registered trademark in the European Union and other countries.

ISBN–13: 978–1–4039–9940–5
ISBN–10: 1–4039–9940–6

This book is printed on paper suitable for recycling and made from fully managed and sustained forest sources.

A catalogue record for this book is available from the British Library.

Library of Congress Cataloging-in-Publication Data
Schaefer, Guido K.
Money, trust, and banking : an integrated approach to monetary theory and banking theory / Guido K. Schaefer.
p. cm.
Includes bibliographical references and index.
ISBN 1–4039–9940–6 (cloth)
1. Money. 2. Monetary policy. 3. Banks and banking. 4. Finance. 5.Financial instruments. I. Title.

HG221.S285 2005
332.4'01–dc22 2005052288

10 9 8 7 6 5 4 3 2 1
14 13 12 11 10 09 08 07 06 05

Printed and bound in Great Britain by
Antony Rowe Ltd, Chippenham and Eastbourne

To Klaudia and Franziska

Contents

List of Figures

1

Introduction

> "Money as means of payment is just a debt. The payment of debt is an exchange of debts. We regard it as payment because the debts have different quality. It is quality from the point of view of the creditor that matters. I pay my creditor with a cheque on a bank: He accepts it because he has more confidence in a debt from the bank than in a debt from me. [...] If I had drawn my cheque on a bank of which he had never heard and which (so far he could tell) might be purely imaginary, he would not have accepted it as a payment."
>
> Sir John Hicks, *A Market Theory of Money* (1989, p. 104).

The goal of this monograph is to provide a formal theoretical outline for an integrated approach to monetary theory and banking theory. Since the early days of Wicksell the role of debt in facilitating exchange has received much attention in monetary economics. Debt claims which are transferable between economic agents allow conducting transactions smoothly without having to engage in burdensome barter. Although contemporary banking theory provides sophisticated analyses of systems of debt claims, research has concentrated on financing and investment problems rather than transaction problems. Also monetary theory has not yet established the analytical linkage between money and the most famous contemporary banking model analyzing debt contracts: the model of banking as delegated monitoring in an information sensitive capital market by Douglas Diamond (1984). Building upon the Diamond model this monograph undertakes to develop an integrated view of money and banking by analyzing contemporary banking theory from a monetary perspective. In the search for efficient solutions to transactions problems the joint microeconomic foundations of money and banking are explored such that more solid ground can be provided for the analysis of money in the economy. The currently existing gap between monetary theory and contemporary banking theory should get narrowed. As suggested by Sir John Hicks the problem of trust between economic transaction partners has a major role in developing such an integrated approach to money and banking.

A unified theory of money and banking is desirable for a number of reasons:

- Modern money mainly exists in the form of bank deposits. Hence this basic empirical fact calls for a clarification of the relationship between money and banking at the theoretical level.
- Monetary policy works through the banking system to a considerable degree. Therefore an integrated theory of money and banking should be more amenable to monetary policy analysis.
- An integrated theory of money and banking helps to clarify better the twin roles of money as a medium of exchange and as a store of value. In most monetary theories these functions are treated separately. Because in today's economies the financial sector has a large and further increasing role, monetary theory should reflect this development by making explicit the links between money and finance.
- An integrated approach provides a monetary foundation for banking theory. It explains why taking deposits and making loans efficiently solves both transaction problems and financing and investment problems in information sensitive markets. Hence banking theory founded upon monetary theory can contribute to a better understanding of the fundamental questions why banks exist and what they do.
- Monetary theory is an analytically challenging field because standard economic models cannot be used and because money is a very flexible financial asset addressing a whole range of different frictions in exchange. It is argued in this monograph that banking theory can provide an analytical focus for monetary theory helping to address those theoretical challenges.
- An integrated approach to money and banking can help to explain better monetary institutions. Just as in contemporary banking theory the structure of monetary institutions is endogenously derived to optimally address the frictions considered. By providing an analytical link between monetary institutions and well established models in banking theory additional explanatory power is gained.
- An integrated approach to money and banking can help to explain better how the monetary sector is embedded in the economy. Recent research has clarified the interactions between informationally sensitive banking markets, macroeconomics, and monetary policy. Hence a monetary interpretation of contemporary banking theory opens up a broad range of potential analytical cross-linkages with other interesting areas in economics. This analysis goes beyond the scope of this monograph but ways of extending the integrated approach into these directions are indicated.

A major problem in both money and banking is lack of trust in transaction partners to fulfil their contractual obligations. This problem of trust which is due to asymmetric information between economic agents provides a key analytical point of departure for integrating monetary theory and contemporary banking theory in this monograph. The analysis shows how a role for money and banks can be explained in dealing efficiently with this friction.

The research approach pursued in this monograph is to analyze a series of formal game theoretical models in which a basic problem of exchange is studied under different transaction technologies. Standard economic models cannot be used for this purpose. They rely on perfect markets in which money has no role because no frictions arise in specific transactions which money could help to address. Hence a novel game theoretical model of an exchange economy with risk-neutral traders is developed as a basic economic framework. The model mimics price-taking behavior of small agents in a large market in the sense that given the equilibrium strategies of other players no single agent has an influence on the prices agreed upon in the market. But unlike in the standard competitive market model specific transactions between agents are well identified. Key terms of the contracts written such as prices and quantities are endogenously explained from the strategic interactions of players in the model. A special matching procedure termed "smart random matching" is introduced in which buyers get matched with the cheapest offers of sellers in the market. Unlike in many existing approaches there is no search, no purely random matching, and no bargaining in the model. A lack of double coincidence of needs and wants exists which creates a motive for trade. Various transaction technologies and frictions in transactions are analyzed within this basic framework.

First, as a benchmark case a pure barter economy is considered in which trade is inconvenient but no problem of trust exists. Then other transaction technologies are studied which all involve some financial element to avoid costly physical exchange of goods. But because agents cannot observe changes in the ability of their transaction partners to fulfil their financial obligations, they cannot be sure to receive value back in exchange and hence a problem of trust arises.

When private agents individually issue debt serving as a medium of exchange it is shown that an underprovision of this medium occurs due to the high incentive cost of issuing such debt. Thereby beneficial trade is hampered. Centralized solutions such as money issued by a central bank or transferable deposits created by a private bank substantially reduce the costs of issuing a medium of exchange. All incentive problems and the associated cost get concentrated in these institutions which are better equipped to deal with them than individual private agents. Hence transactions can be conducted smoothly and trade gets promoted. Private banks are even more efficient at providing a medium of exchange because they create money by making loans. Thereby agents can economize on noninterest bearing cash. Due to the resources saved interest can be paid on loans and deposits. The institutional structure of the bank solving transaction problems is closely related to the institutional structure of banks providing financing and investment services as in the Diamond model of contemporary banking theory. In this sense a monetary foundation for contemporary banking theory is provided and the outline for a formal integrated theory of money and banking starting from the problem of lack of trust in exchange is developed. Thereby a broad field of new research questions opens up whose exploration should help to better understand the role of money and banks in the economy based upon a more solid microeconomic foundation.

Disturbed by the state of monetary theory, in 1935 Sir John Hicks proposed to integrate monetary theory and value theory. At that time in his view value theory was a better developed field than monetary theory due to the advances of neoclassical economics. To achieve more progress in monetary theory a process termed "cross-fertilization" by Hicks should take place between these two fields. Monetary theory should profit from value theory by adopting its basic approach. This research program turned out to be a dead end because it was impossible to explain a role for money in an environment with perfect markets. Money which is supposed to lower transaction barriers between agents had no role if by assumption no transaction barriers existed. In a late book published in 1989 Hicks laid out a fairly different view of money. Money was seen as being essentially high quality debt, motivated by the problem of lack of trust in transactions (see the opening citation by Hicks). Following these ideas it is suggested in this monograph to attempt a cross-fertilization between monetary theory and contemporary banking theory to gain new insights on open research questions in both fields.

I am very grateful to Hanns Abele, Michael Winkler, and Ulrich Berger from Vienna University of Economics and Business Administration for many helpful suggestions and comments on this monograph. Any remaining errors are mine.

2

The Problem of Trust in Monetary Theory

In economic terminology lack of trust is a typical example of a market friction. Frictions only arise in imperfect markets. For example, if a trading partner has an informational advantage about important features of a deal, an agent may fear that the trading partner will exploit this informational advantage. Hence the less informed agent may have reasons not to trust her trading partner. A moral hazard problem exists. In this monograph asymmetric information between transaction partners is considered as the major source of lack of trust in exchange.[1] The goal of this chapter is to discuss the problem of trust in exchange in existing monetary theory. Section 2.2 looks at the development of the concept in former research.

Lack of trust due to asymmetric information is just one of many possible frictions in exchange that have been analyzed in monetary economics. Because frictions are fundamental to explain a role for money in the economy, the development of this concept is briefly reviewed in section 2.1.

2.1 Frictions in transactions as the analytical point of departure in monetary theory

Since the early writings in economics it has been argued that money facilitates exchange by lowering transaction barriers between trading partners. Earlier scholars of monetary theory were graphical in describing a wide range of difficulties which can arise in exchange (e.g., see Monroe, 2001 or Niehans, 1978). Lack of trust is just one such difficulty. In the 20th century neoclassical economics exercised a dominating influence on economic thinking. General equilibrium theory was developed in full mathematical rigor. However, monetary theory stood aside. To develop economics as a unified theory and to provide better guidance for practical questions such as monetary policy, various approaches were pursued to integrate money into general equilibrium theory. Most prominent among these were the "money in the utility function" approach, the "money in the production function" approach, and the Clower constraint. They are still routinely used in macroeconomics to analyze money. The discussion of these approaches is kept brief because their advantages as well as shortcomings are widely known.

Following Walras (1900), Patinkin (1956), and Sidrauski (1967) money was introduced as an additional argument into the utility function. Early on this was seen as a way of incorporating money into general equilibrium theory in a consistent way, allowing to apply well established concepts from value theory to monetary theory (see Hicks, 1935). It was supposed to be a reflection of the general notion that money is useful for agents in exchange. In a straightforward manner a demand for money results from putting money into the utility function. As appealing as this approach may appear, it has serious shortcomings from the point of view of monetary theory. For example, money is demanded and providing utility even if an agent does not exchange goods at all (see Hellwig, 1993). This implication goes against the notion that money is useful in exchange. Because in the "money in the utility function" approach money is not tied to specific transactions, the close correspondence between money and transactions gets lost. Finally, it is not clear what exact properties money in the utility function should have. Should the derivative with respect to money and other consumption goods be positive or negative? Should nonsatiation apply to money holdings (Blanchard and Fischer, 1989)? In a similar way money was introduced into production functions but similar concerns as for money in the utility function apply also in this case.

Clower (1967) suggested to introduce money by requiring it to be used for purchasing goods. This can be achieved by imposing an additional constraint on the decisions of economic agents, the so-called "Clower constraint" which requires that "goods buy money, money buys goods, but goods do not by goods". Therefore individuals need to hold a sufficient amount of money to carry out all the transactions they desire to make. By its very nature the Clower constraint is a technical device taking money as given and assuming away other kinds of payment. It is not an elaborate monetary theory. One major undesirable feature of this constraint is that by imposing additional restrictions on transactions it decreases the welfare of agents rather than increase it which is what money is usually supposed to do (Blanchard and Fischer, 1989). It does not provide answers to the deeper questions of monetary economics due to its mechanical setup. Feenstra (1986) showed that for important cases optimization problems with a Clower constraint can be rewritten as optimization problems with money in the utility function. Therefore similar concerns exist about both approaches.

All three approaches, the money in the utility function approach, the money in the production function approach, and the Clower constraint lack a fundamental economic motivation for introducing money. Agents in those models typically make their decisions in perfect markets. They can trade with each other without incurring any transaction costs. Hence they do not need money to conduct transactions more efficiently because the highest level of efficiency attainable cannot be improved upon. Because there are no frictions which money could help to deal with there is no role for money. Also, the actual structure of transactions is of second order importance. Hence it cannot be seen how money improves the efficiency in specific transactions between individual agents (see Abele, 1970 and 1972). As Walsh (1995) argues, these approaches are theoretical shortcuts for introducing money into general equilibrium theory. For some economic problems these shortcuts may be sufficient. From the perspective of monetary theory these approaches are unsatisfactory because they leave too many fundamental questions open. Money lacks a foundation at the microeconomic level showing its role in specific transaction between individual economic agents. Hence money is either redundant or even inconsistent in these models.

Among others Hahn (1965) argued that only by explicit analysis of transaction costs a monetary theory can be built that is integrated with microeconomic theory. Following this view researchers started to introduce frictions into general equilibrium models (e.g., see Niehans, 1978). However, this early approach of modeling frictions and money often remained close to the general equilibrium framework without frictions. Frictions were introduced as some abstract transaction costs not specified further. Market structures remained similar to the Walrasian setup. Although some insights about efficiency enhancing features of money can be shown in such frameworks, frictions largely remain a black box. The economic consequences of some types of frictions to completely change the entire market setup necessarily have to remain unexplored in this type of analysis. Therefore a more explicit consideration of the nature of frictions and their economic consequences appeared necessary to achieve progress in monetary theory.

By the mid 1960s it was clear that deeper analytical foundations for monetary theory would require a more explicit treatment of transaction barriers. Step by step researchers moved beyond the model of frictionless centralized markets with atomistic agents. However, just as in other areas of economics breaking away from the neoclassical paradigm of perfect markets with perfect competition turned out to be a challenging venture. Once the analytical discipline of a streamlined, highly reduced, internally coherent model of economic interaction is left behind, a myriad of possibilities opens up how agents might deal with each other. Beyond the established paradigm there is always the danger of getting lost in puzzling detail. Results tend to be derived under specific settings of a partial nature such that the overall relevance and logical consistency are harder to gauge. Hence despite many remarkable advances, progress in monetary theory has tended to be tenuous.

The key conclusion from this brief review of the history of monetary economics is that any monetary theory explaining the role of money must start from some market friction which money can address. Lack of trust in exchange is one candidate friction that may give rise to a role for money in the economy. It will be the focus of attention in later chapters.

2.2 Research on money and asymmetric information

In this monograph informational problems between agents are considered as the main source of lack of trust in transactions. Several classical references exist pointing at the importance of private information to explain a role for money in the economy. In an informal manner Alchian (1977) argued that private information was the principal friction underlying monetary exchange. Brunner and Meltzer (1971) pointed out that by using money individuals reduce the amount of information they must acquire, process, and store. Friedman (1960) argued that imperfect information creates a role for the provision of government currency. In earlier times Law (1705), Jevons (1875), and Menger (1892) pointed at the relationship between informational problems in the economy and the role of money. More recent informal discussions of money and information can be found in Hicks (1989), Goodhart (1989), and Stiglitz and Greenwald (2003), for example.

A substantial literature of formal models on money and private information analyzes asymmetric information about the quality of goods, building upon variations of the lemons problem first studied by Akerlof (1970). Banerjee and Maskin (1996) sticking closely to a Walrasian framework show that in an economy with lemons problems the good with the smallest quality uncertainty serves as a medium of exchange. Fiat money eliminates the overproduction of this medium of exchange and thereby enhances welfare.

Many models addressing asymmetric information about the quality of goods are developed within the framework of search and matching in the tradition of Kiyotaki and Wright (1989). E.g., Williamson and Wright (1994) argue that agents who produce high quality refuse to trade these goods against other goods whose quality they cannot recognize. Instead they demand payment in cash. Effectively a cash-in-advance constraint is imposed. This enhances the incentives for producing and trading higher quality goods in the market. Berentsen and Rocheteau (2004) put some of the findings in this literature into perspective. They argue that when the fraction of high quality producers in the economy is endogenized, fiat money can decrease welfare relative to barter. Also, money need not lead to a reduction of information acquisition which may be a complement of money rather than a substitute for it.

Li (1999) studies the coexistence of money and middlemen in an economy with qualitative uncertainty concerning consumption goods. This question arises because both money and middlemen address informational frictions. However, because they are not perfect substitutes but fulfil somewhat different roles, coexistence is possible. Cuadras-Morató (1994) and Li (1995) study lemons problems in which the lemons can be used as a medium of exchange. Trejos (1999) generalizes the search and matching models with asymmetric information about the quality of goods by endogenizing the terms of exchange rather than taking them as given as in most other models.

Other authors look at the role of money in the context of asymmetric information about financial assets. This may matter, for example, to explain the coexistence of fiat money and credit. In a model with spatially separated agents Townsend (1989) argues that money can be used among agents whose histories are not known to one another whereas credit is used in enduring relationships. In a similar vein Bernhardt (1989) argues that credit supports transactions in close-knit economies with enduring trade relationships whereas money is used in larger economies where information concerning repayment diffuses too slowly. However, money and credit can supplement each other to some degree. Taub (1994) provides conditions in a mechanism design framework under which money and credit are equivalent.

In the models discussed so far credit was not extended by financial intermediaries such as banks. Once the analysis includes also this level of financial transactions, a host of complex issues arises. The literature branches out into various directions because besides the question of coexistence of fiat money, private credit, and bank credit – which gets further aggravated in this context – many other issues related to the payments system and the banking system arise even when looking at them just from a monetary perspective. E.g., Aiyagari and Williamson (2000) study money in the context of long-term dynamic credit arrangements when endowments are private information. Random limited participation in the financial market is considered. If a consumer is in contact with a financial intermediary before full information on her current income is available, she may wish to make transactions on the money market to smooth consumption. If participation is unlimited, a pure credit economy arises.

Cavalcanti and Wallace (1999a and b) analyze inside and outside money in a random matching model when a subset of agents called bankers has histories which are public information whereas the histories of other agents are private information. Under the assumption that there are no outside assets bankers optimally issue banknotes as a form of inside money which are also used by nonbankers as a medium of exchange. If outside money exists, only a smaller set of outcomes can be implemented because outside money limits the purchasing capabilities of bankers.

Gorton and Pennacchi (1990) consider a model in which banks or mutual funds protect uninformed financial market agents against losses from trading with better informed insiders by offering liquid investment opportunities whose value is known to everybody.

Finally, in this brief review of models with asymmetric information it should be mentioned that informational questions also play a role for the two workhorses of contemporary monetary theory, the model of spatially separated agents by Townsend (1980)[2] and the search and matching models following Kiyotaki and Wright (1989). Communication between agents and hence information is limited in both models. Agents do not know the full history of transactions in the economy (see Kocherlakota, 1998a, b). Informational issues can be less often found in overlapping generations models which are also frequently analyzed in monetary economics. Wang (1999), however, is one example with asymmetric information of agents about income realizations. This friction creates a role for fiat money whose presence leads to significantly different outcomes than in standard OLG models with money.

When looking at the literature on money and asymmetric information it seems that the problem of asymmetric information about the quality of goods has already been explored quite extensively. Once money is considered within the broader framework of the financial system, the complexity of the problems increases and additional questions open up. Scope for further analyses appears to exist in this area.

The existing research does not emphasize analytical linkages between monetary theory and contemporary banking theory. Notable exceptions are Shreft and Smith (1997, 1998) and Betts and Smith (1997) who integrate the banking model by Diamond and Dybvig (1983) with a model of spatially separated agents as it is frequently used in monetary theory. Still, although debt-based transaction technologies play an important role in monetary economics, the informational frictions in debt contracts analyzed in banking theory tend to be ignored. The research in this monograph attempts to fill this gap by developing an integrated theory of money and banking that has close links with contemporary banking theory.

3 Money, Trust, and Contemporary Banking Theory

Lack of trust between transaction partners is a major market friction in monetary theory as argued in the preceding chapter. However, lack of trust between agents is also an important theme in contemporary banking theory. Still, contemporary monetary theory and banking theory have developed largely separated from each other. Because substantial achievements have been made in banking theory over the last decades the question arises which insights contemporary banking theory can provide for monetary theory. An informal exploration of this question is undertaken in this chapter. First, the relationship between money and banking is analyzed in section 3.1. In section 3.2 major approaches in contemporary banking theory are presented. Finally, in sections 3.3 and 3.4 conclusions are drawn for the development of an integrated theory of money and banking.

3.1 From money to banking

The modern theory of financial intermediation started with Gurley and Shaw's "Money in a Theory of Finance" in 1960. They developed the concept of financial intermediation which is still used today and they emphasized that money has to be analyzed within the broader context of finance. Hence at the origin of the modern theory of financial intermediation there was no separation between the analysis of money and banking.

Historically, money and banking were closely related (Freixas and Rochet, 1997; Kindleberger, 1993; Rajan, 1998). In early times money changing was an important economic activity because different currencies issued by distinct institutions circulated and payments had to be made across currencies. The provision of payment services was closely related to money changing. Accounts developed from storing money safely in early banks. It was also safer and more convenient to make payments by transferring money from one bank account to another rather then taking the risk and the inconvenience of transporting large sums of money as payment from one trader to another. Initially, deposited coins were not lent. Banks started to make loans from deposits in Renaissance Italy. The riskiness of loans increased over time and banks' risk assessment and risk management strategies developed. Therefore it is generally well established in the historical literature that banking developed from relatively simple monetary transaction services to ever more sophisticated deposit and loan making.

The formal analysis of banking typically does not take up the historical link between money and banking. It rather concentrates on the financing and investment services but ignores transaction services (see the following section). The underlying hypothesis is that modern banking can be understood without reference to the monetary origins of banking. As will be argued later, this hypothesis should be subject to further analysis.

Research on monetary policy rather than monetary theory has shown a strong interest in understanding the role between money, banks, and central bank policy. If banks are not just passive agents in the transmission of monetary impulses to the rest of the economy but have an active role, e.g., by setting lending limits such that real economic activity gets affected, understanding what banks do and how they react to monetary policy is key. One problem with the approach of monetary policy to banking is that because of a lack of robust theories of money, the analysis of monetary policy has to proceed without a solid foundation in monetary theory.

Current theories of the bank lending channel emphasize the role of banks in the transmission of monetary policy. But they tend to emphasize the informational disadvantages of banks in the capital market (Stiglitz and Weiss 1981, Bernanke and Gertler, 1989) whereas banking theory emphasizes informational advantages of banks relative to other agents in the capital market (see next section). These two positions need not necessarily be mutually inconsistent because information is a matter of degree and not a zero-one proposition (i.e. banks can be better informed than other agents in the capital market but still they may have less information than lenders themselves). These important questions require a clarification in future research.

Monetary policy research analyzes how banks are embedded into the wider economy. This is a key point to consider also for the development of an integrated theory of money and banking. By linking money to banking also money gets more tightly linked to the rest of the economy. Thereby analytical cross linkages between money, banking, and the rest of the economy can be studied.

Generally speaking, although there is awareness about the close economic relationship between money and banking in existing research, a formal theory establishing an analytical link between the pure theory of money and contemporary banking theory is still in its infancy. Thus the potential for cross-fertilization between monetary theory and banking theory has remained underexplored.

3.2 Contemporary banking theory

At least two elements are required to explain the existence of an intermediary: i) there must be some market friction; ii) an intermediary must have advantages over other agents in dealing with this friction, e.g., cost advantages due to economies of scale or scope (see Freixas and Rochet, 1997). Without a market friction no barrier exists between agents to make transactions. So there is no need to employ an intermediary because agents can enter directly into transactions. Even if there is some market friction but no advantage for an intermediary in dealing with this friction, agents will conduct transactions directly and deal with the friction themselves. The contemporary theory of financial intermediation emphasizes informational frictions in the capital market between agents demanding and supplying capital. Advantages of an intermediary relative to direct transactions between agents can be based, for example, upon benefits from diversification which a financial intermediary enjoys.[3]

Leland and Pyle (1977) were the first to argue for the existence of financial intermediaries in a capital market with asymmetric information. Coalitions of agents could signal the quality of their projects at a lower cost than individual agents. The two most widely studied models in contemporary banking theory are those developed by Diamond and Dybvig (1983) and Diamond (1984). Both models explain qualitative asset transformation by banks such as liquidity transformation, risk transformation, and maturity transformation which are considered to be prime characteristics of banks compared to many other financial intermediaries. These approaches build on earlier work and have been refined and extended by many other researchers (Bhattacharya and Thakor, 1993; Freixas and Rochet, 1997).

3.2.1 The Diamond model: Banking as delegated monitoring

The fundamental friction in the model of Diamond (1984) is asymmetric information between investors and entrepreneurs about the ex post return of a risky project that the entrepreneur wants to undertake with borrowed capital from some group of lenders. The key problem is that the entrepreneur might exploit her informational advantage by claiming a low return due to bad luck although in fact returns unobservable to lenders are high. Hence there is lack of trust in the relationship between the investor and the entrepreneur. Costly monitoring of returns ex post or an incentive debt contract with a nonpecuniary penalty in the case of default can solve the problem of asymmetric information between lenders and borrowers bilaterally. The contractual form is endogenous to the model. The debt contract is shown to be optimal because it maximizes the expected surplus for the debtor but still ensures that the investors get their capital invested plus interest back whenever the entrepreneur is able to pay. Bilaterally, monitoring of ex post returns is supposed to be less costly for agents than using the debt contract. Therefore, without an intermediary, agents would minimize transaction costs by using monitoring for dealing with the market friction.

The major problem with bilateral monitoring as a solution to the problem of asymmetric information is that a single firm gets monitored by each of its many investors individually. This leads to a reduplication of monitoring effort and cost. Monitoring once would be enough to know the true return of an entrepreneur and to discipline firms. Hence by delegating monitoring to an intermediary who monitors an entrepreneur, investors as a group can save on monitoring costs. However, delegation also creates the problem of monitoring the monitor. Once the intermediary has produced the knowledge about the entrepreneurs' unknown returns, she enjoys an informational advantage vis à vis investors which could also be exploited against the interest of investors. Monitoring the intermediary by investors individually is clearly not an efficient solution to the problem of disciplining the intermediary. Monitoring costs would explode. Hence the optimal debt contracts with nonpecuniary penalties are used to solve the incentive problems between the intermediary and investors. Investors deposit their funds with the intermediary and are promised to get them paid back with interest. Such an intermediary performing delegated monitoring and concluding debt contracts with investors can be considered as a bank.

Debt contracts as a way of dealing with the problem of trust between the intermediary and investors do not come without a cost. The bank has to incur the nonpecuniary penalty even if returns from investments are really too low to satisfy all depositors' claims. The bank can lower the burden from the nonpecuniary penalty if the returns from the entrepreneurs' projects are not perfectly correlated because of diversification. At the extreme, if project returns are identically, independently distributed, by increasing its size the bank can almost completely diversify away the risk of going bankrupt. The probability of incurring the nonpecuniary penalty goes towards zero as the bank size increases. Therefore, one implication of the Diamond model is that banks are large and highly diversified financial institutions offering relatively safe investment opportunities.

All incentive problems are solved in this model of a bank. Because of the debt contracts investors are assured that the bank will pay back their capital plus interest whenever returns allow it to do so. Hence they can trust the bank. The bank has an incentive to monitor in order to avoid getting punished. Firms have an incentive to pay because they get monitored by the intermediary.

The debt contract between banks and investors can be interpreted as a deposit contract. Hence an explanation for the specific contractual form of banks is provided starting from only a few basic assumptions and ex post asymmetric information. One issue which remains largely ignored in this analysis is liquidity. The liquidity aspects of debt contracts are not analyzed in the Diamond model. Also any monetary aspects which would have to work through deposits being transferred between different depositors are ignored. Deposits are viewed only as some form of fixed income investment in a capital market with asymmetric information. Thus, the Diamond model concentrates on the financing and investment aspects of banks in a world of frictions but ignores questions of money and liquidity.

One other question raised by the Diamond model is what kind of market form it implies. As size increases diversification, the original version of the model suggests that banking is a natural monopoly. Subsequent research has addressed this aspect. E.g., Millon and Thakor (1985) showed that by considering also internal incentive problems of the intermediary a finite size is optimal which would suggest an oligopolistic market structure rather than a monopolistic one. Other extensions and critical refinements have been suggested (see Bhattacharya and Thakor, 1993). For example, the Diamond model works with deterministic monitoring. But if agents to be monitored are risk averse, stochastic monitoring is better and other contracts than debt contracts may be optimal (see Mookherjee and P'ng, 1989). Other major questions are whether indeed the monitoring of project returns by the bank is perfect. If monitoring is imperfect, all sorts of informational questions and incentive problems arise in the relationship between the bank and borrowers. For example, if unlike in the Diamond model the loan customer can influence the riskiness of her projects during the loan period, moral hazard problems will arise that may lead to screening of loan customers by banks or even credit rationing. Another key aspect is that credit relationships are often dynamic. This feature allows banks and borrowers to structure incentives in a long-term relationship which gives additional leverage to controlling moral hazard. Considering this feature of the bank-borrower relationship leads to models of relationship banking. Still, despite these criticisms and extensions the Diamond model has become a cornerstone of contemporary banking theory.

3.2.2 The Diamond-Dybvig model: Banking as liquidity insurance

Whereas the Diamond model can be seen as a model of risk transformation (i.e., the bank accepts relatively safe deposits and turns them into risky loans), the Diamond-Dybvig model (Diamond and Dybvig, 1983) focuses on liquidity transformation performed by banks. The fundamental friction giving rise to a bank is asymmetric information about the liquidity types of agents and a corresponding market incompleteness which precludes individuals to insure against the risk of having to consume early. If agents have invested their wealth in an illiquid form, the sudden, immediate desire to consume requires liquidating illiquid investments prematurely at a loss. On the other hand, if individuals invested more of their wealth into liquid assets to be better prepared against uninsurable shocks precipitating a sudden need to consume, this would mean that fewer illiquid high yielding, long-term investments can be made. Returns would be lower in all those cases in which no shock occurs. Therefore individuals have to find an optimal balance between investing into liquid assets to be prepared against a shock and investing into illiquid assets to enjoy higher returns if no shock occurs.

It depends upon the economic environment what level of welfare can be expected from the solution to the investment problem in the Diamond-Dybvig model (see Freixas and Rochet, 1997). Under autarky, when each individual is on her own without interacting with other agents, only a relatively low level of welfare can be achieved. Depending upon whether a shock occurs either value is destroyed due to premature liquidation of illiquid investments or value is forgone because individuals have made low yielding liquid investments without actually needing liquidity early. If trade between agents is admitted, those who need funds early can trade illiquid investments with those who also hold liquid funds but do not need them because they have not been hit by a shock. Because of this trade no illiquid investments have to be liquidated at a loss prematurely and nobody has to stick with low yielding liquid assets she does not need. Thus, trade between agents allows to achieve a higher level of welfare.

The key question remaining is whether the market solution achieves already the highest possible level of welfare attainable under the restrictions imposed by the economic environment. As Diamond and Dybvig argue, in general this will not be the case. The utility to be expected for an individual faced with the risk of having to consume early will not correspond to the ex ante Pareto optimum. Thus, welfare can potentially be improved upon the market solution. Due to the market imperfection individuals cannot write contracts contingent upon whether they need to consume early. Hence some special institutional form has to be found that allows agents to attain the welfare maximizing return and consumption levels. At this point a role for a bank offering liquid deposit contracts emerges. The bank can offer rates on the deposit contract for both early withdrawal and late withdrawal which allow agents to achieve consumption levels corresponding to the ex ante Pareto optimum. Because the contract is liquid, the bank does not need to write contracts contingent upon whether agents are hit by a shock. Those who need to consume early can do so by withdrawing funds from their liquid deposits, earning the promised rate for early withdrawal. The others can leave their money in the bank. In this way a bank can implement the ex ante Pareto optimal solution for the liquidity management problem of agents in face of uninsurable shocks that precipitate a need for early consumption. The bank also enjoys benefits of size because uncertainty about liquidity needs for early consumption may either be reduced or get completely eliminated in the aggregate due to diversification.

The Diamond-Dybvig model does not only explain a role for banks in performing socially optimal liquidity management by offering liquid deposit contracts. Inherent to the model is also a critical potential for instability of the bank. If depositors behave strategically, multiple equilibria exist and the bank becomes susceptible to bank runs. If only those depositors who need to consume early withdraw their funds an agent who does not consume early will clearly prefer to leave her money in the bank. At a later consumption date at which illiquid investments mature she will get a higher return. The bank functions well and implements the Pareto-optimal allocation.

Should, however, a depositor who actually wants to consume later expect all other depositors to withdraw their money, then she also wants to withdraw early. The reason is that the bank must go bankrupt if all depositors decide to withdraw. In this case the illiquid investments have to be liquidated prematurely at a loss. This makes it impossible for the bank to honor all depositors' claims. Thus, not withdrawing if everybody else withdraws would mean not to get anything with certainty whereas running to the bank and attempting to withdraw funds means some chance of getting one's deposits out of the bank before it collapses.

Because depository contracts are fully liquid and banks are subject to a sequential servicing constraint, they have to make payments to depositors wishing to withdraw as long as they have funds available. The liquidity of depository contracts is a key element for implementing the Pareto optimal allocation without having to know whether agents are hit by a shock. Therefore, the same contractual feature which makes it possible to implement the Pareto optimum also gives rise to bank fragility. Thus, the Diamond-Dybvig model also shows how bank fragility and market failure arise in a fractional reserve banking system. Thereby it provides a fundamental reason why banks have to be regulated. Regulatory structures such as deposit insurance have to be created in order to eliminate the "bad" bank run equilibrium such that banks can perform their welfare enhancing functions in the "good" ex ante Pareto optimal equilibrium. Despite some criticisms briefly discussed below the Diamond-Dybvig model is by far the most important model to motivate banking regulation (Bhattacharya, Boot, and Thakor, 1998).

The Diamond-Dybvig model has faced some fundamental criticism. E.g., Green and Ping (2000) argue that the ex ante Pareto optimum in the Diamond-Dybvig world can be implemented differently such that a bank and potential bank runs are not necessary to reach the welfare optimum. Jacklin (1987) showed that in some cases not just deposit contracts but also equity can achieve optimal allocations, thus eliminating the bank run problem. Some questions exist about whether banks are stable if they coexist with markets because the Diamond-Dybvig bank offers rates which are different from market rates (see von Thadden, 1998 and 1999). Also, the explanation of banks runs has faced severe criticism. In the Diamond-Dybvig setup bank runs are mere sunspot phenomena. They are not linked to any deterioration of the economic fundamentals of a bank. If everybody believes that the bank will go bankrupt and decides to withdraw a bank run gets started. The failure of the bank is a self-fulfilling prophecy. Empirical work by Calomiris (1993) and Calomiris and Gorton (1991) has shown, however, that bank runs were usually linked to deteriorations of the economic fundamentals of a bank. Bryant (1980), Jacklin and Bhattacharya (1988), Chari and Jagannathan (1988) and Gorton (1988) have developed theoretical models relating bank runs to information about economic fundamentals.

As critical examinations of the Diamond-Dybvig model have attacked the core of the model rather than suggested mere extensions of a basically robust setup, one could argue on these grounds that enough evidence exists to dismiss with the model completely. Neither is the existence of a bank necessary to deal with the market friction considered nor do bank runs seem to be adequately explained. Still, researchers have been very reluctant to arrive at such strong conclusions. It appears that in the eyes of many the model still teaches important lessons about the benefits of liquid demand deposits as an insurance device against uninsurable shocks and about bank fragility due to liquidity transformation.

From a monetary perspective the Diamond-Dybvig model leaves many questions open. It considers a real economy without money. Liquid investments differ from illiquid investments only in their rates of return. The market structures leading to different degrees of marketability of goods remain exogenous. It should be kept in mind, however, that the Diamond-Dybvig model was not designed to explain monetary phenomena in the first place.

3.3 Banking theory providing direction for monetary theory

In the preceding chapter it was argued that monetary theory has to go beyond the standard models in economics to explain a role for money. It is faced with the difficult task of dealing with a large number of theoretically possible approaches. The ultimate goal of developing an integrated theory of money and banking provides a focus for monetary analysis. Thereby monetary issues appear under a more specific angle which helps to guide the analysis.

At a general level models of money and banking share a similar structure. Both depart from some market friction and show how the creation of a financial institution helps to deal with this friction more efficiently. Historically, banking developed from the provision of monetary services, as argued before. Transactions services as well as financing and investment services are provided via the same basic financial instruments, namely deposits and loans. They are used for multiple purposes and are not distinct products. But banking theory focuses on investment and financing services whereas monetary theory emphasizes transaction services. Monetary theory does also analyze the store of value function of money which could have some overlap with the investment services provided by banks. However, monetary theory has traditionally cast this discussion in the framework of a competition between noninterest bearing money and other interest bearing financial assets whose existence questions the need for money (see Hellwig, 1993).

Credit and the problem of lack of trust may be better candidates for analyzing the relationship between money and banking. At least since Wicksell (1936) it has been known in monetary economics that individuals could simply exchange credit claims against each other rather than exchanging money. Such a system of exchange based upon credit also eliminates the need to engage in tedious barter. One key problem with such a credit economy in its simplest form is that it works only if individuals can trust each other. Claims will be accepted only if agents are sure that they can expect sufficiently high repayments. Many complications can arise in an imperfect credit market which lower the expectations for repayment. Banking theory, in particular the Diamond model analyzes credit relationships under market frictions in much depth. Solutions developed in banking theory might therefore also have implications for monetary theory.

Viewing money as credit has a long tradition in monetary economics (see Skaggs, 2000). Apart from the already cited Wicksell, e.g., the late Sir John Hicks argued in his book "A market theory of money" (1989, p. 104):

"Money as means of payment is just a debt. The payment of debt is an exchange of debts. We regard it as payment because the debts have different quality. It is quality from the point of view of the creditor that matters. I pay my creditor with a cheque on a bank: He accepts it because he has more confidence in a debt from the bank than in a debt from me. [...] If I had drawn my cheque on a bank of which he had never heard and which (so far as he could tell) might be purely imaginary, he would not have accepted it as a payment."

These ideas are central to the analysis of money and banking conducted in later chapters. As another example, Dow and Smithin (1999, p. 86) argue:

"Of the various approaches to the reconstruction of monetary theory outlined above, it has been argued here that the approach which emphasizes credit relations represents the best way to cut through the confusion surrounding the role of money in the contemporary market economy. This approach recognises that the majority of market transactions occurring in real time do have the basic characteristic of an exchange of debts, and that completion of the monetary side of the transaction implies a repayment of debt. The economic system therefore rests in an essential way on the need to establish trust and confidence in an uncertain environment. This in turn, in any given system, requires the development of a basic monetary asset which serves both to fix the standard of value and unambiguously represent final payment or settlement."

All these authors argue that the major institutional form under which modern money arises is a debt relationship. They point to the importance of trust in an economy in which money is based upon debt. Debt contracts also play an important role in banking theory. The Diamond model explains how starting from ex post informational asymmetries about the ability of a debtor to repay a bank can solve this problem efficiently by performing delegated monitoring in an institutional structure involving debt. Debt contracts are shown to optimally address this friction. Although debt is a key concept in monetary economics, the friction giving rise to debt contracts has so far hardly been analyzed in formal monetary research. However, the ex post informational asymmetry in the Diamond model about the true return of a borrower's project is akin to the problem of an exchange of I.O.U.s. The investor in the Diamond model lending her funds cannot be sure whether she will be repaid because she cannot observe what the lender does with her money. Similarly, an agent who exchanges her goods against an I.O.U. cannot be sure whether the issuer of the debt claim will indeed repay. Shocks unobservable to the creditor may occur over time such that eventually the debtor may claim to be unable to fulfil her obligations. This close analytical link between monetary theory and banking theory will serve as a starting point in chapter 4 to develop a theory of money integrated with banking theory. Ex post informational asymmetries about the ability of a transaction partner to repay and endogenously arising debt contracts will play a major role. One implication of this approach is that cash must be a backed currency rather than fiat money. In chapter 8 the relationship between backed currency and fiat money will be discussed in more detail.

As a conclusion, contemporary banking theory can provide a research focus for monetary theory by helping to

- identify economically relevant frictions in transactions. Banking theory shows that debt contracts efficiently address asymmetric information about the ability of an agent to repay. But monetary theory typically ignores this type of friction. In the integrated theory of money and banking developed in this monograph this friction plays a central role.
- explain better monetary institutions. Just as in contemporary banking theory the structure of monetary institutions is endogenously derived to optimally address the frictions considered. By providing an analytical link between monetary institutions and well established models in banking theory additional explanatory power is gained.
- explain better how the monetary sector is embedded into the economy as a whole. Recent research has clarified the interactions between informationally sensitive banking markets, macroeconomics, and monetary policy. Hence a monetary interpretation of contemporary banking theory opens up a broad range of potential analytical cross-linkages to other interesting areas in economics.

One major problem exists, however. As Lewis (1991, p.141) puts it: "In most of the new approaches to financial intermediation, the monetary nature of bank liabilities is of no consequence." Basically, money hardly appears in those theories. Therefore a missing link has to be found to bridge the existing gap between monetary theory and banking theory. A candidate for this missing link will be studied in chapter 9.[4]

Cross-fertilization from banking theory may benefit monetary theory. But the integration of those two closely related fields is unlikely to work only into one direction. Also banking theory can gain from stronger ties with monetary theory. One point of interest is to understand better the development from money to banking. Either because monetary theory did not produce models that were amenable to banking theory or because banking theory deemed its monetary origins as less important and therefore ignored them, few formal models exist which integrate monetary theory and contemporary banking theory. None attempts to establish a direct link with the Diamond model, one of the cornerstones of contemporary banking theory.

One interesting aspect about money and banking is that very different economic purposes such as saving, liquidity insurance, or transaction services get served by the same financial instrument, namely deposits. It appears that due to their flexible monetary character the financial instruments issued by banks may allow to reap synergies in performing different economic functions. One instrument achieves several goals, possibly at a lower cost compared to individual stand-alone solutions. This flexible character could also make it harder to state precisely what economic roles a bank actually performs. Once the economic function of banks as institutions reaping financial synergies originating from the moneyness of banks' liabilities has been understood, it is clear that there cannot be just one answer to the question why banks exist. If banking theory does not have a foundation in monetary theory, it will be hard to explain why fairly distinct economic functions such as liquidity insurance or delegated monitoring of informationally opaque loans (and several others) are all performed under one roof in a bank.

4

An Analytical Framework for an Integrated Theory of Money, Trust, and Banking

This chapter provides a synthesis of the reflections in the preceding chapters on monetary and banking theory. The goal is to arrive at an analytical framework for developing an integrated theory of money and banking based upon the problem of trust in exchange. This concept will be implemented in later chapters by developing and analyzing formal models.

Section 4.1 lays out key ideas guiding the development of an integrated theory of money and banking. In section 4.2 basic features of a barter model serving as an analytical point of departure are presented. The focus of the analysis is on financial solutions to transaction problems. Section 4.3 provides the main arguments for such an approach. In section 4.4 requirements for a basic model of exchange are formulated such that the main research ideas put forward in this chapter can be implemented in a consistent framework allowing to study different kinds of transaction technologies.

4.1 Basic building blocks of the analysis

The research approach pursued in this monograph aims at developing an integrated theory of money and banking. The following ideas guide this analysis.

- *Frictions are key to explain a role both for money and for banks.*
  In chapters 2 and 3 it was argued that market frictions are necessary to explain both a role for money and a role for banks. In frictionless economies neither money nor banks can add value to transactions between economic agents and hence they do not have an economically useful role to play.
- *Financial solutions to transaction problems are most efficient.*
  An important strand of the literature on monetary economics focuses on barter with heterogeneous goods to identify key properties of a medium of exchange. Although interesting insights can be gained from this approach, the outcomes are likely to be inefficient relative to financial solutions to transaction prob-

lems because diverting resources from productive uses as in barter entails a welfare loss. Further resources are likely to get lost in the trading process due to frictions. Financial solutions can avoid these losses but they have to deal with frictions arising within financial frameworks.

- *The consistency between frictions, contracts, institutions, and markets is to be pursued.*
  Institutional structures should be designed such that they optimally address the frictions creating a role for money and banks. Otherwise they will be inefficient. A lot of research exists in monetary theory which ignores the link between frictions in transactions and institutions. Monetary theory should not take as given contracts or institutional structures but should derive them endogenously from the frictions considered.
- *The analysis of consistent frictions, contracts, markets, and institutions should be related to banking theory.*
  A growing literature applies mechanism design to monetary economics (see Wallace, 2001). Such approaches allow to develop incentive structures which are consistent with the underlying frictions considered. But typically they ignore possible links between monetary theory and banking theory. It is desirable to see which relationship exists between incentive structures developed in contemporary banking theory and incentive structures in monetary economics.

4.2 Barter as a benchmark

A barter model provides the benchmark against which financial transaction technologies can be compared. The model is set up such that a "best case" scenario for barter can be studied. Only mild frictions in transactions and the simplest possible transaction structures are considered such that barter can still perform relatively well as a transaction technology. Hence the hurdle for financial transactions technologies to cross in efficiency comparisons with barter is set as high as possible.

Without a double coincidence of needs and wants barter requires some traders to acquire goods they do not actually desire in the hope to exchange them later against the desired goods. This is called intermediate exchange of goods. Intermediate exchange is typically burdensome and costly. Hence as a simple market friction in the barter case it is assumed that every round of intermediate exchange reduces the amount of goods available for trade. In the "best case" scenario of barter these losses are small.

Barter implies that goods themselves take over the role of the medium of exchange when they are traded in intermediate exchange. Hence when circulating as a medium of exchange they cannot be used for productive purposes. Also resources are lost in intermediate exchange due to the trading friction. Financial solutions can avoid these losses but they have to deal with frictions arising in a financial framework.

4.3 Debt facilitating exchange

If agents do not exchange physical goods directly to avoid the inconvenience of intermediate exchange, goods must be exchanged against some other asset. If a trader passes her own goods to her transaction partner without receiving a good in exchange, she grants credit to the transaction partner. Essentially, debt of some form is exchanged against physical goods. The trader giving away her good will be willing to accept debt only if eventually the claim resulting from the debt contract can be turned into the goods she desires. Wicksell (1936) was among the first to show that an economy can be based upon credit functioning as a medium of exchange.

Exchange based upon debt contracts in a situation without double coincidence of needs and wants avoids the burdensome intermediate exchange of goods. However, frictions typically arise also in debt relationships. Substantial incentive costs can arise when dealing with these frictions. As Diamond (1984) pointed out, ex post asymmetric information about the ability of an agent to repay is a key friction in credit relationships. This means that after the conclusion of the contract the ability of the debtor to repay is affected by a random shock unobservable to outsiders such that the other agent has an incentive to exploit her informational advantage. She may claim that she has become unable to fulfil her contractual obligations due to the shock although in reality she may very well be able to repay. Hence a moral hazard problem arises between transaction partners.

Diamond also showed that this friction and debt contracts are mutually consistent in the sense that a debt contract with a nonpecuniary penalty can be endogenously derived as the optimal solution for dealing with the ex post informational asymmetry. Diamond did not consider, however, whether such debt contracts could be used as a medium of exchange.

Debt contracts facilitating exchange are studied in a similar market setup as in the barter case. However, the ex post informational friction is introduced into the basic exchange model. Three different variants of debt facilitating exchange are studied within this framework:

1. *Private decentralized solution: Privately issued I.O.U.s*

   In this case individual agents issue I.O.U.s serving as a medium of exchange. These I.O.U.s embody a debt claim against a certain quantity of the good of the issuer. Between the issuing of the I.O.U. and the delivery of the quantity promised a random shock affects the ability of the agent to deliver which is unobservable to the transaction partner. Nonpecuniary penalties ensure, however, that the issuer has proper incentives to deliver whenever she can. Traders can exchange I.O.U.s written on goods rather than the goods themselves and thereby can obtain the goods they desire. The key question in the scenario with privately issued I.O.U.s are the incentive costs associated with the I.O.U.s. If they are too high, agents may not have an incentive to issue as many I.O.U.s as they could, thereby reducing potentially beneficial trade.

2. *Public centralized solution: Money as central bank debt*
   The delicate task of issuing incentive compatible I.O.U.s can be delegated to a central bank. Because the central bank is not affected in the same way as private agents by wealth shocks, the issuing costs which are related to unobservable wealth shocks can potentially be reduced. However, money issued by the central bank incurs an opportunity cost because agents first have to exchange their goods against money, thereby losing returns that would have accrued by keeping their goods longer.
3. *Private centralized solution: The transactions oriented bank*
   The transactions oriented bank can create deposits serving as a medium of exchange by making loans when the funds raised from the loans get redeposited at the bank such that total deposits increase. Because the bank also has an incentive compatible structure such that depositors can be (almost) sure to get their money back, deposits can be transferred between agents as a medium of exchange. By paying interest on deposits from loan income the bank can potentially reduce the opportunity cost of holding money at the bank. Again the key question is how the bank can keep the cost of issuing depository debt contracts functioning as medium of exchange low compared to the other transaction alternatives.

Once barter and the three financial solutions to transaction problems have been analyzed, their efficiency can be compared. It is also interesting to see how the optimal institutional structures designed to solve transaction problems compare with institutional structures in banking theory designed to solve financing and investment problems. The close relationship between the lack of trust in the ability of a transaction partner to repay and the lack of trust in an agent taking out a loan will be key for the development of an integrated theory of money and banking.

As far as existing research on money and banking is concerned, earlier game theoretical work on money and monetary institutions by Shubik (1999) surveyed in Shubik (1990) discusses many ideas which are also analyzed in this monograph. However, much of his work preceded the models by Diamond (1984) and Diamond and Dybvig (1983) and hence does not refer to contemporary banking theory. Also Goodfriend (1991) discusses closely related ideas on the development of money and monetary institutions. However, he does not conduct a formal analysis.

How the underlying economy is modeled in which transactions requiring a transaction technology take place should be consistent with the approach pursued to develop an integrated theory of money and banking based upon the problem of trust in exchange. Standard models of markets cannot be used for this purpose.

- The model must be amenable to the introduction of market imperfections. Standard models typically assume perfect markets.
- Debt contracts require the clear identification of partners to the contract. Under perfect competition, for example, there is just an amorphous mass of agents. Neither transactions nor the agents to the transaction are well identified.
- The terms of the contracts should be explained from the interactions between economic agents. In a perfect market with perfect competition prices can only be explained by the introduction of a fictitious auctioneer.
- Results can be shown most clearly if market power is absent. E.g., bilateral monopoly can be considered as a case where two agents are clearly identifiable. However, the outcomes are highly sensitive to the structure of the market.

To accommodate these requirements a game theoretical model is developed whose structure is appropriate for studying the questions raised in the earlier sections of this chapter. The basic structure of the model is described in the next chapter.

5
A Basic Model of Exchange

To develop an integrated theory of money and banking in an analytically rigorous way, this chapter introduces the basic structure of a formal exchange model capturing essential features of the classical problem of a lack of double coincidence of needs and wants in exchange. The model is a market game between a large number of traders designed to fulfil the requirements for the analysis of an integrated theory of money and banking put forward in the preceding chapter: (i) the model is amenable to the introduction of informational market frictions; (ii) individual deals and partners to a contract can be identified; (iii) the terms of the contract such as quantities and prices are endogenously derived from the economic interactions of traders in the market; (iv) individual agents have no market power in the model. Augmented versions of this model will be used in the following chapters to analyze four different transaction technologies in a common framework: i) barter with intermediate exchange of goods; ii) I.O.U.s as a medium of exchange; iii) money as central bank debt; iv) banks providing transaction services.

As was argued in the preceding chapter standard market models such as perfect competition in a perfect market cannot be used to develop an integrated theory of money and banking. On the other hand it would be desirable to consider models that can be related to standard models such that generalizations of the results and the relationship with other existing research based upon standard models can be studied more easily. Hence the guiding idea behind the development of the basic model of exchange is to develop a model which is close to a standard model but has all the features necessary to analyze the research questions which are the focus of this study.[5] Certainly there is more than one solution fulfilling these requirements. The model described in the following paragraphs is just one attempt among several possible targeting these goals. It is supposed to be close to a perfect market with perfect competition. However, as will be seen later several technical difficulties require to introduce features into the model which somewhat set it apart from this benchmark model.

The starting point of the basic strategic model of exchange is the classical problem of a lack of double coincidence of needs and wants. Agents differ in endowments and preferences such that their welfare can be increased by exchanging goods. Exchange is complicated, however, because no single pair of agents exists for which goods owned and goods desired mutually match. Hence direct barter of goods is not possible. Trading frictions further aggravate the problem of exchange. A transaction technology has to be used that enables agents to deal with the frictions as efficiently as possible such that traders can exhaust the potential for mutually beneficial trade to the fullest extent possible.

Whereas the formal details of the exchange problem will be fully worked out in the subsequent chapters when models with specific transaction technologies are analyzed in full depth, here a sketch of the main characteristics of the exchange problem common to all these different model set-ups is provided. Four types of agents denoted by *A, B, C, D* and four types of goods, *a, b, c, d* exist. The number of agents in each group equals *N*. Hence the total number of agents in the model is $4N$ where *N* is supposed to be a large number. Each agent of type *A* is endowed with one unit of good *a*, each agent of type *B, C*, and *D* is endowed with one unit of goods *b*, *c*, and *d*, respectively.

Agents of type *A* have an advantage at selling goods of type *b* because they can get a higher price by reselling these goods in another market than agents of other types could get. This advantage is due to lower transportation costs compared to other agents which are not reflected in market prices because the group of agents of type *A* is small in the market. Similarly, agents of type *B, C*, and *D* have an advantage at selling goods of type *c*, *d*, and *a*, respectively, because they can resell these goods at higher prices in another market than agents of other types could sell. Agents of type *A* therefore have a demand for goods of type *b*, agents of type *B, C*, and *D*, respectively, have a demand for goods of type *c, d*, and *a* provided that they can acquire these goods at sufficiently attractive terms relative to the benefits from reselling them. No pair of agents can be found for which the type of the endowment good and the type of the good to be acquired for advantageous resale mutually match. Because no production takes place and because the goal of an agent is to acquire a good to resell it at a higher price, agents can be considered as traders seeking to maximize their wealth by entering into exchange arrangements. They are assumed to be risk-neutral.

In the basic strategic model of exchange there are always two clearly identifiable groups of economic agents, sellers and buyers. First, each seller offers a certain amount of her goods simultaneously with other sellers at a certain price. In a second step buyers get randomly matched with these offers and decide how much to buy by exchanging the goods they own. Hence individual deals and the partners to a deal are always well identified. The specific transaction technology to be considered matters how exactly buyers pay for the goods they acquire. The matching procedure considered is not a simple random matching process. Rather, buyers get matched with the cheapest offers in the market. Hence the matching procedure considered here is termed "smart random matching".

The rules of the smart random matching procedure are as follows: At the beginning the matching technology identifies the offers with the most favorable prices for buyers. The pool of buyers to be matched consists of all those who have not submitted zero demands in the past. A buyer is randomly matched from this pool with the best offer where all buyers are equally likely to be drawn. She decides whether to accept the offer or some part of it. The second best offer is then considered. If two offers have the same price, the one with the higher quantity offered gets matched first. If a buyer chooses a quantity of zero or has exchanged all her goods, she drops out of the pool of buyers and will therefore not get matched with any other offers. If she chooses a positive amount, but without fully exhausting her budget, she remains in the pool of buyers and can get matched to other offers later in the matching process. This procedure continues by matching buyers randomly with the next best offer not yet matched until there is no buyer left with positive demand or until buyers have accepted all the offers of sellers. If the quantity offered by sellers at the highest price still to be considered for matching is higher than the quantity demanded by buyers at this price, it is assumed that sellers get deals proportional to the size of their quantities offered. The quantity offered by an agent can be split and the agent can be matched with more than one trader later in the matching process if part of the quantity offered or demanded does not get traded in a match. Hence if a seller can sell only part of her offer, the remaining quantity can get matched with other buyers. If other offers at the same price but with a higher quantity offered exist, they get matched first. Note that because strategies in the models considered are finite, matching processes always end after a finite number of steps.

From the perspective of a buyer the smart random matching procedure implies that an agent never has an incentive to delay advantageous trades. If a buyer gets matched with an offer, it is clear that she will not get any better offer later. Hence, provided that the offer increases her total wealth, a buyer finds it optimal to always accept the offer to the fullest extent possible. This special feature which is inherent in the smart random matching procedure also greatly simplifies the analysis of decision making of buyers because it suffices to check whether the offer is advantageous in a static sense rather than having to consider all the future consequences of decisions within the general dynamic strategic decision problem.

Although one strand of the literature with random matching exists which analyzes the bilateral transactions between sellers and buyers as bargaining problems (see Osborne and Rubinstein, 1990), bargaining is not considered here. Buyers simply get randomly matched with the best deals which are acceptable to them. Also in many real world markets, particularly in mass retailing most deals take place without any negotiations. Sellers just post prices for a certain quantity of goods they offer. Buyers shop around and decide whether to accept one of those offers. There is a tendency for the buyers to look for the best deals in the market. Negotiations and lengthy bargaining over items with low value would be much too costly for the transaction partners. Bargaining rather happens when large, complex deals are struck such that much is at stake for a relatively small group of agents.[6]

In the basic model of exchange the equilibrium price is typically set such that any *M*-1 sellers can satisfy total market demand at this price where *M* is the total number of sellers of a certain good and total market demand is the sum over all goods demanded by buyers at this price. Hence a seller does not have an incentive to bid a higher price because this would mean that the *M*-1 other traders in the market would satisfy total market demand. The quantity she can sell would therefore drop to zero. Provided that trades increase total wealth at the equilibrium price, charging a higher price than the equilibrium price is not optimal. Offering goods at a lower price than the equilibrium price set by the other sellers means that the trader could sell a slightly higher quantity but at a less favorable price. The question is whether the positive quantity effect prevails over the negative price effect. To avoid infinite undercutting of traders by infinitely small price reductions it is assumed that prices are discrete. The minimum price step is chosen such that the negative price effect always outweighs the positive quantity effect of offering goods at a lower price. The size of the discrete price steps can be made arbitrarily small by increasing the total number of traders in the market. The description of the basic logic of the equilibrium shows that key features of the transactions between traders such as the prices and the quantities of a deal are determined from the economic interactions of agents in the model.

From the considerations above follows that to discipline sellers it is necessary that in equilibrium a certain quantity of goods remains unsold. This excess supply has the role of a strategic threat to keep traders from charging too high a price. Depending upon the number of buyers and sellers this excess supply can be very small relative to the total size of the market. From the perspective of the buyer this means that she is never faced with empty shelves when shopping for goods such that she could always buy more. From this feature of the basic model of exchange its name is derived. Because buyers are always facing some oversupply (even though it may be small), the model is called "shopper's paradise model". The shopper's paradise model provides the basic economic framework within which transaction technologies are studied in the following chapters.

It should be noted that the market power of both buyers and sellers is quite limited. Buyers behave as price takers, i.e. they only decide how much to buy given some offer they receive in a smart random matching process. Sellers do set prices, but because of the large number of players and the strategic logic of the game an individual seller does not have an influence on the market price either. Whatever her strategy is, the equilibrium prices of deals concluded in the market are independent from her actions given the equilibrium play of other players. In this sense the model mimics price-taking behavior.

It should be noted that a market clearing price in the sense that all endowments are traded could not be sustained as an equilibrium price. If all other sellers in the market offer their goods at the market clearing price, one seller considering her best response to those strategies will realize that she is left in the market with buyers who have no other alternative but buying from her because all other traders are sold out as their offers get fully matched with buyers. She will therefore exploit this position as a virtual monopolist relative to the only remaining buyer(s). Hence charging such a market-clearing price is not a best response to other traders charging the equilibrium price. Still, the equilibrium of the shopper's paradise model is very close to the outcome of a market clearing model if the number of traders is large but individual traders are small such that the excess supply gets small relative to total supply.

Some technical problems in the analysis of the game arise when off the equilibrium path markets exist with only very few active participants and low trading volumes. The shopper's paradise model is specified for large numbers of traders actively dealing in a market. Difficulties arise if these numbers shrink. E.g., minimum discrete price steps become large and the amount of oversupply in the market may be large relative to the total quantity traded. Hence the model has to be specified to ensure that on any possible path there is always enough trading volume such that the basic logic of the shopper's paradise model still carries through. This is achieved by introducing minimum and maximum prices and minimum quantities to be acquired which are consistent with these prices. The economic interpretation of the minimum and maximum prices is straightforward. The market of traders can be considered as a segment within a bigger market. Trading outside the market segment is costly, however, which is reflected in the external prices from the perspective of traders within the market segment. Still, the outside market narrows down the price range within which traders can make deals because unattractive deals get rejected in favor of trading externally at more favorable prices. Play along the equilibrium path is not sensitive with respect to how these external prices are set provided that the admissible price range allows the existence of a symmetric equilibrium in the market segment. Only play along the equilibrium paths will be considered for comparing transaction technologies in later chapters.

The shopper's paradise model has a fairly flexible structure. As will be seen from off equilibrium play, it can deal with asymmetric agents. Also it is possible to accommodate several rounds of exchange. Even concave objective functions can be handled as will be seen in chapter 7 although under most scenarios traders have simple linear objective functions. The model serves the purpose of providing a consistent economic framework within which various transaction technologies can be studied. It fulfils all the requirements in chapter 4 for the development of an integrated theory of money and banking. Traders and deals are well identified in the model. Traders correspond to the players in the game. Deals arise as a consequence of the interactions between the players during the game. Key terms of the contracts between traders such as prices and quantities of deals are explained endogenously from the model. Informational market frictions can be introduced into a game. Finally, due to the large number of traders and the specific logic of economic interactions none of the traders in the model has any significant market power. The formal details of the model and the modifications necessary to accommodate the various transaction technologies will be explained in the following chapters.

As far as presentation style is concerned some redundancies in the description of the models are to be found in the following chapters. This choice of presentation style has deliberately been made to keep individual chapters self-contained. Another reason is that when going beyond the standard Walrasian models some effort has to be taken in terms of notation to describe the full structure of transactions even in relatively simple models. Due to this feature there is a danger of puzzling readers too much by making many cross-references between various parts of models in different chapters.

6

Barter with Intermediate Exchange of Goods

This chapter prepares the ground for the analysis of advanced transaction technologies by developing a barter model with intermediate exchange of goods. If there exists a lack of double coincidence of needs and wants, barter implies that at least some traders have to acquire goods temporarily which they do not actually desire. Accepting goods in exchange which an agent does not actually desire for trading them against the desired goods is called intermediate exchange of goods.[7]

Another major purpose of the model presented in this chapter is to analyze the shopper's paradise model introduced in the preceding chapter in full formal detail. The friction considered in the barter case is relatively simple such that the shopper's paradise model can be studied without much interference from more sophisticated transaction technologies.

Barter transactions make up only a minor share of total transactions in a modern economy. This is not to say that barter cannot become an important transaction technology if due to a major crisis other transactions technologies collapse. After wars or other major disruptions of economic activity economies may fall back on barter to conduct economic transactions for a certain period of time. But the goal of this chapter is not to explain real world barter transactions in the first place or to conduct a historically accurate study of the development of transaction technologies. The goal is rather to establish a basic theoretical benchmark. Because of its basic character barter is a useful point of departure to start monetary analysis. In later chapters the search for more efficient transaction technologies can be motivated by relating the benefits of those technologies to this benchmark.

Barter also provides an interesting starting point for the development of an integrated theory of money and banking based upon the problem of trust in exchange. In a barter economy in which goods are traded on the spot no problem of trust in the ability of a transaction partner to repay arises provided that agents are fully informed about the goods to be exchanged.[8] Hence the problem of trust must be related to specific transaction technologies that will be studied in later chapters. It will be interesting to see under what circumstances this problem arises.

If it were possible to barter goods without cost at market clearing prices no need would exist to introduce money or other transaction technologies into an economy. Intermediate exchange of goods would be sufficient for agents to obtain the goods they want. Therefore, if other forms of conducting transactions are to be beneficial, some cost must exist which makes intermediate exchange of goods burdensome. Such costs are typically tied to market frictions. To show at this introductory stage a simple example of a friction hampering trade it is assumed that the intermediate exchange of goods involves some physical cost. The quantity of a good to be exchanged gets reduced in every round of intermediate exchange.[9] In such a situation market clearing prices and/or quantities depend upon the structure how transactions are conducted in the economy. The more intermediate transactions take place, the more the quantity of goods available in exchange gets reduced. This loss reduces trading volume and may even affect relative prices.

One key problem which arises is the multitude of theoretically possible barter structures. Although for some distribution of endowments, preferences, and transaction costs the general solution to the problem of optimizing transaction structures may be difficult to obtain, the focus of interest for monetary theory is more specific. Clearly, a total lack of double coincidence of needs and wants requires at least one round of intermediate exchange for a subgroup of agents. In the scenario of the following subsection with symmetric transaction costs and a given distribution of goods and preferences the most efficient way of conducting transactions is one round of intermediate exchange. It can be considered as a "best case" benchmark because in general more than one round of intermediate exchange is necessary, incurring higher transaction costs and making intermediate exchange a less attractive transaction method.

6.1 The formal structure of the barter model with intermediate exchange

There are four types of agents denoted by *A, B, C,* and *D* and five types of goods, denoted by *a, b, c, d,* and *x*. A total number of *N* traders exist in each group, i.e. there is a total of 4*N* traders in the model. *N* is supposed to be a large number. The analysis focuses on the case in which *N* goes towards infinity. Each agent of type *A* is endowed with quantity $a_0 + \varepsilon^A$ of good *a*, each agent of type *B, C,* and *D* is endowed with quantities b_0, $c_0 + \varepsilon^C$, and d_0 of goods *b*, *c*, and *d*, respectively ($a_0 = b_0 = c_0 = d_0 = 1$). The basic goal of traders is to exchange their endowments among each other in order to acquire goods which they can profitably resell in an external resale market. Thereby their wealth can be increased compared to just keeping their endowment. Because there does not exist any money in the model, good a is taken as a numeraire good whose price is set to one.

Agents can deal in three different types of markets: the market of traders, the external market, and the resale market. Transporting goods between markets incurs a transportation cost. This cost creates some scope for autonomous price formation as will be explained below. The strategic analysis focuses on the market of traders.

The market of traders: In the market of traders the agents can exchange endowments among each other in two rounds of trading. In the first round goods of type a are exchanged against goods of type b and goods of type c are exchanged against goods of type d. In the second round goods of type a and type c are exchanged. Prices and quantities are derived endogenously from the strategic interactions between traders. The shopper's paradise model provides the basic setup for the market. Conclusions about transaction technologies will be drawn by comparing the outcomes in this market.

The external market: The market of traders can be considered as a segment in a bigger market in which the same goods are traded as in the other markets. This market is called the external market. Trading in this market is costly for the agents from the market of traders because of transportation costs. These costs are reflected in the prices for selling and buying goods (including transportation costs) as viewed by the agents in the market of traders. The structure of the market is similar to the market of traders in the sense that in the first round goods of type a are exchanged against goods of type b and goods of type c are exchanged against goods of type d. In the second round goods of type a and type c are exchanged. However, unlike in the market of traders no strategic interactions are considered in the external market. It is just assumed that agents can buy and sell there at the exogenously given prices. Hence the market of traders is supposed to be small relative to the external market.

In the external market goods of type a can be sold at a price $\overline{p}_a$ and can be acquired at a price $\widetilde{p}_a$ by agents from the market of traders where due to the transportation cost it holds that $\widetilde{p}_a > 1 > \overline{p}_a$. Note that because good a is the numeraire good its price is also one in the external market. However, as viewed from the perspective of agents in the market of traders, prices including transportation costs are different from one. Similarly, goods of type b, c, and d can be sold externally at prices[10] $\overline{p}_b$, $\overline{p}_c$, and $\overline{p}_d$ whereas they can be acquired at prices $\widetilde{p}_b$, $\widetilde{p}_c$, and $\widetilde{p}_d$. Again it holds that $\widetilde{p}_b > 1 > \overline{p}_b$, $\widetilde{p}_c > 1 > \overline{p}_c$, and $\widetilde{p}_d > 1 > \overline{p}_d$. Further it is assumed that $\widetilde{p}_a = \widetilde{p}_b = \widetilde{p}_c = \widetilde{p}_d$ and $\overline{p}_a = \overline{p}_c < \overline{p}_b = \overline{p}_d$. These prices in the external market narrow down the range of prices that can be agreed upon in the market of traders. An agent is willing to accept a deal in the market of traders only if she cannot get a better deal in the external market. The condition $\overline{p}_a = \overline{p}_c < \overline{p}_b = \overline{p}_d$ ensures that constraints on equilibrium prices do not become binding as will be shown in the appendix at stage 2a). Thereby the analysis can be concentrated on the market of traders which is of primary interest because transaction technologies are studied in this market.

Finally, the external market also provides an opportunity to exchange goods of type x acquired in the resale market against goods of type a (see below). Note that the introduction of goods of type x is necessary such that also traders of type D can resell the numeraire goods of type a at a price which is effectively higher than one.

The resale market: Traders of the same type in the market of traders have special access to a third market where they can profitably sell a certain type of goods which is different from the type of their endowment good. Hence they have to acquire goods of the required type to resell them. This explains why the third market is called resale market. Traders of type A have a special advantage at selling goods of type b in the resale market. Traders of type B, C, and D have a special advantage at selling goods of type c, d, and a, respectively. The advantage is due to the ability of traders to transport costlessly these goods from the market of traders to the resale market.

The resale market is supposed to import goods of type a, b, c, and d from the external market and from the market of traders. The prices of these goods include a substantial cost for transporting goods from the external market to the resale market. As the market of traders is small relative to the external market, agents from the market of traders potentially have the benefit of selling goods in the resale market at the high price reflecting the transportation costs between the external market and the resale market without actually having to pay this cost.

In exchange agents from the market of traders receive goods of type x in the resale market. These type x goods are valued at the price at which they can be sold in the external market against goods of type a, net of the cost of transporting the goods from the resale market to the external market. One unit of a good of type a can be exchanged at a relative price of p^{aR}/p_x against goods of type x in the resale market. In the external market one unit of good x can be exchanged at a relative price p_x/p_a against good a. Taking into account also a transportation cost T per unit of goods of type x to be transported from the resale market to the external market, one unit of a good of type a that a trader of type D sells in the resale market has a value of $(p^{aR}/p_x)(p_x/p_a)-T=p^a$. It is assumed that $p^a>\widetilde{p}_a$. In an analogous way also goods of other types can be exchanged in the resale market by agents from the market of traders against goods of type x such that agents of type B, C, and D having an advantage at selling goods of type c, d, and a, respectively, because they can trade at prices p^c, p^d, and p^a. For the relationship between these prices it also holds that $p^a=p^b=p^c=p^d$ and $p^b>\widetilde{p}_b$, $p^c>\widetilde{p}_c$, and $p^d>\widetilde{p}_d$.

Arbitrage between the external market and the market of traders performed by agents in the market of traders is limited because the benefit from exploiting price differences is supposed to be too small relative to the transaction costs stemming from transporting goods from the external market to the market of traders and from the cost of writing incentive compatible debt contracts (see the next chapter). Hence borrowing and trading on price differences between the external market and the resale market is not profitable due to transaction costs. Still an incentive may exist for agents in the market of traders to exchange endowments among each other to resell them profitably, thereby enjoying the transportation cost advantage. If all traders want to trade, a lack of double coincidence of needs and wants exists in the market of traders.

The only way how traders can obtain the goods in the market of traders which they actually desire to resell is for some group of agents to engage in intermediate exchange of goods. The case is considered in which in the first round of transactions traders of type A sell their goods to traders of type B and traders of type C sell their goods to traders of type D. Trading occurs within the framework of the shopper's paradise model introduced in the preceding chapter as will be seen in more detail below. Clearly, traders of type A and type C are satisfied with these deals because they acquire the types of goods they can resell profitably. Traders of type B acquire goods of type a although they can profitably resell goods of type c. Traders of type D acquire goods of type c although they can profitably resell goods of type a. Hence traders of type B and D have an incentive to deal with each other in a second round of exchange to acquire the goods they actually desire provided the terms are sufficiently attractive. Also in the second round of exchange trading takes place within the framework of the shopper's paradise model.

Alternatively, traders of type A and D as well as B and C could meet in the first round of trades. In this case, agents from groups A and C would have to engage in intermediate trade, but the whole trading process in the market could also get completed after the second round. If agents of type A and C as well as B and D met in the first round, everybody would have to enter into a second round of transactions which is inefficient if intermediate trade is costly. We will focus on the case where A and B as well as C and D meet in the first round of trades because this is sufficient to show the basic logic behind the transactions which also applies in an analogous way to the other efficient situations.

As argued before, the intermediate exchange of goods is costly. Traders of type B and traders of type D lose a share of $1-\rho$ of the quantity of goods they have acquired in the first round of trades ($0<\rho<1$) because of the trading friction in intermediate exchange. In the second round of trades they can trade only ρ times the quantity of goods acquired.

Formally, the barter model with intermediate exchange corresponds to a game in extensive form. The sequence of trades and events is described below.

1) First round of trades in the market of traders

1a) Supply

- Simultaneously with other traders of her type each trader of type A offers strategically a certain quantity of good a from her endowment at a certain price to be exchanged against goods of type b from traders of type B.
- Simultaneously with traders of type A and other traders of type C also each trader of type C strategically submits an analogous offer for goods of type d from traders of type D.

1b) Smart random matching and demand

- Traders of type B get randomly matched with the cheapest offers submitted by traders of type A.
- Given some price which trader i of type B gets offered in the matching process, she optimally chooses a certain quantity of good b from her endowment to be exchanged against good a.
- Traders of type D get randomly matched with the cheapest offers submitted by traders of type C.
- Given an offer that she receives in the matching process trader i of type D optimally chooses a certain quantity of good d to be exchanged against good c at some offered relative price.

2) Second round of trades in the market of traders

2a) Supply

- Depending upon prior play each trader of type B offers strategically a certain quantity of good a acquired in the first round of trades at a certain relative price simultaneously with other traders of her type.

2b) Smart random matching and demand

- Traders of type D get randomly matched with the cheapest offers submitted by traders of type B. Given a price offer which trader i of type D receives in the matching process, she optimally chooses the quantity of good c from the goods acquired in the first period to be exchanged against a good of type a.

3) Resale

- All traders sell the goods they have acquired for resale in the resale market.

A simplified sketch of the game tree is shown in figure 6.1. As argued in chapter 5 the shopper's paradise model is designed to capture behavior in markets with many participants. But off the equilibrium path there could exist small numbers of active traders (i.e., agents trading nonzero quantities) in markets with low trading volumes. Restrictions on quantities and prices ensure some minimum trading activity also off the equilibrium path. Minimum prices and maximum prices are pinned down by alternative trading opportunities in the external market. Minimum quantities to be traded are chosen to ensure a certain aggregate volume of trading such that individual buyers at stage 1b) have no impact on equilibrium prices at stage 2a) determined by the aggregate volumes of goods traded in the first round. All these restrictions will be described below in more detail when the specific decision problems of individual traders at the various stages of the game are discussed.

Agents decide about the quantities of their goods to be exchanged. If they are sellers, they also have to determine the price at which they sell. In the first round of trades agents decide about exchanging their endowments. In the second round of trades traders decide how much to exchange of the goods they have acquired in the first period. The goal of all traders is to maximize total expected wealth. The decision problems of traders are described below. Note that whereas the notation here describes only the general structure of the decision problem at each stage of the game without referring to specific information sets of a trader, the notation will be analogous in the following sections. Only superindex T will be added when complete strategies for determining play at all the information sets of a trader at a certain stage of the game will be discussed because it will suffice to consider just one representative path through the game to show the equilibrium. Hence given a specific information set in the game variables with superindex T refer to i) variables determined or consistently expected in prior play on the path leading to the information set, (ii) variables determined at the information set, and (iii) optimally anticipated variables in future play following the information set considered.

At the end of the game total wealth for trader i of type A can be represented as follows:

$$p^b b_i^A + (a_0 + \varepsilon^A - a_i^{AS})\overline{p}_a. \qquad 6.1$$

By offering an amount a_i^A of her endowment $a_0 + \varepsilon^A$ at a price p_{ai}^A / p_{bi}^A at stage 1a) of the game the trader actually sells a quantity a_i^{AS} in the following smart random matching process at stage 1b). The relative price p_{ai}^A / p_{bi}^A indicates how many units of good b are to be exchanged against one unit of good a. The restriction on the choice of a_i^A is described by the following relationship imposing lower and upper boundaries on this variable:

$$a_{\min}^A \le a_i^A \le a_0 + \varepsilon^A. \qquad 6.2$$

The constant $a_{\min}^A$ is the minimum amount of the good of type a to be exchanged. For the quantity of the endowment $1 + \varepsilon^A$ it holds that the incremental value above one ε^A shrinks as the size of the population of traders grows:

$$\varepsilon^A = 1/(N-1). \qquad 6.3$$

As N goes towards infinity, the incremental value vanishes completely.

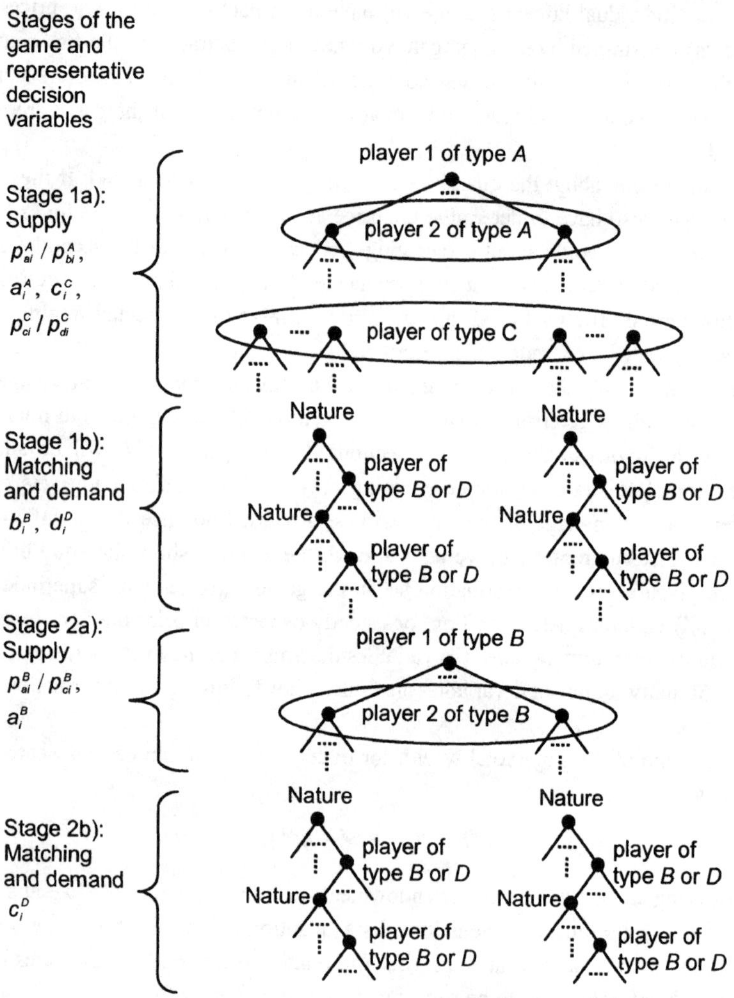

Figure 6.1 The sketch of a game tree for the model of barter with intermediate exchange

Note: The dots indicate a reduplication of the structure of the tree to which the dots refer.

The quantity of good a which trader i can actually exchange after matching is denoted by a_i^{AS}. It is a function of the decision variables of all traders of type A and it is determined according to the matching rules in the subgames starting at stage 1b). In one matching process the matching rules can be formulated as restrictions on the decision making of traders as shown below (indices are defined as follows: j=1…N across all traders of type B; s: all traders of type A for whom $p_{as}^A/p_{bs}^A \leq p_{ai}^A/p_{bi}^A$; k: all traders of type A for whom $p_{ak}^A/p_{bk}^A < p_{ai}^A/p_{bi}^A$; g: all traders of type A for whom $p_{ag}^A/p_{bg}^A = p_{ai}^A/p_{bi}^A$):

$$a_i^{AS} = \begin{cases} a_i^A \text{ if } \sum_j a_j^B \geq \sum_s a_s^A, \\ 0 \text{ if } \sum_j a_j^B \leq \sum_k a_k^A, \\ (a_i^A / \sum_g a_g^A)(\sum_j a_j^B - \sum_k a_k^A) \text{ if } \sum_j a_j^B > \sum_k a_k^A \text{ and } \sum_j a_j^B \leq \sum_s a_s^A \end{cases} \qquad 6.4$$

The quantity actually exchanged by trader i of type A after matching equals zero if there are enough more attractive bids for buyers in the matching process to satisfy total demand. If the price submitted by trader i of type A is among the most attractive bids in the matching process as consistently expected and optimally anticipated by the trader, all her quantity offered is matched with buyers. If the trader's bid is marginally attractive, i.e. if it is the highest bid which still gets matched with buyers, the remaining unsatisfied demand by traders of type B is split up among the sellers offering this price in proportion to the size of their bids. The randomization in the matching process occurs only across buyers. Sellers know with certainty the amount a_i^{AS} they can sell in the matching process. $\sum a_j^B$ is total demand by traders of type B for good a as optimally anticipated by trader i of type A at the information set at which she decides. In equilibrium this aggregate amount is independent from the actions of trader i of type A.

A sale of a_i^{AS} translates into an amount b_i^A purchased of good b according to the following relationship

$$b_i^A = (p_{ai}^A / p_{bi}^A) a_i^{AS}. \qquad 6.5$$

This amount is resold at price p^b. No resale decision is explicitly modeled because resale always increases wealth. Note that the part of the endowment which remains unsold is valued at the price $\overline{p}_a < 1$ at which these goods can be sold in the external market. This implies a requirement for traders to eventually move all their goods to the external market because otherwise these traders would not have an incentive to reduce the amount of the numeraire good which they own by the transportation cost. This assumption is made for reasons of symmetry with other traders who can value their goods only at the prices in the external market.

Traders of type A can submit their price offerings p_{ai}^A / p_{bi}^A only in discrete steps of σ^A. Prices chosen in equilibrium are assumed to be always part of the admissible price scale. The step size can be made arbitrarily small by increasing the number of traders. This is a technical assumption which is necessary to avoid infinite undercutting in infinitely small steps by traders such that no equilibrium would exist (see the appendix, stage 1a, for the derivation of σ^A).

$$\sigma^A > (1 - \overline{p}_a / p^b)/N. \tag{6.6}$$

As described before, lower and upper boundaries on prices are determined by the condition that neither buyers nor sellers should have an incentive to conduct transactions in the external market rather than in the market of traders. A trader of type A could sell her goods in the external market at price $\overline{p}_a$ and she could acquire goods of type b for resale at price $\widetilde{p}_b$. Hence a trader of type A will not be willing to trade at a relative price lower than $\overline{p}_a / \widetilde{p}_b$ in the market of traders. Her trading partner of type B could sell her goods outside the market of traders at price $\overline{p}_b$ and she could acquire goods of type a for resale at price $\widetilde{p}_a$. For simplicity it is assumed that also in the external market a trader of type B would have to engage in the same intermediate exchange of goods and would incur the same loss. Hence a trader of type B will not be willing to trade at a relative price higher than $\widetilde{p}_a / \overline{p}_b$. From these considerations one can conclude that the following relationship must hold: $\overline{p}_a / \widetilde{p}_b \leq p_{ai}^A / p_{bi}^A \leq \widetilde{p}_a / \overline{p}_b$.

The decision of a trader of type C is analogous to the decision of a trader of type A. Replacing in the discussion above any a by c, A by C, b by d, B by D and replacing $\sigma^A > (1 - \overline{p}_a / p^b)/N$ by $\sigma^C > 1/N - (\overline{p}_c(N-1)/(N^2 p^d))$ yields a discussion of the decision of trader i of type C.

Traders of type B are buyers in the first round of exchange and sellers in the second round. As compared to the decision problem of a trader of type A a trader of type B faces more complicated constraints which are related to transactions because she has to engage in intermediate exchange. Goods of type a acquired in the first round have to be exchanged again in the second round against goods of type c to obtain the goods for resale. At the end of the game total wealth for trader i of type B for all i=1...N looks as follows:

$$p^c c_i^B + (\rho a_i^B - a_i^{BS})\overline{p}_a + (b_0 - b_i^B)\overline{p}_b. \tag{6.7}$$

At stage 1b) trader i of type B decides how much of her endowment to exchange against goods of type a at the offered prices. In one random matching process she chooses a total quantity of b_i^B goods of her endowment to be exchanged against a total amount a_i^B of good a at an average price of $\dddot{p}_{bi}^B / \dddot{p}_{ai}^B$ for which the prices of individual deals accepted get weighted by the quantities of her goods exchanged. Note that this total quantity and average price result from all the decisions taken by the trader in a matching process as will be analyzed in detail in the appendix to this chapter. In this same matching process she has to obey the restrictions at stage 1b) that she cannot offer more than her endowment and less than the minimum amount required $b^B_{\min}$:

$$b^B_{\min} \leq b^B_i \leq b_0, \tag{6.8}$$

$$a^B_i = b^B_i (\dddot{p}^B_{bi} / \dddot{p}^B_{ai}). \tag{6.9}$$

If goods do not get sold, they are valued at the exogenously specified price $\overline{p}_b$ at which traders of type B could sell goods of type b in the market outside the market of traders. Note that when deciding about the quantity to be acquired at stage 1b) a trader of type B cannot influence equilibrium prices in the second round of trades because she is too small relative to the total market for N going towards infinity.

Depending upon prior play trader i of type B decides in any of the subgames starting at the beginning of stage 2a) about the amount of good a to be offered at some relative price in exchange for good c. In one subgame she offers an amount a^B_{i2} which cannot exceed the total amount of good a acquired at stage 1b) reduced by the loss due to intermediate exchange.

$$0 \leq a^B_{i2} \leq a^B_i \rho. \tag{6.10}$$

The minimum amount to be chosen is zero here because there is no further trading round for which a positive minimum quantity would have to be ensured. The relative price player i of type B offers in one subgame is p^B_{ai} / p^B_{ci}. It indicates how many goods of type c trader i of type B is ready to exchange against one unit of goods of type a. Also here discrete price steps denoted by σ^B are considered. The derivation of σ^B is explained in the appendix at stage 2a). The minimum price step goes towards zero as N goes towards infinity.

Because of the condition that prices have to lie within the range where both sellers and buyers do not have an incentive to trade their goods in the external market, the relative price offered by trader i of type B is bounded from above and below as follows:

$$\overline{p}_a / \widetilde{p}_c \leq p^B_{ai} / p^B_{ci} \leq \widetilde{p}_a / \overline{p}_c. \tag{6.11}$$

The random matching process determines how much of the amount offered can be actually exchanged. Because the randomization is over individual buyers but not over the total amount sold in the market, the trader knows with certainty how much she can sell. The quantity actually sold in the random matching process following the subgame equals a^{BS}_i. This amount determines what amount c^B_i of good c trader i of type B can acquire.

$$c_i^B = (p_{ai}^B / p_{ci}^B) a_i^{BS}. \tag{6.12}$$

The basic rules of the smart random matching process as viewed by the seller can be described by the following restrictions. The sum $\sum a_j^B$ is total demand by traders of type *D* for good *a* as optimally anticipated by trader *i* of type *B* which is independent from her decision (indices are defined as follows: *j*=1...*N* across all traders of type *D*; *s*: all traders of type *B* for whom $p_{as}^B/p_{cs}^B \leq p_{ai}^B/p_{ci}^B$; *k*: all traders of type *B* for whom $p_{ak}^B/p_{ck}^B < p_{ai}^B/p_{ci}^B$; *g*: all traders of type *B* for whom $p_{ag}^B/p_{cg}^B = p_{ai}^B/p_{ci}^B$.

$$a_i^{BS} = \left\{ \begin{array}{l} a_{i2}^B \text{ if } \sum_j a_j^D \geq \sum_s a_{s2}^B, \\ 0 \text{ if } \sum_j a_j^D \leq \sum_k a_{k2}^B, \\ (a_{i2}^B / \sum_g a_{g2}^B)(\sum_j a_j^D - \sum_k a_{k2}^B) \text{ if } \sum_j a_j^D > \sum_k a_{k2}^B \text{ and } \sum_j a_j^D \leq \sum_s a_{s2}^B \end{array} \right\} \tag{6.13}$$

If goods of type *a* do not get sold, they are valued at the exogenously specified price $\overline{p}_a$ at which traders of type *B* can sell goods of type *a* outside the market of traders. Again this implies a requirement for unsold goods to be transported to the external market. Also here this assumption is made for reasons of symmetry with other goods and traders.

Traders of type *D* are buyers in both rounds of transactions. At the end of the game total wealth for trader *i* of type *D* looks as follows (*i*=1...*N*):

$$p^a a_i^D + (pc_i^D - c_{i2}^D)\overline{p}_c + (d_0 - d_i^D)\overline{p}_d. \tag{6.14}$$

At stage 1b) trader *i* of type *D* decides how much of her goods to exchange at the offered prices against goods of type *c* in the smart random matching processes. In one random matching process she chooses a total amount d_i^D of goods from her endowment to be exchanged against a total amount c_i^D of good *c* at an average price of $\dddot{p}_{di}^D / \dddot{p}_{ci}^D$ for which the prices of individual deals accepted get weighted by the quantities of her goods exchanged. In this same matching process she has to obey the restrictions at stage 1b) that she cannot offer more than her endowment and less than the minimum amount required $d_{\min}^D$. Note that this total quantity and average price result from all the decisions taken by the trader in a matching process as will be analyzed in detail in the appendix to this chapter. If goods do not get sold, they are valued at the exogenously specified price $\overline{p}_d$ at which traders of type *D* could sell goods of type *d* in the external market.

$$d_{\min}^D \leq d_i^D \leq d_0, \tag{6.15}$$

$$c_i^D = (\dddot{p}_{di}^D / \dddot{p}_{ci}^D) d_i^D. \tag{6.16}$$

At stage 2b) depending upon prior play trader i of type D decides in smart random matching processes how much to exchange of her goods of type c acquired in the first round of exchange against goods of type a offered in the matching processes. In one random matching process she chooses a total quantity c_{i2}^D of goods of type c acquired in the first round of exchange to be exchanged against a total amount a_i^D of goods a at an average price of $\ddot{p}_{ci}^D / \ddot{p}_{ai}^D$ for which the prices of individual deals accepted get weighted by the quantities of her goods exchanged. In this same matching process she has to obey the restrictions at stage 2b) that she cannot offer more than the goods of type c acquired in 1b) reduced by the loss due to the trading friction:

$$0 \leq c_{i2}^D \leq c_i^D \rho, \qquad 6.17$$

$$a_i^D = (\ddot{p}_{ci}^D / \ddot{p}_{ai}^D) c_{i2}^D. \qquad 6.18$$

Again, if goods do not get sold, they are valued at the exogenously specified price $\overline{p}_c$ at which traders of type D could sell goods of type c in the external market. The resale decision is not explicitly modeled but resale always increases wealth in the model.

For all traders it holds that minimum amounts to be exchanged in the first round of trading have to be large enough to ensure a sufficiently large trading volume on any path in the game. In particular, the trading volume must be large enough such that the impact which traders in the first round of trading can have on the equilibrium price in the second round of trading goes towards zero as N approaches infinity. Minimum amounts have to be consistent with each other in the sense that if all suppliers offer minimum amounts at maximum prices, buyers have to be able to purchase these amounts by offering their minimum amounts. This implies that the following conditions must hold:

$$b_{\min}^B = a_{\min}^A \tilde{p}_a / \overline{p}_b, \qquad 6.19$$

$$d_{\min}^D = c_{\min}^C \tilde{p}_c / \overline{p}_d. \qquad 6.20$$

It is assumed that these conditions can be fulfilled such that minimum quantities are greater than zero but less than one. It is further assumed that minimum quantities to be traded have the following properties ensuring that equilibrium prices do not hit the price constraints as is shown in the appendix to this chapter at stage 2a):

$$b_{\min}^B \overline{p}_b \geq \overline{p}_c, \qquad 6.21$$

$$d_{\min}^D \overline{p}_d \geq \overline{p}_a. \qquad 6.22$$

As a final technical assumption discrete quantities for goods are introduced. Hence both quantities and prices in the model are discrete. This feature allows to apply sequential equilibrium which will be used as an equilibrium concept in the next section such that all beliefs off the equilibrium part can be restricted. For continuous strategies substantial technical difficulties arise such that sequential equilibrium is usually applied only in the case of discrete strategies (see e.g., Fudenberg and Tirole, 1991, p. 345). However, several problems result from the introduction of discrete prices and quantities. As will be seen in the next section, equilibrium prices in the second round of trading are derived from the total quantities of goods traded in the first round. The scales for prices and quantities need not be compatible, however. To avoid these problems it is assumed that just like for prices the size of the discrete quantity steps goes towards zero as N goes towards infinity. Because the analysis focuses on this case, in the limit the problem of the incompatibility of price scales and quantity scales "disappears". Hence for specifying expectations in sequential equilibrium the model is analyzed from the point of view of discrete strategies. For analyzing prices and quantities the model is analyzed as if strategies became continuous in the limiting case of N going towards infinity. A more refined mathematical analysis of these technical problems is not undertaken at this point.

6.2 The equilibrium in the barter model with intermediate exchange

In Proposition 1 a symmetric sequential equilibrium in the barter model with intermediate exchange of goods is described. The concept of sequential equilibrium is used because in extensive form the simultaneous move game between sellers in a random matching model becomes a game of imperfect information such that an equilibrium concept with expectation formation is required that restricts beliefs everywhere in the game.

Proposition 1: For a mild trading friction (i.e., for ρ sufficiently high such that $\rho \geq (\overline{p}_b / p^c)$) a symmetric sequential equilibrium with high trading volume exists in which sellers offer all their goods on the equilibrium path and buyers accept any of these offers at prices such that any (N-1) sellers in a market can satisfy the demand of buyers.

Proof: See appendix to chapter 6.

The goal of the analysis here is not to analyze all possible cases in the barter scenario. The main purpose is to take barter with intermediate exchange of goods as a theoretical benchmark against which other transaction technologies can be compared. For this purpose the analysis focuses on a scenario with a mild trading friction and a high trading volume. The basic idea to choose a barter scenario where trade does not get hampered too much had already guided the choice of the trading setup with just one round of intermediate exchange although many more rounds are theoretically possible. If other transaction technologies are superior to barter even in cases where barter is relatively efficient, this clearly shows that barter is dominated by these other transaction technologies.

Also other equilibria exist in the model in which the existence of the trading friction reduces trading volume even more. Consider as a simple example the case of an extreme friction where $\rho = 0$. In this case buyers in the first round of exchange acquire only the minimum amount of goods required. No trade takes place in the second round. More generally speaking, the lower ρ, the more trading volume tends to shrink. Hence cases with low values of ρ in relation to resale prices drastically show how frictions can hamper trade.

The equilibrium referred to in Proposition 1 is described in more detail in the following paragraphs. Because a symmetric equilibrium is considered, it suffices to describe the equilibrium strategy for one representative trader of each type. The following strategies and expectations of players form a sequential equilibrium in the barter model with intermediate exchange:

- Trader *i* of type *A* chooses $a_i^{A*} = a_0 + \varepsilon^A$ and $p_{ai}^{A*} / p_{bi}^{A*} = 1$, expecting to be at the point in her information set where other traders of type *A* before her have made the same choices as her own equilibrium choice at stage 1a) of the game.
- Trader *i* of type *C* chooses $c_i^{C*} = c_0 + \varepsilon^C$ and $p_{ci}^{C*} / p_{di}^{C*} = 1$, expecting to be at the point in her information set where other traders of type *C* before her have made the same choices as her own equilibrium choice and traders of type *A* have chosen their equilibrium strategy at stage 1a) of the game.
- Trader *i* of type *B* chooses the maximum possible amount of goods offered at her information sets at stage 1b) if the following condition is satisfied: $\rho > (\overline{p}_b / p^c)(p_{ai}^{BT} / p_{bi}^{BT})(p_{ci}^{BT} / p_{ai}^{BT})\Sigma a_j^{BT} / (\Sigma a_j^{BT} - a_{\max}^{BT})$ (see the exact meaning of variables and the derivation in the appendix). Otherwise she chooses the minimum amount possible. At stage 2a) player *i* of type *B* optimally chooses $a_{i2}^{B*} = a_i^{BT} \rho$ and $p_{ai}^{BT*} / p_{ci}^{BT*} = \Sigma c_n^{DT} / ((\Sigma a_j^{BT}) - a_{\max}^{BT})$ in any of the matching subgames starting at the beginning of stage 2a) where for one specific subgame considered the variables denoted by superindex *T* have all been determined in previous play leading to the subgame. In any of the subgames starting at the beginning of stage 2a) trader *i* of type *B* expects other traders of her own type deciding before her to choose the same equilibrium decisions as her own.
- Trader *i* of type *D* chooses the maximum amount possible of good *c* at any of her information sets at stage 1b) if $\rho \geq (\overline{p}_d / p^a)(p_{ai}^{DT} / p_{ci}^{DT})(p_{ci}^{DT} / p_{di}^{DT})$ (see the appendix to this chapter for an exact definition of the variables). If this condition is not fulfilled the trader optimally chooses the minimum amount possible of good *d* to be traded. Trader *i* of type *D* optimally chooses the maximum amount possible of good *a* at any of her information sets at stage 2b).

The equilibrium path of the game is as follows:

- Each trader of type A optimally chooses $a_i^{AT*} = a_0 + \varepsilon^A$, $p_{ai}^{AT*} / p_{bi}^{AT*} = 1$.
- Each trader of type B optimally chooses $b_i^{BT*} = b_0$, $a_{i2}^{B*} = a_0 \rho$, and the price $p_{ai}^{BT*} / p_{ci}^{BT*} = N/(N-1)$.
- Each trader of type C optimally chooses $c_i^{CT*} = c_0 + \varepsilon^C$, $p_{ci}^{CT*} / p_{di}^{CT*} = 1$.
- Each trader of type D optimally chooses $d_i^{DT*} = d_0$, $c_{i2}^{DT*} = c_0 \rho$.

On the equilibrium path for $N \to \infty$ total wealth equals p^b for a trader of type A and p^d for a trader of type C. It equals ρp^c for a trader of type B and ρp^a for a trader of type D.

The economic logic behind the equilibrium follows from the basic incentive to trade due to the differences of traders in endowments and reselling opportunities. The market environment of the shopper's paradise model, the trading friction, and the transaction technology determine how these basic incentives to trade are translated into specific economic interactions between traders.

Traders of type A maximize their expected wealth in the first round by offering all their endowments in exchange for goods of type b which they can resell at a high price. At the equilibrium price buyers of type B can buy only one unit of good a whereas sellers offer one unit plus ε^A. Hence ε^A is the excess supply of each trader of type A in equilibrium. Because total supply of traders of type A exceeds total demand of traders of type B in equilibrium and because all sellers offer the same price each seller gets matched with a share of $1/N$ of total demand. According to the smart random matching procedure this means that each trader of type A gets matched with one trader of type B. The trader of type B exchanges all her endowment whereas the trader of type A exchanges one unit of her endowment and keeps ε^A. Hence a bilateral structure of trades emerges on the equilibrium path where each trader meets with only one other trading partner.

The size of ε^A is such that N-1 traders of type A can satisfy the equilibrium demands of traders of type B. This excess supply has an important strategic role in equilibrium. If such excess supply did not exist and all other traders sold all their goods, a trader would realize that given the equilibrium strategies of the other players she is virtually alone in the market with one buyer. This buyer is ready to accept any offer up to a certain level. Hence the seller would have an incentive to deviate from the equilibrium and charge this higher price. This reasoning shows that a situation where supply gets fully exhausted could not be an equilibrium. Because of the excess supply in the market a seller will never have an incentive to offer her goods at a price higher than the equilibrium price because this would imply that the N buyers satisfy their demand by getting matched with the N-1 other sellers. The seller would just keep her endowment and miss the opportunity to acquire goods of type b which she could resell at a high price. Note that the excess supply per seller necessary in equilibrium to deter the exploitation of market power goes towards zero as the number of traders approaches infinity.

Bidding a lower price than the equilibrium price means that the buyer can increase the quantity of goods sold because her offer is the best offer in the market and the entire quantity offered gets matched with buyers. However, the price to be achieved is lower and the question arises whether the positive quantity effect prevails over the negative price effect. Note that if ε^A is small the quantity effect will also be small. Still, in principle the seller could always bid an infinitely smaller price than the other traders such that the quantity effect would dominate the price effect. Such infinite undercutting in infinitely small steps of prices is ruled out in the model by the assumption of discrete steps for price bids. If the difference between the discrete prices is large enough relative to ε^A undercutting will not be profitable any more because the negative price effect will dominate the positive quantity effect of undercutting other sellers. The size of σ^A ensures that this is the case. If neither undercutting the equilibrium price nor bidding a price higher than the equilibrium price is optimal, offering goods at the equilibrium price is best and hence indeed the strategy in Proposition 1 is an equilibrium strategy for traders of type *A* in the first round as is also shown formally in the appendix to this chapter. Again the step size of the discrete values for prices goes towards zero as *N* goes towards infinity. The same decision logic as for a trader of type *A* also holds true for a seller of type *C*.

In the first round of transactions traders of types *B* and *D* have an incentive to exchange all their endowments on the equilibrium path. The prices charged by sellers make it attractive for the buyers to enter into intermediate exchange of goods such that they finally obtain those goods which they can resell at a profit. Off the equilibrium path players are confronted with different prices that make an offer acceptable only if the terms are sufficiently attractive. When considering the appeal of an offer a trader anticipates that at stage 2a) she will resell the good at a sufficiently attractive price. She also anticipates that traders of type *D* will accept this offer except for some small strategic oversupply which has the same key role of disciplining traders as on the equilibrium path. If accepting an offer at stage 1b) leads to a lower total wealth than just keeping her endowment and selling it externally, the trader will buy as little as possible.

In the second round of exchange in the market of traders agents of type *B* are sellers whereas traders of type *D* are buyers. Hence their strategic opportunities and incentives differ. The economic logic behind their interactions is determined by the shopper's paradise model in a similar way as in the shopper's paradise model in the first round of trades. One key difference on the equilibrium path is that in the second round both buyers and sellers have the same quantity of goods to be traded whereas in the first round sellers had slightly more goods than buyers. Because excess supply of sellers is still necessary for strategic reasons to deter the exploitation of market power in bilateral exchange, the price must be such that some excess supply exists. Hence in equilibrium the goods of type *a* and *c* cannot be exchanged one for one but the price for goods of type *a* has to be slightly higher than the price for goods of type *c* such that any *N*-1 traders of type *B* can satisfy market demand at this price. Again sellers neither have an incentive to charge higher prices because this would exclude them from exchange nor do they want to offer a lower price because the negative price effect outweighs the positive quantity effect due to discrete price steps. Finally, at the equilibrium prices offered by traders of type *B* in the second round of transactions buyers of type *D* have again an incentive to trade all their goods acquired in the first round.

Also off the equilibrium path at stage 2a) the price has to take over the role of creating some small excess supply to keep any trader from gaining market power. Because off the equilibrium path traders are heterogeneous, owning different amounts of goods to be exchanged, the excess supply must be high enough to cover even the amount of good *a* owned by the biggest trader of type *B* in the market.

6.3 Conclusions from the barter model with intermediate exchange

The model of barter with intermediate exchange presented in this chapter allows to analyze explicitly the role of a basic transaction technology in a fully specified strategic market framework mimicking price-taking behavior of agents. A benchmark solution for a barter economy without money or finance could be derived. Other, potentially more efficient solutions obtained in the following chapters from other transaction technologies can be compared against this benchmark.

In the context of the following chapters it is interesting to see how barter with intermediate exchange addresses key issues that typically arise in the context of exchange and will reappear also in later models. A clear profile of the strengths and weaknesses of barter with intermediate exchange emerges.

- Because all transactions in the barter model with intermediate exchange are spot transactions a trader giving away her good can be sure to receive other goods in return. Problems of trust in the ability of a trading partner to repay do not arise.
- Intermediate exchange of goods is burdensome. For some goods the cost of intermediate exchange may become prohibitively high such that no exchange takes place at all. Also intermediate exchange requires a good to be storable. For instance services cannot be exchanged at all. Hence the problem of a lack of double coincidence of needs and wants does not get addressed in an efficient manner. A transaction technology which does not require intermediate exchange could save the cost of intermediate exchange and enable more trade.
- Intermediate exchange of goods uses potentially productive resources as a rudimentary medium of exchange. Transaction technologies not requiring to leave productive resources idle can avoid this problem. In a way this aspect of

intermediate exchange can also be seen as a cost of lack of trust. By exchanging her good against the good of the transaction partner on the spot a trader can avoid issues of trust to arise. But thereby she also forgoes the benefit of keeping the goods and earning additional returns before selling them to the other traders who actually want to acquire them.

- The problem of a lack of double coincidence of needs and wants does not get addressed by intermediate exchange of goods.

In more general cases with more types of goods and traders as well as heterogeneous preferences, endowments, and transactions costs the problem of a lack of double coincidence of needs and wants can become much more difficult to solve through intermediate exchange of goods. Hence the current scenario shows a situation in which intermediate exchange of goods is a relatively efficient way of conducting transactions. If other transaction technologies are still more efficient, the inferiority of barter is clearly shown.

In the context of the literature on money and barter it is key for the results of the model in this chapter that symmetric losses due to barter were assumed. If some goods yielded lower losses than others, those would be candidates for becoming a medium of exchange. Some monetary theories focus on such asymmetric losses to derive money endogenously as a medium of exchange. This line of reasoning is not pursued further in this monograph because the focus here is on financial solutions to transaction problems. The underlying presumption is that financial solutions are always more efficient than barter solutions. For example, even if one assumes in the model with symmetric losses that the loss due to intermediate exchange is very small such that any good in the economy could be used as medium of exchange (i.e., if ρ is close to one), still it will be shown in later chapters that financial solutions lead to better outcomes for traders.

Appendix to Chapter 6: Proof of Proposition 1

In the sequential equilibrium considered in Proposition 1 beliefs are derived which are consistent with the strategies of players. Because a symmetric equilibrium in pure strategies is considered in a game which is a simultaneous move game represented in extensive form, agents expect other traders deciding "before" them to choose the same equilibrium strategies as their own equilibrium strategies. This result can also be obtained by considering a sequence of completely mixed strategies which approach the equilibrium strategies in the limit such that beliefs consistent with strategies can be derived everywhere in the game by applying Bayes' rule. Given this system of beliefs the sequential rationality of the strategies of players is analyzed in the following paragraphs. Note that any indices in summation signs run from 1 to N in the derivations below (for example, index k for a good of type y in Σy_k).

At stage 2b) any of her information sets trader i of type D at has knowledge about variables which have been determined in prior play and she anticipates future optimal play. Without loss of generality consider one specific information set. Variables from prior play determined on the path to this information set, the variable(s) about which a decision has to be made at the information set, and anticipated optimal future variables on the path following the information set are all defined as in section 6.1 but are marked with superindex T. Hence at a specific information set the trader knows d_i^{DT}, c_i^{DT} and the price $p_{ci}^{DT} / p_{ai}^{DT}$ offered to her in the matching procedure. Consider the decision of a player at the very bottom of the tree where she is the last trader in the matching process who gets offered some deal. The price of this last sale is known with certainty. The decision problem of trader i of type D at the very bottom of a matching process looks as follows:

$$\begin{aligned}&\max\ c_{i2}^{DT}(p^a p_{ci}^{DT} / p_{ai}^{DT} - \overline{p}_c) + \rho c_i^{DT}\overline{p}_c + (d_0 - d_i^{DT})\overline{p}_d + c_{i2}^{DT\leftarrow}(p^a p_{ci}^{DT\leftarrow} / p_{ai}^{DT\leftarrow} - \overline{p}_c)\\ &\text{s.t. } 0 \le c_{i2}^{DT} \le \min[c_i^{DT}\rho - c_{i2}^{DT\leftarrow}, c_u^{BT}].\end{aligned} \qquad \text{A 6.1}$$

The coefficient on the decision variable c_{i2}^{DT} is a constant.[11] Hence the sign of the coefficient determines the optimal choice. If $p_{ci}^{DT} / p_{ai}^{DT} \ge \overline{p}_c / p^a$ the trader finds it optimal to exchange the maximum amount possible which is $\min[c_i^{DT}\rho - c_{i2}^{DT\leftarrow}, c_u^{BT}]$. This condition always holds because $p_{ci}^{DT} / p_{ai}^{DT} \ge \overline{p}_c / \tilde{p}_a$ according to the restriction on prices to be offered. Because $p^a > \tilde{p}_a$ it holds that $p_{ci}^{DT} / p_{ai}^{DT} \ge \overline{p}_c / p^a$. Note that $c_{i2}^{DT\leftarrow}$ is the total amount of good c which the trader has already exchanged at prior information sets in the matching procedure. The average price (weighted by the quantities of her goods exchanged) of those trades is $p_{ci}^{DT\leftarrow} / p_{ai}^{DT\leftarrow}$. The variable c_u^{BT} is the maximum quantity which the trader of type B who has been matched with the trader of type D would be willing to exchange at the offered price.

At decision sets which are reached before the end of the matching process trader i of type D has to solve a dynamic strategic decision problem. Anticipating future optimal play she must decide how much of an offer to accept now or whether to keep some of her funds to exchange them in future trades. The logic of the smart random matching process at a specific information set at which the agent has to decide is key in this context. Any future offer in a matching process is made at the same price or at a more unfavorable price from the perspective of the buyer and any future quantity offered will be equal to or less than the quantity offered now. Hence the trader will accept any deal offered to the fullest extent possible if the optimality condition is fulfilled and otherwise will acquire the minimum amount required.

To show this argument more formally, suppose that an agent finds it statically optimal to choose a quantity c_{i2}^{DT*} at some information set prior to the end of the matching procedure (i.e., ignoring the impact of the decision on future play). Consider the impact on expected total wealth of reducing this quantity by Δ_i^D and leaving it for trading at future information sets. Original expected total wealth is bigger than expected total wealth with more Δ_i^D to be traded in the future if

$$\begin{aligned}&(c_{i2}^{DT*})(p^a p_{ci}^{DT} / p_{ai}^{DT} - \overline{p}_c) + \pi_i^{1D} c_{i2}^{1DT*}(p^a p_{ci}^{1DT} / p_{ai}^{1DT} - \overline{p}_c) + \\ &+ \pi_i^{2D} c_{i2}^{2DT*}(p^a p_{ci}^{2DT} / p_{ai}^{2DT} - \overline{p}_c) + \ldots \geq (c_{i2}^{DT*} - \Delta_i^D)(p^a p_{ci}^{DT} / p_{ai}^{DT} - \overline{p}_c) + \\ &+ \pi_i^{1D} c_{i2\Delta}^{1DT}(p^a p_{ci}^{1DT} / p_{ai}^{1DT} - \overline{p}_c) + \pi_i^{2D} c_{i2\Delta}^{2DT}(p^a p_{ci}^{2DT} / p_{ai}^{2DT} - \overline{p}_c) + \ldots\end{aligned} \qquad \text{A 6.2}$$

where π_i^{1D} is the probability of reaching price $p_{ci}^{1DT} / p_{ai}^{1DT}$, π_i^{2D} is the probability of reaching price $p_{ci}^{2DT} / p_{ai}^{2DT}$ etc. and c_{i2}^{1DT*} is the quantity of good c optimally chosen at price $p_{ci}^{1DT} / p_{ai}^{1DT}$, c_{i2}^{2DT*} is the quantity of good c optimally chosen at price $p_{ci}^{2DT} / p_{ai}^{2DT}$ when Δ_i^D has not been subtracted from c_{i2}^{DT*} etc. These quantities are obtained from backwards induction. Furthermore, $c_{i2\Delta}^{1DT}$ is the quantity of good c optimally chosen at price $p_{ci}^{1DT} / p_{ai}^{1DT}$, $c_{i2\Delta}^{2DT}$ is the quantity of good c optimally chosen at price $p_{ci}^{2DT} / p_{ai}^{2DT}$ when Δ_i^D has been subtracted from c_{i2}^{DT*} etc. Again the quantities are obtained from backwards induction. Note that due to the linearity of decision rules any state which is reached when Δ_i^D has not been subtracted is also reached when Δ_i^D has been subtracted but the reverse need not be true because the upper boundary on the quantity to be exchanged is tighter in the first case than in the second case. Rearranging terms yields

$$\begin{aligned}&\pi_i^{1D} c_{i2}^{1DT*}(p^a p_{ci}^{1DT} / p_{ai}^{1DT} - \overline{p}_c) + \pi_i^{2D} c_{i2}^{2DT*}(p^a p_{ci}^{2DT} / p_{ai}^{2DT} - \overline{p}_c) + \ldots \\ &\geq -\Delta_i^D(p^a p_{ci}^{DT} / p_{ai}^{DT} - \overline{p}_c) + \pi_i^{1D}(c_{i2}^{1DT*} + \Delta_i^{1D})(p^a p_{ci}^{1DT} / p_{ai}^{1DT} - \overline{p}_c) + \\ &+ \pi_i^{2D}(c_{i2}^{2DT*} + \Delta_i^{2D})(p^a p_{ci}^{2DT} / p_{ai}^{2DT} - \overline{p}_c) + \ldots\end{aligned} \qquad \text{A 6.3}$$

Δ_i^{1D} is the amount by which an agent chooses a different amount than the formerly optimal amount in state one, where again superindices refer to states. Subtracting yields

$$\Delta_i^D(p^a p_{ci}^{DT} / p_{ai}^{DT} - \overline{p}_c) \geq \pi_i^{1D}\Delta_i^{1D}(p^a p_{ci}^{1DT} / p_{ai}^{1DT} - \overline{p}_c) + \pi_i^{2D}\Delta_i^{2D}(p^a p_{ci}^{2DT} / p_{ai}^{2DT} - \overline{p}_c) + \ldots \qquad \text{A 6.4}$$

It must hold that the sum of all probabilities is less than or equal to one as in general agents cannot be sure to receive another offer. Because the sum of $\Delta_i^{1D} + \Delta_i^{1D} + \ldots \leq \Delta_i^D$ as an agent cannot be sure whether she will indeed be able to trade all the additional quantity shifted into the future, it must hold that $\Delta_i^D \geq \pi_i^{1D}\Delta_i^{1D} + \pi_i^{2D}\Delta_i^{2D} + \ldots$. Further note that the weighted sum of future prices also cannot be larger than the current price due to the smart random matching process starting with the most favorable price for the buyer. Hence the above inequality must be fulfilled and shifting any quantity that could be favorably traded today into the future reduces total expected wealth. The best deal the trader can get is the one currently offered at the information set at which the trader has to decide. Hence the solution to the static decision problem at the information set ignoring future trading options is also part of the backwards induction solution of the dynamic problem. This implies that the optimal decision at a particular information set can simply be found as the solution to the static problem at this information set. Hence the optimal solution for the decision problem at information sets prior to the end of the matching process can be found in the same way as for an information set at the end of the matching process. The only differences are the price offered and the maximum quantity to be exchanged. Therefore the same condition $p_{ci}^{DT} / p_{ai}^{DT} \geq \overline{p}_c / p^a$ which determines play at the end of the matching process also determines in the same way decisions taken during the matching process. It is also fulfilled under the price restrictions in the model as before.

At stage 2a) player i of type B decides about trade, knowing from prior play the aggregate quantities of good a, Σa_j^{BT}, and good c, Σc_f^{DT}, to be traded after exchange at stage one. In each of the subgames starting at the beginning of stage 2a) player i of type B has exactly one information set. Consider one specific information set in one specific subgame and denote the variables pertaining to it with superindex T (i.e., variables determined or consistently expected on the path leading to the information set as well as variables determined at the information set and anticipated future optimal variables). Trader i of type B expects other traders of her own type choosing before her to have taken the same decision as her equilibrium decision The trader has to decide what quantity a_{i2}^{BT} of good a she is going to offer at what price $p_{ai}^{BT} / p_{ci}^{BT}$. She anticipates that any offer within the admissible price range will be accepted by traders of type D. Agents interact in the market of traders according to the following strategic logic:

(i) *Wealth of trader i of type B from playing the equilibrium strategy*: W_i^{BT*}. The trader anticipates that she will be able to actually sell in the matching process

$$a_i^{BST*} = [(a_i^{BT} / \Sigma a_j^{BT}) \rho (\Sigma c_f^{DT} p_{ci}^{BT*} / p_{ai}^{BT*})] \qquad \text{A 6.4}$$

which can be further simplified by inserting for the equilibrium price to

$$a_i^{BST*} = a_i^{BT} \rho [1 - a_{\max}^{BT} / \Sigma a_j^{BT}]. \qquad \text{A 6.5}$$

The variable $a_{\max}^{BT}$ is the biggest amount of good a offered by a trader of type B on the game path considered (i.e., on the consistenly expected path before the player or on the optimally anticipated path after the player). Using this expression for the quantity actually sold a_i^{BST*} to derive total expected wealth yields

$$a_i^{BT} [1 - a_{\max}^{BT} / \Sigma a_j^{BT}][p^c p_{ai}^{BT*} / p_{ci}^{BT*} - \overline{p}_a] + \rho a_i^{BT} \overline{p}_a + (b_0 - b_i^{BT}) \overline{p}_b. \qquad \text{A 6.6}$$

Inserting for the equilibrium price and simplifying finally yields a level of wealth for trader i of type B which is equal to

$$W_i^{BT*} = a_i^{BT} \rho [(p^c \Sigma c_f^{DT} + a_{\max}^{BT} \overline{p}_a) / \Sigma a_j^{BT}] + (b_0 - b_i^{BT}) \overline{p}_b. \qquad \text{A 6.7}$$

Note that bidding a lower quantity than the equilibrium quantity at the equilibrium price would reduce total expected wealth and therefore cannot be optimal.

(ii) *Wealth of trader i of type B from charging a higher price than the equilibrium price in the second round of exchange*: W_{iH}^{BT}. In this case trader i of type B places the most expensive offer. Because the other traders of type B can satisfy the total demand of traders of type D for goods of type a in the second round of trades even if trader i of type B offers the biggest quantity of all traders of her type, the matching procedure does not match trader i of type B with a trader of type D. Hence a_i^{BST} equals zero. Total wealth of trader i of type B in this second case is therefore $W_{iH}^{BT} = \rho a_i^{BT} \overline{p}_a + (b_0 - b_i^{BT}) \overline{p}_b$. It holds that $W_i^{BT*} > W_{iH}^{BT}$ if $p^c \Sigma c_f^{DT} + a_{\max}^{BT} p_a \geq \Sigma a_i^{BT} p_a$. This condition can be further simplified to obtain the inequality $p^c / \overline{p}_a \geq p_{ci}^{BT*} / p_{ai}^{BT*}$. It is fulfilled because $p^c / \overline{p}_a > \tilde{p}_c / \overline{p}_a \geq p_{ci}^{BT} / p_{ai}^{BT}$.

(iii) *Wealth of trader i of type B from charging a price lower than the equilibrium price in the second round of exchange*: W_{iL}^{BT}. Consider the case in which trader i of type B offers all her goods of type a at a price of $p_{ai}^{BT} / p_{ci}^{BT} - \sigma_i^{BT}$ where σ_i^{BT} is the minimum discrete price step on the path considered which is necessary for the equilibrium to obtain. As in this case she offers the lowest price in the market in the second round of exchange, her total quantity offered gets matched with traders of type *D*. Hence a_i^{BST} equals $a_i^{BT}\rho$. As a consequence total wealth for trader *i* of type *B* in this case can be expressed as follows:

$$W_{iL}^{BT} = \rho a_i^{BT} p^c [\Sigma c_f^{DT} /(-a_{\max}^{BT} + \Sigma a_j^{BT}) - \sigma_i^{BT}] + (b_0 - b_i^{BT})\overline{p}_b . \quad \text{A 6.9}$$

For $W_{iL}^{BT} < W_i^{BT*}$ to hold the following condition on the minimum size of bidding steps for prices must be fulfilled: $\sigma_i^{BT} > (p_{ai}^{BT*} / p_{ci}^{BT*} - p_a / p^c)(a_{\max}^{BT} / \Sigma a_j^{BT})$. The step size σ^B referred to in the chapter is the maximum over the σ_i^{BT} at all information sets at stage 2a). Note that $p_{ai}^{BT*} / p_{ci}^{BT*} - \overline{p}_a / p^c$ is positive. The minimum step size goes towards zero because $(a_{\max}^{BT} / \Sigma a_j^{BT})$ goes towards zero as *N* goes towards infinity: $\sigma^B \to 0$ as $N \to \infty$. If σ^B is set at a value as derived above then indeed it holds that $W_{iL}^{BT} < W_i^{BT*}$ and charging a lower price than the equilibrium price cannot be optimal. Offering a lower quantity at a lower price than the equilibrium price would further reduce any advantageous quantity effect for a trader and is not optimal either.

Finally, it is shown that under the assumptions made equilibrium prices do not hit the price constraints. Consider first one polar case where traders of type *D* have exchanged minimum amounts of their endowment at maximum unfavorable prices at stage 1b) and where traders of type *B* have acquired the maximum amount possible. The equilibrium price $p_{ai}^{BT*} / p_{ci}^{BT*}$ in this case is greater than the lower boundary for prices if the inequality holds that $[\rho N d_{\min}^D \overline{p}_d / \tilde{p}_c]/[\rho(N-1)] \geq \overline{p}_a / \tilde{p}_c$. For *N* going towards infinity this condition reduces to the assumption about minimum quantities to be traded at the end of section 6.1, $d_{\min}^D \overline{p}_d \geq \overline{p}_a$. Similarly, if traders of type *B* have exchanged minimum amounts of their endowment at maximum unfavorable prices at stage 1b) and where traders of type *D* have acquired the maximum amount possible. The equilibrium price $p_{ai}^{BT*} / p_{ci}^{BT*}$ in this case is below the upper boundary for prices if it holds that the following condition is fulfilled: $\rho N /[\rho(N b_{\min}^B \overline{p}_b / \tilde{p}_a - \tilde{p}_b / \overline{p}_a)] \leq \tilde{p}_a / \overline{p}_c$. For *N* going towards infinity this condition reduces to the assumption about minimum quantities at the end of section 6.1, $b_{\min}^B \overline{p}_b \geq \overline{p}_c$.

At stage 1b) trader *i* of type *D* at any of her information sets has knowledge about variables which have been determined in prior play. Hence at a specific information set she knows $\sum a_j^{BT}$ from prior play and she knows the price $p_{di}^{DT} / p_{ci}^{DT}$ offered to her in a match. She anticipates that by acquiring some quantity of good *c* now she will take part in a matching process in the second round of transactions where traders of type *B* all bid the same equilibrium price at which all traders of type *D* can profitably exchange their goods of type *c* to acquire goods of type *a* for reselling. Just as at stage 2b) also here an argument can be made that because of the logic of the smart random matching process a trader of type *D* always finds it optimal to acquire as much as possible if she gets an offer which increases her expected total wealth and she never finds it optimal to delay the acquisition of some minimum amount required because future offers are never more favorable for the buyer. Hence at any information set at stage 1b) trader *i* of type *D* solves a simple static optimization problem whose solution is also part of the dynamic strategic solution:

$$\begin{aligned} &\max\ d_i^{DT}[p^a(p_{ci}^{DT} / p_{ai}^{DT})(p_{di}^{DT} / p_{ci}^{DT})\rho - \overline{p}_d] + \\ &\quad + d_i^{DT\leftarrow}[p^a(p_{ci}^{DT} / p_{ai}^{DT})(p_{di}^{DT\leftarrow} / p_{ci}^{DT\leftarrow})\rho - \overline{p}_d] + d_0\overline{p} \qquad \text{A 6.10} \\ &\text{s.t. } \max[0, \min[d_{\min}^D - d_i^{DT\leftarrow}, d_j^{BT}]] \leq d_i^{DT} \leq \min[d_0 - d_i^{DT\leftarrow}, d_j^{BT}]. \end{aligned}$$

The variable d_j^{BT} is the amount of good *d* that the matching partner of type *B* offers to buy at the price she bids. Again the sign of the coefficient on the decision variable d_i^{DT} is key.[12] It is greater than zero if $\rho \geq (\overline{p}_d / p^a)(p_{ai}^{DT} / p_{ci}^{DT})(p_{ci}^{DT} / p_{di}^{DT})$. If the sign is positive the agent chooses the maximum amount possible at the information set, if it is negative she chooses the minimum amount possible. Using this inequality and inserting for the equilibrium price yields the condition $\rho \geq (\overline{p}_d / p^a)(N/(N-1))$ which is the same as in Proposition 1 for N going towards infinity. Note that $d_i^{DT\leftarrow}$ is the total amount of good d already chosen by trader i of type B earlier in the matching procedure and $p_{di}^{DT\leftarrow} / p_{ci}^{DT\leftarrow}$ is the corresponding average price weighted by the quantities of her goods exchanged. In the objective function above also $p_{ci}^{DT} / p_{ai}^{DT}$ depends upon d_i^{DT}. The impact is weak, however, and goes towards zero as N goes towards infinity. Hence this impact is ignored in the analysis.

At stage 1b) trader i of type B at any of her information sets has knowledge about variables which have been determined in prior play. Hence at a specific information set she knows the price of the deal offered to her $p_{bi}^{BT} / p_{ai}^{BT}$ from prior play leading to the information set. She anticipates that by acquiring some quantity of good c now she will take part in a matching process in the second round of transactions where traders of type B all bid the same equilibrium price at which all traders of type D can profitably exchange their goods of type c to acquire goods of type a for reselling. Just as at stage 2b) also here an argument can be made that because of the logic of the smart random matching process a trader of type B always finds it optimal to acquire as much as possible if she gets an offer which increases her expected total wealth and she also never finds it optimal to delay the acquisition of some required amount under the minimum trading regime because future offers are less favorable for the buyer. Hence at any information set at stage 1b) trader i of type B solves a simple static optimization problem whose solution is part of the solution to the dynamic strategic decision problem she faces:

$$\begin{aligned} \max\ & b_i^{BT}\{(p_{bi}^{BT} / p_{ai}^{BT})[(1-a_{\max}^{BT} / \Sigma a_j^{BT})p^c p_{ai}^{BT} / p_{ci}^{BT}] - \overline{p}_b\} + b_0 \overline{p}_b + \\ & + b_i^{BT\leftarrow}\{(p_{bi}^{BT\leftarrow} / p_{ai}^{BT\leftarrow})[(1-a_{\max}^{BT} / \Sigma a_j^{BT})p^c p_{ai}^{BT} / p_{ci}^{TB}] - \overline{p}_b\} \qquad \text{A 6.11} \\ \text{s.t. }\ & \max[0, \min[b_{\min}^{B} - b_i^{BT\leftarrow}, b_j^{AT}]] \leq b_i^{BT} \leq \min[b_0 - b_i^{BT\leftarrow}, b_j^{AT}]. \end{aligned}$$

The variable b_j^{AT} is the amount of good b that the trader of type A in the match considered offers to buy at the price she bids. Again the sign of the coefficient on the decision variable b_i^{BT} is the key determinant for the decision of the trader.[13] The sign is positive if the following condition holds:

$$\rho > (\overline{p}_b / p^c)(p_{ai}^{BT} / p_{bi}^{BT})(p_{ci}^{BT} / p_{ai}^{BT})\Sigma a_j^{BT} / (\Sigma a_j^{BT} - a_{\max}^{BT}). \qquad \text{A 6.12}$$

If the sign is positive the agent chooses the maximum amount possible at the information set, if it is negative she chooses the minimum amount possible. Note that $b_i^{BT\leftarrow}$ is the total amount of good b already chosen by trader i of type B earlier in the smart random matching process and $p_{bi}^{BT\leftarrow} / p_{ai}^{BT\leftarrow}$ is the corresponding average price weighted by the quantities of her goods exchanged. On the equilibrium path of the game this condition can be expressed as $\rho \geq \overline{p}_b / p^c$. For N going towards infinity this is the same condition as for traders of type D at stage 1b) and hence the same condition as stated in Proposition 1. Note that in the objective function above also $p_{ai}^{BT} / p_{ci}^{BT}$ depends upon b_i^{BT}. The impact is weak and goes towards zero as N goes towards infinity. Hence this impact is ignored in the analysis.

At stage 1a) for traders of type A neither bidding a higher price than the equilibrium price nor bidding a lower price than the equilibrium price yields a higher total wealth. Hence the best response of trader i of type A to the equilibrium strategies of the other traders is to play also the equilibrium strategy. At stage 1a) traders of type A anticipate that when playing their equilibrium strategies players of type B will accept the offer they receive in the matching process such that one unit of good a can be sold.

(i) *Wealth of trader i of type A from playing the equilibrium strategy:* W_i^{A*}. From $a_i^{A*} = a_0 + \varepsilon^A$, $p_{ai}^{A*} / p_{bi}^{A*} = 1$ follows that the actual quantity sold by trader i of type A after

matching a_i^{AS} equals 1 because $Na_0(a_0+\varepsilon^A)/(N(a_0+\varepsilon^A))=1$. Hence b_i^A equals 1. Inserting these equilibrium values into the objective function yields a total equilibrium wealth $W_i^{A*}=p^b+\overline{p}_a(1/(N-1))$. Clearly, exchanging a lower quantity then the equilibrium quantity of good a at the equilibrium price would lower total wealth and cannot be optimal.
(ii) *Wealth of trader i of type A from charging a higher price than the equilibrium price:* W_{iH}^A. In this case trader i of type A places the most expensive offer. Because it holds that $(N-1)(a_0+\varepsilon^A)=N$ such that the N-1 traders can satisfy the total demand of traders of type B for goods of type a the matching procedure does not match trader i of type A with a trader of type B. Hence a_i^{AS} equals zero. Total wealth of trader i of type A in this second case is therefore $W_{iH}^A=\overline{p}_a(a_0+\varepsilon^A)=\overline{p}_a(1+1/(N-1))$. Because $p^b>\overline{p}_a$ it is clear that $W_{iH}^A<W_i^{A*}$. Therefore charging a higher price than the equilibrium price is not a best response to other traders' strategies. Offering a lower quantity of good a at a price lower than the equilibrium price also leads to a wealth of W_{iH}^A and cannot be optimal either.
(iii) *Wealth of trader i of type A from charging a price lower than the equilibrium price*: W_{iL}^A. Consider the case in which trader i of type A offers all her endowment (i.e., $a_0+\varepsilon^A$) at a price of $1-\sigma^A$. As in this case she offers the lowest price in the market, her total quantity offered gets matched with traders of type B. Hence a_i^{AS} equals $a_0+\varepsilon^A$. As a consequence total wealth in this case becomes $W_{iL}^A=p^b(1-\sigma^A)(1+\varepsilon^A)$. For $W_{iL}^A<W_i^{A*}$ to hold the following condition on the minimum size of bidding steps must be fulfilled: $\sigma^A>(1-\overline{p}_a/p^b)/N$. This constraint is the same as in the optimization problem such that indeed $W_{iL}^A<W_i^{A*}$ and charging a lower price than the equilibrium price cannot be optimal. Offering a lower quantity at a lower price than the equilibrium price would further reduce the advantageous quantity effect for a trader and is not optimal either.

At stage 1a) for traders of type C neither bidding a higher price than the equilibrium price nor bidding a lower price than the equilibrium price yields a higher total wealth. The proof for the optimality of the equilibrium strategy of a trader of type C is similar to the proof for a trader of type A except for that $p_{ci}^{C*}=(N-1)/N$ rather than one. Neither bidding a higher price than the equilibrium price nor bidding a lower price than the equilibrium price yields a higher total wealth for a trader of type B than the wealth attained by playing the equilibrium strategy. At stage 1a) traders of type C anticipate that when playing their equilibrium strategies players of type D will accept any offer they receive in the matching process such that one unit of good b can be sold.
(i) *Wealth of trader i of type C from playing the equilibrium strategy*: W_i^{C*}. In this case the wealth of trader i of type C equals $W_i^{C*}=p^d+\overline{p}_c\varepsilon^C(N-1)/(N)$. Clearly, exchanging a lower quantity then the equilibrium quantity of good a at the equilibrium price would lower total wealth and cannot be optimal.
(ii) *Wealth of trader i of type C from charging a higher price than the equilibrium price*: W_{iH}^C. In this case wealth of trader i of type C equals $W_{iH}^C=\overline{p}_c(1+\varepsilon^C)(N-1)/N$ which is clearly less than W_i^{C*}. Offering a lower quantity of good a at a price lower than the equilibrium price also leads to a wealth of W_{iH}^C and cannot be optimal either.
(iii) *Wealth of trader i of type C from charging a price lower than the equilibrium price*: W_{iL}^C. Consider the case in which trader i of type C offers all her endowment (i.e., $c_0+\varepsilon^C$) at a price of $1-\sigma^C$. In this case her total wealth equals $W_{iL}^C=p^d(1-\sigma^C)(1+\varepsilon^C)$. For $W_{iL}^C<W_i^{C*}$ to hold the following condition on the minimum size of bidding steps must be fulfilled: $\sigma^C>1/N-\overline{p}_c(N-1)/(N^2p^d)$. This constraint is the same as in the optimization problem such that indeed $W_{iL}^C<W_i^{C*}$. Offering a lower quantity at a lower price than the equilibrium price would further reduce the advantageous quantity effect for a trader and is not optimal either.

7

Privately Issued I.O.U.s as a Medium of Exchange

A fundamental problem for any agent wishing to exchange her goods is to ensure that she receives value back when she abandons control over her goods. In a barter economy with intermediate exchange agents are sure to receive value in return because goods are exchanged on the spot.[14] However, as was argued in the preceding chapter, barter with intermediate exchange is costly and burdensome if there is a lack of double coincidence of needs and wants. Hence, if physical goods are not to be exchanged directly between agents for cost reasons, some other asset has to take over the role of a medium of exchange. The quality of this asset will be a prime determinant of how certain an agent can be to receive adequate value in return.

If intermediate exchange of physical goods is to be avoided, privately issued I.O.U.s can serve as a medium of exchange. In this case the buyer does not deliver a physical good on the spot. She just issues a debt note embodying a claim against a certain amount of goods to be delivered later to the owner of the note. Essentially, by accepting an I.O.U. in exchange for some good a seller extends credit payable in real goods to the buyer. This credit gets securitized in the I.O.U. Supposing that an I.O.U. as a financial asset can be stored at no cost, the seller of a good accepting an I.O.U. in exchange can avoid the loss of intermediate exchange. However, she has to find a buyer for the I.O.U. who offers goods the seller wants to acquire in exchange for the I.O.U. Hence privately issued I.O.U.s written on specific goods do not solve the problem of a lack of a double coincidence of needs and wants.

The issuer of the I.O.U. can benefit from the credit extended by the seller by generating additional returns with her endowment goods until she has to deliver them to fulfil the obligations from the I.O.U. Therefore I.O.U.s do not only help to avoid losses from intermediate exchange. By extending credit they also allow to use goods productively rather than letting them merely circulate as a means of payment.

The considerations above suggest that I.O.U.s are a more efficient way of conducting transactions than barter with intermediate exchange of goods. Sometimes they are discussed in the literature as a possible alternative to money. It should be noted, however, that in most treatments I.O.U.s as debt contracts are simply imposed on transactions ad hoc. They do not arise endogenously from the models as the solution to a contract design problem and hence lack a fundamental economic explanation. The solution to such a contract design problem also properly shows the costs of dealing with the incentive problems. These costs have to be taken into account when analyzing the attractiveness of privately issued I.O.U.s as a medium of exchange. This chapter provides a formal analysis of I.O.U.s in which contracts are optimally designed to deal with the underlying frictions and incentive costs can be derived.

If an I.O.U. is used as a medium of exchange, before the conclusion of the deal the seller of a good will check the ability and the incentives of her transaction partner issuing the I.O.U. to make sure that the I.O.U. will be honored with a sufficiently high probability. Supposing that a privately issued I.O.U. entails some risk of default, the seller's assessment will depend upon her knowledge about the uncertain prospects for delivery by the buyer. Symmetric information between the buyer and the seller ex ante, i.e. before the resolution of the uncertainty about the buyer's ability to deliver will help to agree on a common basic assessment of the economic viability of a deal. But the key issue remains whether the debtor will have incentives to deliver whenever she can. This ability of the issuer to deliver can change over time if she is exposed to random shocks. If ex post asymmetric information exists about the realization of a random factor affecting the ability to deliver, the issuer of the I.O.U. might exploit her informational advantage and claim that a negative shock has made it impossible to fulfil her contractual obligations. The seller of the good is unable to verify this claim. Hence a moral hazard problem exists between the buyer and the seller, undermining the usefulness of I.O.U.s to serve as a medium of exchange. The ex post informational asymmetry between the seller and the buyer about the buyer's ability to fulfil her obligations is a key element for developing an integrated theory of money and banking in this monograph because it critically matters in both contexts.

Contract theory poses the question what contractual form is the best way of structuring the interaction between economic agents in a given economic environment. Diamond (1984) showed that in a situation with ex post informational asymmetry about the ability of an agent to repay, a debt contract with a nonpecuniary penalty equal to the shortfall is the best solution. His argument follows pioneering work by Townsend (1979) on costly state verification and debt contracts. Hence considering I.O.U.s and ex post informational asymmetries about the ability of agents to repay is an internally consistent theoretical approach. This fundamental point has been mostly neglected in monetary research.

I.O.U.s with a nonpecuniary penalty are incentive compatible because the issuer of the I.O.U. has no advantage from understating her wealth and defaulting. She gets punished such that any advantage from nonpayment is wiped out exactly. The welfare cost for the issuer of the I.O.U. arises from the contractual feature that she even gets punished if due to an adverse shock she is really unable to fully repay. Hence issuing incentive compatible I.O.U.s is costly which reduces their attractiveness as a transaction technology.

The model of trade with privately issued I.O.U.s is developed in a strategic market setting allowing to study transaction structures. A version of the shopper's paradise model is used to determine prices and quantities directly from the strategic interactions of agents. Hence the model of trade with privately issued I.O.U.s as a transaction technology has a similar underlying structure as the model of barter with intermediate exchange. The transaction technology is the main difference between these two models which makes it possible to compare the results within one consistent framework.

7.1 The formal structure of the model of exchange with privately issued I.O.U.s

There are four types of agents denoted by *A, B, C,* and *D* and five types of goods, *a, b, c, d,* and *x*. A total number of *N* traders exist in each group, i.e. there is a total of 4*N* traders in the model. *N* is supposed to be a large number. The analysis focuses on the case in which *N* goes towards infinity. Each agent of type *A* is endowed with quantity a_0 of good *a*, each agent of type *B, C,* and *D* is endowed with quantities b_0, c_0, and d_0 of goods *b*, *c*, and *d*, respectively (the following relationship holds: $a_0 = b_0 = c_0 = d_0 = 1$). The basic goal of traders is to exchange endowments and I.O.U.s written on endowments among each other in order to acquire those goods which they can profitably resell in an external resale market. Thereby their expected wealth can be increased compared to just keeping their endowment. Because there does not exist money in the model, good *a* is taken as a numeraire good whose price is set to one.

Agents can deal in three different types of markets: the market of traders, the external market, and the resale market. Transporting goods between markets incurs a transportation cost. This cost creates some scope for autonomous price formation in a market as will be explained below. The strategic analysis focuses on the market of traders.

The market of traders: In the market of traders the agents can exchange endowments and I.O.U.s among each other in two rounds of trades. In the first round I.O.U.s written on goods of type *a* are exchanged against goods of type *b* and I.O.U.s written on goods of type *c* are exchanged against goods of type *d*. In the second round I.O.U.s written on goods of type *a* and type *c* are exchanged. Prices and quantities are derived endogenously from the strategic interactions between traders. The shopper's paradise model provides the basic setup for the market.

The external market: The market of traders can be considered as a segment in a bigger market in which the same goods are traded as in the other markets. This market is called the external market. Trading in this market is costly for the agents from the market of traders because of transportation costs. These costs are reflected in the prices for selling and buying goods (including transportation costs) as viewed by the agents in the market of traders. The structure of the market is similar to the market of traders in the sense that in the first round I.O.U.s written on goods of type *a* are exchanged against goods of type *b* and I.O.U.s written on goods of type *c* are exchanged against goods of type *d*. In the second round I.O.U.s written on goods of type *a* and type *c* are exchanged. However, unlike in the market of traders no strategic interactions are considered in the external market. It is just assumed that agents can buy and sell there at the exogenously given prices. Hence the market of traders is supposed to be small relative to the external market.

In the external market goods of type *a* can be sold at a price $\overline{p}_a$ and can be acquired at a price $\widetilde{p}_a$ by agents from the market of traders[15] where due to the cost of trading externally it holds that $\widetilde{p}_a > 1 > \overline{p}_a$. Note that because good *a* is the numeraire good its price is also one in the external market. However, as viewed from the perspective of agents in the market of traders, prices including transportation costs are different from one. Similarly, goods of type *b*, *c*, and *d* can be sold externally at prices $\overline{p}_b$, $\overline{p}_c$, and $\overline{p}_d$ whereas they can be acquired at prices $\widetilde{p}_b$, $\widetilde{p}_c$, and $\widetilde{p}_d$. Again it holds that $\widetilde{p}_b > 1 > \overline{p}_b$, $\widetilde{p}_c > 1 > \overline{p}_c$, and $\widetilde{p}_d > 1 > \overline{p}_d$. Further it is assumed that $\widetilde{p}_a = \widetilde{p}_b = \widetilde{p}_c = \widetilde{p}_d$ and $\overline{p}_a = \overline{p}_c < \overline{p}_b = \overline{p}_d$. These prices in the external market narrow down the range of prices that can be agreed upon in the market of traders. Thereby the analysis can be concentrated on the market of traders which is of primary interest because transaction technologies are studied in this market. An agent is willing to accept a deal in the market of traders only if she cannot get a better deal in the external market. The condition $\overline{p}_a = \overline{p}_c < \overline{p}_b = \overline{p}_d$ is required to ensure later that all equilibrium prices do not violate the restrictions imposed upon them. Finally, the external market also provides an opportunity to exchange goods of type *x* acquired in the resale market against goods of type *a* (see below).

Resale markets: Traders of the same type in the market of traders have special access to a third market where they can profitably sell goods of a certain type which is different from the type of their endowment good. Hence they have to acquire goods of the required type to resell them. This explains why the third market is called resale market. Traders of type *A* have a special advantage at selling goods of type *b* in the resale market. Traders of type *B*, *C*, and *D* have a special advantage at selling goods of type *c*, *d*, and *a*, respectively. The advantage is due to the ability of traders to transport these goods costlessly from the market of traders to the resale market.

The resale market is supposed to import goods of type *a*, *b*, *c*, and *d* from the external market and from the market of traders. The prices for importing these goods include a substantial cost for transporting goods from the external market to the resale market. As the market of traders is small relative to the external market, agents from the market of traders potentially have the benefit of selling goods in the resale market at the high price reflecting the transportation costs between the external market and the resale market without actually having to pay this cost.

In exchange agents from the market of traders receive goods of type *x* in the resale market. These type *x* goods are valued at the price at which they can be sold in the external market against goods of type *a*, net of the cost of transporting the goods from the resale market to the external market. One unit of a good of type *a* can be exchanged at a relative price of p^{aR} / p_x into goods of type *x* in the resale market. In the external market one unit of good *x* can be turned at a relative price p_x / p_a into units of good *a*. Taking into account also a transportation cost *T* per unit of goods of type *x* to be transported from the resale market to the external market, one unit of a good of type *a* that a trader of type *D* sells in the resale market has a value of $(p^{aR} / p_x)(p_x / p_a) - T = p^a$. It is assumed that $p^a > \widetilde{p}_a$. In an analogous way also goods of other types can be exchanged in the resale market by agents from the market of traders against goods of type *x* such that agents of type *B*, *C*, and *D* having an advantage at selling goods of type *c*, *d*, and *a*, respectively, can trade at prices p^c, p^d, and p^a. It also holds that $p^a = p^b = p^c = p^d$ and $p^b > \widetilde{p}_b$, $p^c > \widetilde{p}_c$, and $p^d > \widetilde{p}_d$.

Arbitrage between the external market and the market of traders performed by agents in the market of traders is limited because the benefit from exploiting price differences is supposed to be too small relative to the transaction costs stemming from transporting goods from the external market to the market of traders and from the cost of writing incentive compatible debt contracts. Hence borrowing and trading on price differences between the external market and the resale market is not profitable due to transaction costs. Still an incentive may exist for agents in the market of traders to exchange endowments among each other to resell them, thereby enjoying the transportation cost advantage. If this exchange takes place at sufficiently attractive prices, agents can profit by reselling those goods which they can transport costlessly at a higher price. If all traders want to trade, a lack of double coincidence of needs and wants exists in the market of traders.

Trading in the market of traders takes place within the framework of the shopper's paradise model. In the first round traders of type *A* and *C* are sellers. They obtain their desired goods already in the first round of transactions. In exchange they issue I.O.U.s written on their endowment goods such that no intermediate exchange of physical goods is necessary. An I.O.U. is a debt security promising the delivery of a certain amount of a good. For simplicity it is assumed that I.O.U.s do not pay interest.[16] Traders of type *A* issue I.O.U.s written on goods of type *a,* traders of type *C* issue I.O.U.s written on goods of type *c.*

Traders of type *D* and *B* are buyers in the first round of exchange. A buyer of type *B* acquires I.O.U.s written on goods of type *a* but actually wants to obtain goods of type *c.* A buyer of type *D* acquires I.O.U.s written on goods of type *c* but actually wants to obtain goods of type *a.* Hence traders of type *B* and *D* have a motive to trade with each other in a second round of trades. Unlike in the preceding chapter the intermediate exchange of I.O.U.s is not supposed to reduce the amount of I.O.U.s because it involves just financial transactions.

After all trades have been completed, a stochastic shock affects the total wealth of traders of type *A* and *C* who have issued the I.O.U.s in the first round of trades. Also the endowment of these traders is affected by the shock and hence their ability to deliver the goods promised in the I.O.U. The realization of the shock is not observable to the owners of the I.O.U.s, i.e. to traders of type *B* and *D.* If contracts were simple debt contracts without any further provisions, the better informed traders would have an incentive to exploit their informational advantage. They could claim that the adverse shock has made it impossible for them to deliver the goods promised. However, the debt contracts considered in this model result from a contract design problem such that the better informed traders have no incentive to misrepresent their true wealth.

Diamond (1984) showed in a banking context that a debt contract with a nonpecuniary penalty emerges as the optimal solution to a contract design problem with ex post informational asymmetry about the ability of a debtor to fulfil her obligations from the contract. The contract has the property to maximize the surplus from the transaction for the debtor and to ensure a certain minimum amount for the lender. In the context of trade with I.O.U.s as a medium of exchange this means that the expected difference between the gross wealth after trading and the burden due to the contract such as deliveries and nonpecuniary penalties is maximized. The constraints in the optimization problem take into account that the issuer of the contract behaves opportunistically choosing always the best payments for her and that the acquirer of the contract must be guaranteed a certain minimum expected value from the transaction. The optimal contract is shown to be a debt contract in the sense that the debtor pledges to deliver a certain fixed value of goods of a certain type. If she does not deliver the full amount, a nonpecuniary penalty is imposed on her which is equal to the value of the shortfall. Whereas in the Diamond model the project size and hence the contract size is fixed, in the trading model the issuers of the I.O.U.s themselves decide how much debt they want to issue. Appendix 2 to this chapter shows the formal relationship between the contract design problem in the Diamond model and the model analyzed in this chapter.

As another important feature of the model traders of type A and C issuing an I.O.U. do not have to abandon control over their goods prematurely to let them circulate as a medium of exchange. Physical goods do not function as a medium of exchange as in the case of intermediate exchange. Rather, a basic financial structure provides the functions of the medium of exchange. Hence the endowment goods can be used to generate returns before they have to be delivered to the owners of I.O.U.s. It is assumed that the endowment grows by a rate of $1+r$. This return may be considered as productive storage, for example. It accrues only, however, if credit is explicitly extended to an agent. If goods simply remain unsold in the trading process no interest accrues. Rather they are simply sold off in the external market.

Formally, the model of trade with privately issued I.O.U.s as a transaction technology corresponds to a game in extensive form. The exact sequence of trades and events is described below. The notation in this description outlines only the general structure of the decision problems at the various stages of the game without referring to all the specific information sets of a trader at a certain stage. Still, the notation will be analogous in the following sections. Only superscript T will be added when complete strategies for all the information sets of a trader at a certain stage of the game will be discussed.

1) First round of trades in the market of traders

1a) Supply

- Type A traders: Simultaneously with other traders of her type each trader of type A strategically offers a certain amount of I.O.U.s written on goods of type a at a certain price. The quantity offered by trader i of type A is denoted as h_i^A where i=1...N indexes all traders of the same type. Note that the amount pledged in the I.O.U. h_i^A (i.e., the face amount of the debt issued by a trader of type A) and the expected amount to be delivered can be used interchangeably to characterize a specific I.O.U. because there is an unequivocal relationship between the two. Hence there exists an invertible function $h_i^A(\Omega_{ai}^A)$ which describes this relationship. In the following the expected value Ω_{ai}^A is frequently used to characterize the amount of an I.O.U. The trader exchanges her I.O.U. against a certain quantity b_i^A of goods of type b from transaction partners of type B. The relative price offered by trader i of type A to exchange units of good b against one expected unit of good a equals p_{ai}^A / p_{bi}^A.
- Type C traders: Simultaneously with traders of type A each trader of type C strategically offers her I.O.U.s written on goods of type c in exchange for goods of type d. Ω_{ci}^C is the expected quantity of good c which trader i of type C offers at relative price p_{ci}^C / p_{di}^C. This relative price indicates how many units of good d are exchanged against one expected unit of good c. The trader receives d_i^C goods of type d.

1b) Smart random matching and demand

- Traders of type B get randomly matched with the cheapest offers submitted by traders of type A.
- Traders of type D get randomly matched with the cheapest offers submitted by traders of type C.
- Given an average price $\dddot{p}_{ai}^{B} / \dddot{p}_{bi}^{B}$ (weighted by the quantities of her goods exchanged) which trader i of type B gets offered, she chooses a total quantity b_i^B of her endowment to be exchanged against a certain expected value Ω_{ai}^{B} of goods of type a securitized as I.O.U.s issued by traders of type A.
- Also trader i of type D chooses a total quantity d_i^D of her endowment to be exchanged against a certain expected value Ω_{ci}^{D} of goods of type c pledged in I.O.U.s issued by traders of type C at an average price $\dddot{p}_{ci}^{D} / \dddot{p}_{di}^{D}$ (weighted by the quantities of her goods exchanged) which trader i of type D gets offered.

2) Second round of trades in the market of traders

2a) Supply

- Type B traders: Simultaneously with other traders of her type each trader of type B strategically offers a certain quantity of I.O.U.s written on good a acquired in the first round of trades at a certain price. The expected quantity of good a securitized as an I.O.U. offered by trader i of type B to be exchanged against I.O.U.s written on goods of type c is denoted as Ω_{ai2}^{B}. The relative price offered by trader i of type B to exchange expected units of good c against one expected unit of good a equals p_{ai}^{B} / p_{ci}^{B}.

2b) Smart random matching and demand

- Traders of type D get randomly matched with the cheapest offers submitted by traders of type B.
- Type D traders: Given some average price $\dddot{p}_{ai}^{D} / \dddot{p}_{ci}^{D}$ (weighted by the expected quantities of her goods exchanged) which trader i of type D gets offered in a matching process, she optimally chooses a total expected quantity Ω_{ci2}^{D} of goods of type c securitized as I.O.U.s to be exchanged against I.O.U.s written on good a.

3) Random shocks, deliveries, and nonpecuniary penalties

- Traders of type A and C resell the acquired goods at prices p^b and p^d, respectively.
- Additional returns on the endowment for traders of type A and C are realized. These returns result from productively using the endowments before delivery has to be made to the owners of I.O.U.s. The return equals r per unit of endowment.
- After all trades have been completed, individual random shocks hit the total wealth of each trader of type A and C. Trader i of type A is affected

by the random variable $\tilde{\psi}_i^A$, trader j of type C is affected by the random variable $\tilde{\psi}_j^C$ ($\tilde{\psi}_i^A$ denotes the random variable whereas ψ_i^A is a realization of the random variable). All random variables are identically, independently distributed with expectation 1. Any possible realizations lie between zero and 2. Density functions are assumed to be symmetric, bell-shaped functions. For each trader of type A or C the initial endowment plus any wealth from trading get multiplied by the individual shock term. Hence in the two extreme cases, the wealth of a trader can either get doubled or completely annihilated.

- After the shock each trader of type A and C has to decide how much she is going to deliver when a claim from an I.O.U. she has issued is made against her. Because the random shock is not observable to the other traders, in principle she can decide to deliver less than the quantity due in the I.O.U. even if she were able to deliver more goods. However, the debt contract is designed such that she has no incentive to do so. Because delivery always (weakly) dominates nondelivery once the optimal contracts have been imposed, the choice of the amount to be delivered will not be modeled explicitly.
- Traders who are unable to deliver because they have been hit by an adverse shock get punished. These nonpecuniary punishments are necessary to maintain incentives but reduce the welfare of the traders issuing I.O.U.s.[17] The welfare reductions are due to the informational frictions between traders and represent part of the cost of using privately issued I.O.U.s as a transaction technology.
- Traders of type B and D resell the acquired goods at prices p^d and p^a.

The prices and quantities of goods to be traded in the market of traders are simultaneously determined in equilibrium. Because there is no money in the model, a numeraire has to be chosen. I.O.U.s written on goods of type a are taken as numeraire good. An I.O.U. with an expected value of one has a price of one.[18]

A sketch of the game in extensive form is shown in figure 7.1. As argued in chapter 5 the shopper's paradise model is designed to capture behavior in markets with many participants. But off the equilibrium path there could exist small numbers of active traders (i.e., agents trading nonzero quantities) in markets with low trading volumes. Restrictions on quantities and prices ensure some minimum trading activity also off the equilibrium path. As in the preceding chapter minimum prices and maximum prices are pinned down by alternative trading opportunities in the external market. Minimum quantities to be traded are chosen to ensure a certain aggregate volume of trading such that at stage 1b) individual buyers have no impact on equilibrium prices at stage 2a) determined by the aggregate

Stages of the
game and
representative
decision
variables

Stage 1a):
Supply
p^A_{ai} / p^A_{bi},
Ω^A_{ai}, Ω^C_{ci},
p^C_{ci} / p^C_{di}

Stage 1b):
Matching
and demand
b^B_i, d^D_i

Stage 2a):
Supply
p^B_{ai} / p^B_{ci},
Ω^B_{ai2}

Stage 2b):
Matching
and demand
Ω^D_{ci2}

Stage 3):
Stochastic
Shock
$\widetilde{\psi}^A_i$, $\widetilde{\psi}^C_i$

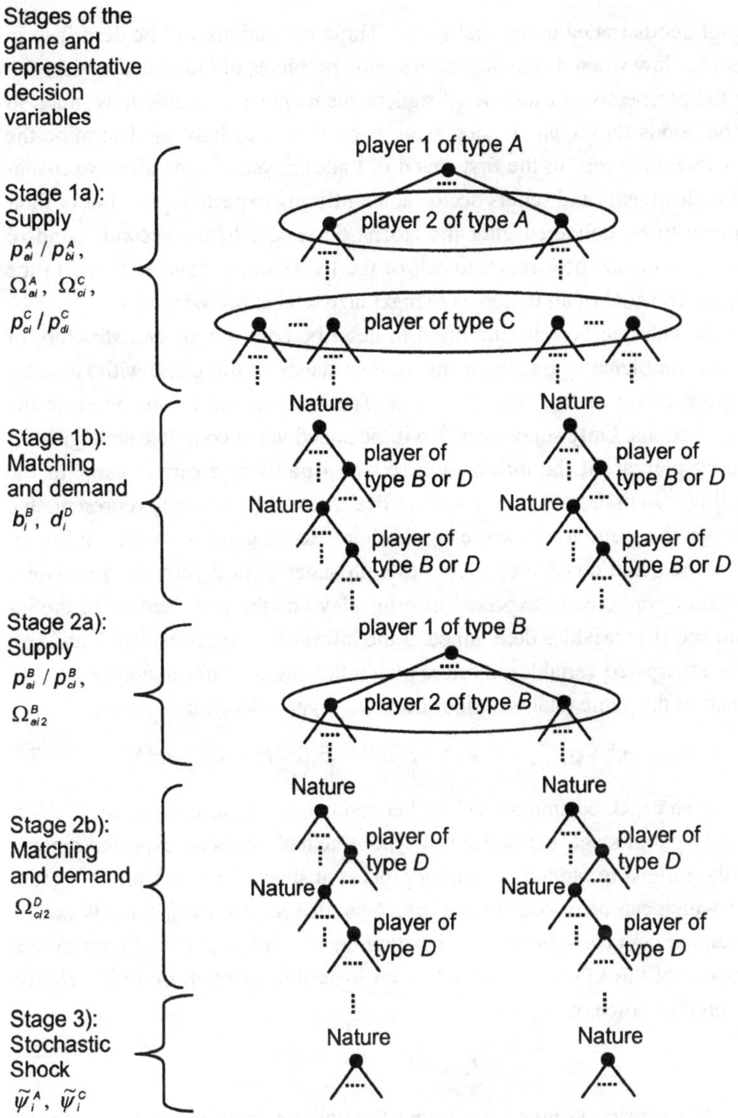

Figure 7.1 The sketch of a game tree for the model of trade with privately issued I.O.U.s

Note: The dots indicate a reduplication of the structure of the tree to which the dots refer.

volumes of goods traded in the first round. These restrictions will be described in more detail below when discussing the decision problems of individual traders.

From the perspective of individual traders agents have to decide how much to sell of the goods they own. If they are sellers, they also have to determine the price at which they sell. In the first round of trades buyers decide about exchanging their endowments and sellers decide about offering expected quantities of their endowments to be delivered after the stochastic shock. In the second round of trading traders decide how much to sell of the I.O.U.s they have acquired in the first period. The goal of all traders is to maximize total expected wealth.

Again the notation here is simplified to describe only the general structure of the decision problems of traders at the various stages of the game without referring to specific information sets of a trader. The notation will be analogous in the following sections. Only superscript *T* will be added when complete strategies for determining play at all the information sets of a trader at a certain stage of the game will be discussed because it will suffice to consider just one representative path through the game to show the equilibrium. Hence given a specific information set in the game considered variables with superscript *T* refer to i) variables determined or consistently expected in prior play on the path leading to the information set, (ii) variables determined at the information set considered, and (iii) optimally anticipated variables in future play following the information set.

At the end of the game total wealth of trader *i* of type *A* looks as follows:

$$\psi_i^A p^b b_i^A + \psi_i^A \overline{p}_a a_0(1+r) - \overline{p}_a a_i^{AS} - \overline{p}_a \phi_i^A(h_i^A(\Omega_{ai}^{AS}), a_i^{AS}). \qquad 7.1$$

By offering an expected amount Ω_{ai}^A of her endowment securitized as an I.O.U. at a price p_{ai}^A / p_{bi}^A at stage 1a) trader *i* of type *A* actually sells an expected amount Ω_{ai}^{AS} in the following random matching process at stage 1b) to acquire b_i^A goods of type *b* which can be resold at price p^b. Note that for each Ω_{ai}^A there is exactly one corresponding face value of h_i^A denoting the amount of goods of type *a* owed by the issuer of the I.O.U. Hence h_i^A is an invertible function of Ω_{ai}^{AS}. The restriction on the choice of Ω_{ai}^A is

$$\Omega_{a\min}^A \le \Omega_{ai}^A \le a_0. \qquad 7.2$$

Note that this restriction presupposes that the trader cannot promise the delivery of I.O.U.s beyond her own expected endowment. Also, additional returns earned on the endowment accruing at a rate of *r* are not assumed to be traded. The minimum amount to be offered by a trader of type *A* in 1a) is denoted as $\Omega_{a\min}^A$ (see the discussion of minimum amounts at the end of this section). Sales of Ω_{ai}^A translate into purchases of good *b* as follows:

$$b_i^A = (\Omega_{ai}^A p_{ai}^A / p_{bi}^A). \qquad 7.3$$

The expression $\overline{p}_a a_0(1+r)$ reflects the additional returns earned on the endowment good before delivery has to be made to the owners of I.O.U.s. It is one of the key benefits for the issuer of the I.O.U. from the credit extended by the buyers of I.O.U.s. These returns are also subject to the stochastic shock variable $\widetilde{\psi}_i^A$.

The expected quantity of good a that trader i of type A can actually exchange in the matching process is denoted as Ω_{ai}^{AS}. It is a function of the decision variables of all traders of type A and is determined according to the matching rules in the subgames starting at stage 1b). In one matching process the matching rules can be formulated as restrictions on the trader's decisions as follows (definition of indices: m=1…N across all traders of type B; s: all traders of type A for whom $p_{as}^A / p_{bs}^A \le p_{ai}^A / p_{bi}^A$; k: all traders of type A for whom $p_{ak}^A / p_{bk}^A < p_{ai}^A / p_{bi}^A$; g: all traders of type A for whom $p_{ag}^A / p_{bg}^A = p_{ai}^A / p_{bi}^A$):

$$\Omega_{ai}^{AS} = \begin{Bmatrix} \Omega_{ai}^A \text{ if } \sum_m \Omega_{am}^B \ge \sum_s \Omega_{as}^A, \\ 0 \text{ if } \sum_m \Omega_{am}^B \le \sum_k \Omega_{ak}^A, \\ (\Omega_{ai}^A / \sum_g \Omega_{ag}^A)(\sum_m \Omega_{am}^B - \sum_k \Omega_{ak}^A) \text{ if } \sum_m \Omega_{am}^B > \sum_k \Omega_{ak}^A \text{ and } \sum_m \Omega_{am}^B \le \sum_s \Omega_{as}^A \end{Bmatrix} \qquad 7.4$$

$\Sigma\Omega_{am}^B$ is the total market demand of traders of type B as optimally anticipated by traders of type A. It does not depend upon the choice of trader i of type A.

Trader i of type A can submit price offerings p_{ai}^A / p_{bi}^A only in discrete steps of σ^A. Prices chosen in equilibrium are assumed to be always part of the admissible price scale on a certain path. Discrete price steps are a technical assumption which is necessary to avoid infinite undercutting in infinitely small steps by traders such that no equilibrium would exist. The step size can be made arbitrarily small by increasing the number of traders. The derivation is explained in the appendix (stage 1a).

As in chapter 6 lower and upper boundaries on prices are determined by the condition that neither buyers nor sellers should have an incentive to conduct transactions in the external market rather than in the market of traders. In the external market a trader of type A could sell an I.O.U. written on one expected unit of good a at price $\overline{p}_a$. She could acquire goods of type b for resale at price $\widetilde{p}_b$. Hence a trader of type A will not be willing to trade at a relative price lower than $\overline{p}_a / \widetilde{p}_b$ in the market of traders. Her trading partner of type B could sell her goods outside the market of traders at price $\overline{p}_b$ and she could acquire I.O.U.s embodying a claim against one expected unit of goods a at price $\widetilde{p}_a$. Hence a trader of type B will not be willing to trade at a relative price higher than $\widetilde{p}_a / \overline{p}_b$. From these considerations follows that

$$\overline{p}_a / \widetilde{p}_b \le p_{ai}^A / p_{bi}^A \le \widetilde{p}_a / \overline{p}_b . \qquad 7.5$$

The multiplicative shock term $\widetilde{\psi}_i^A$ affects both the revenue from reselling goods of type a as well as the initial endowment plus the return earned on it. The agent delivers an amount a_i^{AY} which is valued at the externally set price $\overline{p}_a$ when the I.O.U. is presented to her after all trades and the shocks have taken place. Because the optimally designed nonpecuniary penalty[19] $\phi_i^A = \overline{p}_a \max(h_i^A - a_i^{AY}, 0)$ is constructed such that any delivery below the contractually promised amount a_i^{AY} triggers a punishment corresponding to the value of this shortfall, it holds that $\overline{p}_a[a_i^{AY} + \phi_i^A(h_i^A(\Omega_{ai}^{AS}), a_i^{AY})]$ equals $\overline{p}_a h_i^A(\Omega_{ai}^{AS})$. Hence total wealth at the end of the game reduces to $\psi_i^A p^b b_i^A + \psi_i^A \overline{p}_a a_0(1+r) - \overline{p}_a h_i^A(\Omega_{ai}^{AS})$. For a bell-shaped density function of $\widetilde{\psi}_i^A$ the function h_i^A representing the face value is convex.[20] Because of the convexity of h_i^A the wealth function is concave (see appendix 1, stage 1a). The amount delivered a_i^{AY} is actually a strategic variable. However, as can be seen from above, once the optimal contract with the nonpecuniary penalty is in place, the welfare of a trader becomes independent of a_i^{AY}. Hence the strategic choice of a_i^{AY} is not considered. Delivery always weakly dominates nondelivery. Therefore the trader delivers whenever she can. Also the reselling decision is not explicitly modeled because once an agent has acquired a good for reselling it is always optimal to sell the maximum amount possible because resale prices are higher than the value of selling goods elsewhere. Note that the rest of the endowment which is not delivered to owners of I.O.U.s is valued at the price $\overline{p}_a < 1$ at which these goods can be sold in the external market. This implies a requirement for traders to eventually move all their goods to the external market because otherwise these traders would not have an incentive to reduce the amount of the numeraire good which they own by the transportation cost. This assumption is made for reasons of symmetry with other traders who can value their goods only at the prices in the external market.

The decision problem of a trader of type C is analogous to the decision problem of a trader of type A. Replacing in the optimization problem of a trader of type A any a by c, A by C, b by d, and B by D yields the decision problem for trader i of type C.

Traders of type B are buyers in the first round and sellers in the second round of exchange. At the end of the game total expected wealth of trader i of type B looks as follows:

$$p^c \Omega_{ci}^B + (\Omega_{ai}^B - \Omega_{ai}^{BS})\overline{p}_a + (b_0 - b_i^B)\overline{p}_b. \qquad 7.6$$

At stage 1b) trader i of type B decides how much of her endowment goods to exchange against I.O.U.s written on goods of type a at the offered prices. In one random matching process starting at the beginning of stage 1b) she chooses a total amount of b_i^B goods of her endowment to be exchanged against a total expected amount Ω_{ai}^B of good a securitized as an I.O.U. at an average price of $\dddot{p}_{bi}^B / \dddot{p}_{ai}^B$ for which the prices of individual deals accepted get weighted by the quantities exchanged by the agent. Note that this total quantity and average price result from all the decisions taken by the trader in a matching process as will be analyzed in detail in the appendix to this chapter. In this same matching process she has to obey the restrictions at stage 1b) that she cannot offer more than her endowment and less than the minimum amount required $b^B_{\min}$ (see the end of this section for a discussion of minimum amounts).

$$b^B_{\min} \leq b^B_i \leq b_0, \tag{7.7}$$

$$\Omega^B_{ai} = b^B_i (p^B_{bi} / p^B_{ai}). \tag{7.8}$$

If goods do not get sold, they are valued at the exogenously specified price $\overline{p}_b$ at which traders of type B could sell goods of type b in the external market.

Depending upon prior play trader i of type B decides in any of the subgames starting at the beginning of stage 2a) about the amount of I.O.U.s written on good a to be offered at some relative price in exchange for I.O.U.s written on good c. In one subgame she offers an expected amount of good a denoted as Ω^B_{ai2} which cannot exceed Ω^B_{ai} being the total expected amount of good a securitized as an I.O.U. that was acquired at stage 1b).[21]

$$0 \leq \Omega^B_{ai2} \leq \Omega^B_{ai}. \tag{7.9}$$

The relative price player i of type B offers in one subgame is p^B_{ai} / p^B_{ci}. Also here discrete price steps denoted by σ^B around the equilibrium prices are considered. The derivation of σ^B is explained in appendix 1 to this chapter (stage 2a). Again, the step size can be made arbitrarily small by increasing the number of traders.

Because of the condition that prices have to lie within the range in which both sellers and buyers do not have an incentive to trade their goods externally, the relative price offered by trader i of type B is bounded from above and below as follows:

$$\overline{p}_a / \widetilde{p}_c \leq p^B_{ai} / p^B_{ci} \leq \widetilde{p}_a / \overline{p}_c. \tag{7.10}$$

Smart random matching determines how much of the amount offered can be actually exchanged. The expected quantity sold by trader i of type B in a random matching process following the subgame equals Ω^{BS}_{ai}. This amount determines which expected amount Ω^B_{ci} of good c securitized as an I.O.U. trader i of type B can acquire.

$$\Omega^B_{ci} = (p^B_{ai} / p^B_{ci})\Omega^{BS}_{ai}. \tag{7.11}$$

The basic rules of the smart random matching process can be described from the perspective of the seller by the following restrictions (definition of indices: m=1…N across all traders of type D; s: all traders of type B for whom it holds that

$p^B_{as} / p^B_{cs} \le p^B_{ai} / p^B_{ci}$; *k*: all traders of type *B* for whom $p^B_{ak} / p^B_{ck} < p^B_{ai} / p^B_{ci}$; *g*: all traders of type *B* for whom $p^B_{ag} / p^B_{cg} = p^B_{ai} / p^B_{ci}$). It should be noted that Ω^{BS}_{ai} can be anticipated by the seller with certainty because the randomization occurs only across buyers:

$$\Omega^{BS}_{ai} = \left\{ \begin{array}{l} \Omega^B_{ai2} \text{ if } \sum\limits_m \Omega^D_{am} \ge \sum\limits_s \Omega^B_{as2}, \\ 0 \text{ if } \sum\limits_m \Omega^D_{am} \le \sum\limits_k \Omega^B_{ak2}, \\ (\Omega^B_{ai2} / \sum\limits_g \Omega^B_{ag2})(\sum\limits_m \Omega^D_{am} - \sum\limits_k \Omega^B_{ak2}) \text{ if } \sum\limits_m \Omega^D_{am} > \sum\limits_k \Omega^B_{ak2} \text{ and } \sum\limits_m \Omega^D_{am} \le \sum\limits_s \Omega^B_{as2} \end{array} \right\} \qquad 7.12$$

$\Sigma\Omega^D_{am}$ is the total market demand of traders of type *D* as optimally anticipated by traders of type *B*. It does not depend upon the choice of trader *i* of type *B*.

If I.O.U.s on goods of type *a* do not get sold, they are valued at the exogenously specified price $\overline{p}_a$ at which traders of type *B* can sell I.O.U.s on goods of type *a* in the external market. This presupposes a requirement for traders of type *B* to sell any remaining goods of type *a* in the external market. Otherwise such a trader would want to keep the numeraire good which by definition has a price of one rather than selling it in the external market at a price of less than one after considering also transportation costs.[22] For reasons of symmetry with other traders this assumption is made. Note also that the resale decision is not explicitly modeled because resale always increases wealth.

Traders of type *D* are buyers in both rounds of transactions. At the end of the game total wealth for trader *i* of type *D* looks as follows (*i*=1...*N*):

$$p^a \Omega^D_{ai} + (\Omega^D_{ci} - \Omega^D_{ci2})\overline{p}_c + (d_0 - d^D_i)\overline{p}_d. \qquad 7.13$$

At stage 1b) trader *i* of type *D* decides how much of her goods to exchange in the smart random matching processes against I.O.U.s written on goods of type *c* at the offered prices. In one random matching process she chooses a total quantity of d^D_i goods of her endowment to be exchanged against a total expected amount Ω^D_{ci} of good *c* securitized as an I.O.U. at an average price of $\dddot{p}^D_{di} / \dddot{p}^D_{ci}$ (the prices of individual deals accepted by the buyer get weighted by the quantities of her goods exchanged). Note that this total quantity and average price result from all the decisions taken by the trader in a matching process as will be analyzed in detail in the appendix to this chapter. In this matching process she has to obey the restrictions that she cannot exchange more than her endowment and less than the minimum amount required $d^D_{\min}$:

$$d^D_{\min} \le d^D_i \le d_0, \qquad 7.14$$

$$\Omega^D_{ci} = (\dddot{p}^D_{di} / \dddot{p}^D_{ci}) d^D_i. \qquad 7.15$$

If goods do not get sold, they are valued at the exogenously specified price $\overline{p}_d$ at which traders of type *D* could sell goods of type *d* in the external market.

At stage 2b) depending upon prior play trader *i* of type *D* decides in smart random matching processes how much to exchange of her I.O.U.s written on goods of type *c* acquired in the first round of exchange against I.O.U.s on goods of type *a*. In one random matching process she chooses a total expected quantity Ω_{ci2}^{D} of goods of type *c* securitized as I.O.U.s and acquired in the first round of trades to be exchanged against a total expected amount Ω_{ai}^{D} of goods of type *a* securitized as I.O.U.s at an average price of $\ddot{p}_{ci}^{D} / \ddot{p}_{ai}^{D}$ for which the prices of individual deals accepted get weighted by the quantities of her goods exchanged. In this same matching process she has to obey the restrictions at stage 2b) that she cannot offer more than the I.O.U.s written on goods of type *c* acquired in 1b):

$$0 \leq \Omega_{ci2}^{D} \leq \Omega_{ci}^{D}, \tag{7.16}$$

$$\Omega_{ai}^{D} = (p_{ci}^{D} / p_{ai}^{D})\Omega_{ci2}^{D}. \tag{7.17}$$

Again, if goods do not get sold, they are valued at the exogenously specified price $\overline{p}_c$ at which traders of type *D* could sell goods of type *c* in the external market. The resale decision is not explicitly modeled but resale is always more advantageous than keeping unsold goods that could be resold.

Minimum amounts to be exchanged in the first round of trading have to be large enough to ensure sufficiently large trading volume on any path in the game. In particular, trading volume must be large enough such that the impact which in the first round of trading traders can have on the equilibrium price in the second round of trading goes towards zero as *N* approaches infinity. Minimum amounts have to be consistent in the sense that if all suppliers offer minimum amounts at maximum prices, buyers have to be able to purchase these amounts by offering their minimum amounts. This implies that the following conditions must hold:

$$b_{\min}^{B} = \Omega_{a\min}^{A} \tilde{p}_a / \overline{p}_b, \tag{7.18}$$

$$d_{\min}^{D} = \Omega_{c\min}^{C} \tilde{p}_c / \overline{p}_d. \tag{7.19}$$

It is assumed that these conditions can be fulfilled such that minimum quantities are greater than zero but less than one. It is further assumed that minimum quantities to be traded have the following properties ensuring that equilibrium prices do not hit the price constraints as is shown in the appendix to this chapter at stage 2a):

$$b_{\min}^{B} \overline{p}_b \geq \overline{p}_c, \tag{7.20}$$

$$d_{\min}^{D}\,\overline{p}_{d} \geq \overline{p}_{a}. \qquad 7.21$$

Just as in chapter 6 as a final technical assumption discrete quantities for goods are introduced. Hence both quantities and prices in the model are discrete. This feature allows to apply sequential equilibrium which will be used as an equilibrium concept in the next section (see e.g., Fudenberg and Tirole, 1991, p. 345). However, several problems result from the introduction of discrete prices and quantities. As will be seen in the next section, equilibrium prices in the second round of trading are derived from the total quantities of goods traded in the first round. The scales for prices and quantities need not be compatible, however. To avoid these problems it is assumed that just like for prices the size of the discrete quantity steps goes towards zero as N goes towards infinity. Because the analysis focuses on this case, in the limit the problem of the incompatibility of price scales and quantity scales "disappears". Hence for specifying expectations in sequential equilibrium the model is analyzed from the point of view of discrete strategies. For analyzing prices and quantities the model is analyzed as if strategies became continuous in the limiting case of N going towards infinity. A more refined mathematical analysis of these technical problems is not undertaken at this point.

7.2 The equilibrium in the model of exchange with privately issued I.O.U.s

In Proposition 2 a symmetric sequential equilibrium in the model with I.O.U.s as a medium of exchange is described. As in chapter 6 the concept of sequential equilibrium is used because in extensive form the simultaneous move game between sellers in a random matching model becomes a game of imperfect information such that an equilibrium concept with expectation formation is required restricting all beliefs on and off the equilibrium path.

Proposition 2: For sufficiently low risk of the privately observable random shock variable in the sense of second order stochastic dominance and for sufficiently attractive reselling opportunities such that $p^{a} / \overline{p}_{d} \geq 1/\Omega^{A*}$ a symmetric sequential equilibrium with high trading volume on the equilibrium path exists. In this equilibrium traders of type A and C exchange I.O.U.s written on their endowments below the maximum possible amount but above half this amount at a price such that any N-1 sellers of a good have an incentive to satisfy total market demand for this good at this price. On the equilibrium path traders of type B and D exchange all their endowments against the I.O.U.s offered in the first round of trading. In the second round traders of type B offer all their I.O.U.s on goods of type a at a price such that any N-1 traders can satisfy total market demand by traders of type D who find it optimal to exchange all their I.O.U.s of type c at these prices.

Proof: See appendix 1 to chapter 7.

The equilibrium considered reflects the case of a relatively mild friction just as in chapter 6 such that the transaction technology can be studied in actual trading processes. If severe frictions existed and transactions technologies were relatively inefficient, transaction costs would become so high that no trading would take place at all (see the appendix, stage 1a, case (ii)).

The severity of the ex post asymmetric information problem constituting the key friction in this chapter can be judged from the perspective of the degree of risk associated with the unobservable shock variable. If the variance of the random shock variable is zero, the case of symmetric information is obtained. In this scenario $h_i^A(\Omega_{ai}^{AS})$ is a 45 degree line and sellers of type A and C have an incentive to exchange their total expected endowment as I.O.U.s. For a non-zero variance h_i^A becomes vertical as Ω_{ai}^{AS} approaches one. Hence selling some additional amount of the expected future endowment requires bigger and bigger increases in the face value of the I.O.U. Because close to one it becomes almost completely unlikely that an agent will actually be able to deliver the additional amount, the additional face value required goes towards infinity. Because the additional benefits from selling an additional unit of expected I.O.U.s are limited but the additional cost increases beyond any limits as Ω_{ai}^{AS} approaches one, it is never optimal for an agent to sell her complete endowment as I.O.U.s. The discontinuity of the optimal amount of I.O.U.s issued with respect to risk is worth noting. For zero risk the trader issues the maximum amount of I.O.U.s whereas for small risk the amount issued gets significantly reduced.

The equilibrium referred to in the Proposition is described in full detail in the paragraphs below. Because a symmetric equilibrium is considered, it suffices to describe the equilibrium strategy for one representative trader of each type. The following strategies of players form a symmetric sequential equilibrium in pure strategies in the model of privately issued I.O.U.s as a transaction technology.

- Trader i of type A optimally chooses $\Omega_{ai}^{A*} = a_0$ and $p_{ai}^{A*} / p_{bi}^{A*} = N/[(N-1)\Omega^{A*}]$ as derived from the two equations $\partial h_i^A / \partial\Omega^A = (p^b / \overline{p}_a) p_{ai}^{AT} / p_{bi}^{AT}$ and $p_{ai}^{AT} / p_{bi}^{AT} = N/[(N-1)\Omega^A]$ where $p_{ai}^{A*} / p_{bi}^{A*}$ and Ω^{A*} are the solutions determined by this system. She expects to be at the point in the information set where players of her own type before her have chosen the same decision as her own equilibrium decision at stage 1a). The random shock variable must have sufficiently low risk in the sense of second order stochastic dominance such that $p^b > \overline{p}_a h_i^A(\Omega_{ai}^{AS*})$. It holds that $0.5 < \Omega_{ai}^{A*} < 1$.
- Trader i of type C optimally chooses $\Omega_{ci}^{C*} = c_0$ and $p_{ci}^{C*} / p_{di}^{C*} = N/[(N-1)\Omega^{C*}]$ as derived from the two equations $\partial h_i^C / \partial\Omega^C = (p^d / \overline{p}_c) p_{ci}^{CT} / p_{di}^{CT}$ and $p_{ci}^{CT} / p_{di}^{CT} = N/[(N-1)\Omega^C]$ where $p_{ci}^{C*} / p_{di}^{C*}$ and Ω^{C*} are optimally determined by this system. She expects to be at the point in the information set where players of her own type have chosen the same decision as her own equi-

librium decision at stage 1a) before her and where also all players of type A have chosen their equilibrium decision at this stage. It holds that $0.5 < \Omega_{ci}^{C*} < 1$.

- Trader i of type B optimally chooses to exchange the maximum possible amount of her endowment at any of her information sets at stage 1b) if $p^c / \overline{p}_b \geq (p_{ai}^{BT} / p_{bi}^{BT})(p_{ci}^{BT} / p_{ai}^{BT})$. Otherwise she chooses the minimum possible amount of her endowment. The relative prices denoted by hats are determined on the path leading to a specific information set at which the trader decides and on the optimally anticipated path following the information set. At stage 2a) player i of type B optimally chooses the variables $\Omega_{ai2}^{BT*} = \Omega_{ai}^{BT}$ and $p_{ai}^{BT*} / p_{ci}^{BT*} = \Sigma\Omega_{cq}^{DT} /((\Sigma\Omega_{aj}^{BT}) - \Omega_{a\max}^{BT})$ in any of the matching subgames starting at the beginning of stage 2a). The variables denoted by superscript T refer to the information set of the trader at one specific subgame, i.e., they are either determined or consistently expected on the path prior to this information set or they are optimally anticipated on the path following the information set (see appendix 1 to this chapter for details). The trader expects other players of type B before her to have made the same choices as her own equilibrium decision at this stage of the game.
- Trader i of type D optimally chooses the maximum amount possible of her endowment good d at any of her information sets at stage 1b) if it holds that $p^a / \overline{p}_d \geq (p_{ai}^{DT} / p_{ci}^{DT})(p_{ci}^{DT} / p_{di}^{DT})$. Otherwise she chooses the minimum amount possible of her endowment good. The relative prices denoted by hats are determined on the path leading to a specific information set at which the trader decides and on the optimally anticipated path following the information set. Trader i of type D optimally chooses the maximum amount possible of I.O.U.s written on good a at any of her information sets at stage 2b).

The equilibrium path of the game is as follows:

- Each trader of type A chooses as optimal variables an expected amount $\Omega_{ai}^{A*} = a_0$ and a price $p_{ai}^{A*} / p_{bi}^{A*} = N/[(N-1)\Omega^{A*}]$.
- Each trader of type B optimally chooses $b_i^{B*} = b_0$, $\Omega_{ai2}^{B*} = \Omega^{A*}(N-1)/N$, $p_{ai}^{B*} / p_{ci}^{B*} = (N\Omega^{C*})/[(N-1)\Omega^{A*}]$.
- Each trader of type C chooses as optimal variables an expected quantity $\Omega_{ci}^{C*} = c_0$ and a price $p_{ci}^{C*} / p_{di}^{C*} = N/[(N-1)\Omega^{C*}]$.
- Each trader of type D optimally chooses $d_i^{D*} = d_0$, $\Omega_{ci2}^{D*} = \Omega^{C*}(N-1)/N$.

The economic logic behind the equilibrium is similar to the model in the preceding chapter. The results follow from the basic incentive to trade due to the differences of traders in endowments and reselling opportunities. The market environment of the shopper's paradise model and the transaction technology determine how these basic incentives to trade are translated into specific economic interactions between traders.

In the second round of exchanges traders of type D profit most by exchanging all their I.O.U.s on good c acquired in the first round of trades against as many as possible I.O.U.s on good a offered by traders of type B in the matching process. It never pays for a trader to postpone the acquisition of some quantity to a later offer in the matching process because the terms of such an offer can never be better than those of the current offer.

At stage 2a) traders of type B anticipate that traders of type D will accept their offers within the admissible price range. According to the logic of the shopper's paradise game sellers have no incentive to bid a higher price than the equilibrium price because this would mean that their demand drops to zero. Bidding less than the equilibrium price is unattractive because the gain from selling a higher quantity does not compensate for the loss due to the negative price effect resulting from lowering the price by one price step below the equilibrium price. This holds even for the biggest trader in the market having the largest amount of I.O.U.s written on goods of type a.

At stage 1b) traders of type B and D anticipate the optimal play in the second round of trades described above. They have to consider whether despite the reduced supply by traders of type A and C the terms of deals are still attractive enough to exchange more than the required minimum amounts. Under the condition in the Proposition this is the case on the equilibrium path.

In the first round traders of type A and C have to consider how the disadvantage of selling an additional unit of expected goods of type a due to more debt and nonpecuniary punishment compares to the additional benefit from acquiring and reselling more goods of type b. Unlike in all the other cases the wealth function of a trader of type A or C is concave rather than linear, thus changing somewhat the logic of strategic decision making in the shopper's paradise model.

Given the equilibrium price a trader optimally offers all her endowment in the form of I.O.U.s. This leads to an equal splitting up of total market demand. It would never be optimal for the trader to actually sell all the I.O.U.s offered because the function h_i^A gets vertical as Ω_{ai}^{AS} approaches one. This reflects the fact that the additional benefits from selling an additional unit of expected I.O.U.s are limited but the additional cost in terms of additional goods that have to be promised increases beyond any limits as Ω_{ai}^{AS} approaches one as the probability of being able to actually deliver the additional promised goods goes towards zero. Hence it is never optimal for an agent to sell her complete endowment as an I.O.U.

The equilibrium price offered is set such that sellers can almost exchange the amount for which the marginal benefit from reselling equals the marginal disadvantage from higher nonpecuniary penalties at the equilibrium price. Summed over (N-1) traders the small amounts by which sellers actually exchange less than their optimal quantities are equal to the amount which one trader exchanges in equilibrium. Because of this feature no trader has an incentive to bid a higher price than the equilibrium price as in this case the other traders would be able and willing to sell this amount. Hence there is again some small strategic oversupply in the market to deter prices higher than the equilibrium price. Offering prices lower than the equilibrium price is not optimal either because minimum steps for discrete prices are such that the benefit from selling a slightly higher quantity is undone by the negative price effect. Hence even in the case of a concave objective function the same basic logic of decision making in the shopper's paradise model carries through.

It should be noted that the additional return which traders of type A and C derive from not having to exchange their goods prematurely increases their wealth and hence their capacity to pay back debt. For simplicity it is not assumed, however, that these additional goods are also traded. Still the additional returns which traders earn on their endowments are a source of welfare gains relative to barter with intermediate exchange of goods as considered in the previous chapter.

7.3 Conclusions from the model of exchange with privately issued I.O.U.s

The key result of this chapter is that a debt-based private decentralized system for the creation of a medium of exchange runs into difficulties if ex post asymmetric information about the ability of transaction partners to repay exists. The fundamental friction to be analyzed is the problem that the ability of the issuer of a debt contract to honor her obligations can randomly change over time in a manner unobservable to outside agents. This informational friction endogenously gives rise to a debt contract with a nonpecuniary penalty which can be considered as an incentive compatible I.O.U. Individual agents issue I.O.U.s as a medium of exchange only on part of their endowments to limit the sharply rising incentive costs. Because of this underprovision of a medium of exchange beneficial trade between agents gets lost. This central result goes beyond the analysis of Diamond (1984) who considered debt contracts of fixed size and did not analyze the use of such contracts for transaction purposes. It is also interesting to see that once they have been issued, the debt contracts can be smoothly exchanged in the second round of trading due to their incentive compatible structure and their financial nature.

The analysis of privately issued I.O.U.s as a transaction technology is key in this monograph because it lays out the basic theoretical framework with informational frictions that leads to a role for money and banks. I.O.U.s may be seen as a rudimentary financial structure that makes exchange possible without costly intermediate exchange of goods. The exchange of debt contracts written on physical goods replaces the unnecessary and burdensome barter. Hence privately issued debt is shown to have a role in facilitating exchange. But to make this financial structure incentive compatible significant penalties are required which lead to an underprovision of the medium of exchange and depress trade. Because a return to intermediate exchange of physical goods in order to avoid these welfare losses is not an attractive option, more efficient financial transaction technologies have to be found. The following two chapters analyze such alternatives.

Exchange with privately issued I.O.U.s as a transaction technology is interesting from the perspective of analytical cross-fertilization between monetary theory and banking theory. First, following a long tradition in monetary economics it was argued in chapter 6 that pure barter is burdensome. Hence a rationale was given to look for alternative transaction technologies. Privately issued I.O.U.s were introduced as one such alternative. Ex post informational asymmetry about the ability of a debtor to fulfil her obligations was shown to be a key issue in an exchange context, endogenously creating a need for debt contracts such as I.O.U.s. Thereby an internally consistent analysis between frictions and debt contracts becomes possible. This step in the analysis was inspired by the Diamond banking model which analyzes similar frictions. In the formal analysis of the model with privately issued I.O.U.s it was shown that the friction and the corresponding contracts shed light on the viability of a debt-based private decentralized system of exchange, pointing at the underprovision of the medium of exchange by private agents. Ex post asymmetric information about the ability of an agent to repay appears to be a key element for the development of an integrated theory of money and banking as will be argued further in the following chapters.

A brief overall assessment of privately issued I.O.U.s as a transaction technology leads to the following conclusions:

- Privately issued I.O.U.s save the cost of physical intermediate exchange of goods.
- Privately issued I.O.U.s as a decentralized individual solution for the creation of a medium of exchange leads to an underprovision of such a medium because of the high incentive costs necessary to make the contracts credible when asymmetric information about the ability of transaction partners to repay exists.
- Trading volume shrinks as a consequence of the informational friction.
- Privately issued I.O.U.s provide issuers the benefit of keeping control longer over their goods such that they can generate additional returns.
- Privately issued I.O.U.s do not solve the problem of a lack of double coincidence of needs and wants because they are written on specific goods.

Appendix 1 to Chapter 7: Proof of Proposition 2

For the sequential equilibrium considered in Proposition 2 beliefs are derived which are consistent with the strategies of players. Because a symmetric equilibrium in pure strategies is considered in a game which is a simultaneous move game represented in extensive form, agents expect other traders deciding "before" them to choose their equilibrium strategies. This result can also be obtained by considering a sequence of completely mixed strategies which approach the equilibrium strategies in the limit such that beliefs consistent with strategies can be derived everywhere in the game by applying Bayes' rule. Given this system of beliefs the sequential rationality of the strategies of players is analyzed in the following paragraphs. Note that any indices in summation signs run from 1 to N in the derivations below (e.g., index k for some good of type y in Σy_k).

At stage 2b) at any of her information sets trader i of type D has knowledge about variables which have been determined in prior play. The variables pertaining to this information set are denoted with superscript T (i.e., variables determined in prior play leading to the information set). Hence at a specific information set she knows the variables d_i^{DT}, Ω_{ci}^{DT}, and the price $p_{ci}^{DT} / p_{ai}^{DT}$ currently offered to her in the matching process. Consider first the decision of a player at the very end when she is the last trader in a specific matching process who gets offered a deal. In this case the trader is not restricted by the quantity offered, i.e. she can exchange all her remaining goods to acquire goods for reselling. Also the price of this last sale is known with certainty because if the trader decides to exchange only part of her goods she will get the same price offered again due to the rules of the smart random matching procedure. The decision problem of trader i of type D at the end of a matching process looks as follows:

$$\begin{aligned} \max \quad & \Omega_{ci2}^{DT}(p^a p_{ci}^{DT} / p_{ai}^{DT} - \overline{p}_c) + \Omega_{ci}^{DT}\overline{p}_c + (d_0 - d_i^{DT})\overline{p}_d + \Omega_{ci2}^{DT\leftarrow}(p^a p_{ci}^{DT\leftarrow} / p_{ai}^{DT\leftarrow} - \overline{p}_c) \\ \text{s.t. } & 0 \le \Omega_{ci2}^{DT} \le \Omega_{ci}^{DT} - \Omega_{ci2}^{DT\leftarrow}. \end{aligned} \qquad \text{A 7.1}$$

The coefficient on the decision variable Ω_{ci2}^{DT} is a constant.[23] The sign of the coefficient determines the optimal choice. If $p^a p_{ci}^{DT} / p_{ai}^{DT} - \overline{p}_c \ge 0$ the trader finds it optimal to exchange the maximum amount possible which is $\Omega_{ci}^{DT} - \Omega_{ci2}^{DT\leftarrow}$. Because it holds that $p^a / \overline{p}_c > \tilde{p}_a / \overline{p}_c \ge p_{ai}^{DT} / p_{ci}^{DT}$ this condition is always fulfilled. Note that $\Omega_{ci2}^{DT\leftarrow}$ is the total amount of good c which the trader has already exchanged at prior information sets in the matching procedure. The quantity weighted average price of those trades is $p_{ci}^{DT\leftarrow} / p_{ai}^{DT\leftarrow}$.

At decision sets which are reached before the end of the matching process trader i of type D has to solve a dynamic strategic decision problem by backwards induction. Anticipating future optimal play she must decide how much of an offer to accept now or whether to keep some of her funds to exchange them in future trades. Any future offer in a matching process is made at the same price or at a less favorable price from the perspective of the buyer and any future quantity offered will be the same or lower than the quantity offered now. Hence the best deal the trader can get is the one currently offered at the information set at which the trader has to decide. This implies that the optimal decision at a particular information set can simply be found as the solution to the static problem at this information set which is also optimal from the perspective of the dynamic strategic problem. For a more formal treatment of this argument see the appendix to chapter 6, stage 2b). Therefore the optimal solution for decision problems at information sets prior to the end of the matching process can be found in the same way as for an information set at the end of the matching process. The only differences between the two decision problems are the price offered and the maximum quantity to be exchanged. The latter is either the remaining quantity not exchanged yet $\Omega_{ci}^{DT} - \Omega_{ci2}^{DT\leftarrow}$ or the quantity Ω_{cj}^{BT} trader *j* of type *B* being matched with trader *i* of type *D* is ready to exchange given her offer.

$$\begin{aligned} &\max \; \Omega_{ci2}^{DT}(p^a p_{ci}^{DT} / p_{ai}^{DT} - \overline{p}_c) + \Omega_{ci}^{DT}\overline{p}_c + (d_0 - d_i^{DT})\overline{p}_d + \Omega_{ci2}^{DT\leftarrow}(p^a p_{ci}^{DT\leftarrow} / p_{ai}^{DT\leftarrow} - \overline{p}_c) \\ &\text{s.t. } 0 \le \Omega_{ci2}^{DT} \le \min[\Omega_{ci}^{DT} - \Omega_{ci2}^{DT\leftarrow}, \Omega_{cj}^{BT}]. \end{aligned} \quad \text{A 7.2}$$

Therefore the same condition $p^a p_{ci}^{DT} / p_{ai}^{DT} - \overline{p}_c \ge 0$ which determines play at the end of the matching process also determines decisions taken during the matching process.

At stage 2a) player *i* of type *B* decides about trade, knowing from prior play the aggregate quantities of I.O.U.s written on goods *a* and *c* to be traded after exchange at stage one. In each of the subgames starting at the beginning of stage 2a) player *i* of type *B* has exactly one information set. Consider one specific information set in one specific subgame and denote the variables pertaining to it with a superscript *T* (i.e., variables determined in prior play and consistently expected prior play leading to the information set and variables from anticipated optimal future play following the information set). The trader has to decide what expected quantity Ω_{ai2}^{BT} of good *a* securitized as I.O.U.s she is going to offer at what price $p_{ai}^{BT} / p_{ci}^{BT}$.

(i) *Wealth of trader i of type B from playing the equilibrium strategy*: W_i^{BT*}. The trader anticipates that she will be able to actually sell in the matching process an amount of I.O.U.s equal to

$$\Omega_{ai}^{BST*} = [(\Omega_{ai}^{BT} / \Sigma\Omega_{aj}^{BT})(\Sigma\Omega_{cq2}^{DT} p_{ci}^{BT*} / p_{ai}^{BT*})] \quad \text{A 7.3}$$

which can be further simplified to

$$\Omega_{ai}^{BST*} = \Omega_{ai}^{BT}[1 - \Omega_{a\max}^{BT} / \Sigma\Omega_{aj}^{BT}] \quad \text{A 7.4}$$

by inserting for the equilibrium price ($\Omega_{a\max}^{BT}$ is the biggest amount of I.O.U.s of type *a* acquired by a trader of type *B* on the consistently expected path leading to the matching process or on the optimally anticipated following path). Using this expression to derive the total wealth of trader *i* of type *B* yields

$$\Omega_{ai}^{BT}[(1 - \Omega_{a\max}^{BT} / \Sigma\Omega_{aj}^{BT})(p^c p_{ai}^{BT*} / p_{ci}^{BT*} - \overline{p}_a) + \overline{p}_a] + (b_0 - b_i^{BT})\overline{p}_b. \quad \text{A 7.5}$$

Inserting for the equilibrium price and simplifying this expression finally yields as total wealth

$$W_i^{BT*} = \Omega_{ai}^{BT}[(p^c \Sigma\Omega_{cf}^{DT} + \overline{p}_a \Omega_{a\max}^{BT}) / \Sigma\Omega_{aj}^{BT}] + (b_0 - b_i^{BT})\overline{p}_b. \quad \text{A 7.6}$$

Note that bidding a lower quantity than the equilibrium quantity at the equilibrium price would reduce total wealth by reducing the benefits from reselling and therefore cannot be optimal.

(ii) *Wealth of trader i of type B from charging a price higher than the equilibrium price in the second round of exchange*: W_{iH}^{BT}. In this case trader *i* of type *B* places the most expensive offer. Because the other traders of type *B* can satisfy the total demand of traders of type *D* for goods of type *a* in the second round of trades even if trader *i* of type *B* offers the biggest quantity of all traders of her type, the matching procedure does not match trader *i* of type *B* with a trader of type *D*. Hence Ω_{ai}^{BST} equals zero. Total wealth of trader *i* of type *A* in this second case is therefore $W_{iH}^{BT} = \Omega_{ai}^{BT}\overline{p}_a + (b_0 - b_i^{BT})\overline{p}_b$. It holds that $W_i^{BT*} > W_{iH}^{BT}$ if the following inequality is fulfilled:

$$(p^c / \overline{p}_a)(\Sigma\Omega_{cf}^{DT} / \Sigma\Omega_{aj}^{BT}) + \Omega_{a\max}^{BT} / \Sigma\Omega_{aj}^{BT} > 1. \qquad \text{A 7.7}$$

This condition can be simplified to $p^c / \overline{p}_a > p_{ci}^{BT} / p_{ai}^{BT}$. The inequality is always fulfilled because it holds that $p^c / \overline{p}_a > \tilde{p}_c / \overline{p}_a \geq p_{ci}^{BT} / p_{ai}^{BT}$.

(iii) *Wealth of trader i of type B from charging a price lower than the equilibrium price in the second round of exchange*: W_{iL}^{BT}. Consider the case in which trader *i* of type *B* offers all her goods of type *a* at a price $p_{ai}^{BT} / p_{ci}^{BT} - \sigma_i^{BT}$ where σ_i^{BT} is the minimum necessary discrete price step on the path considered for the equilibrium to obtain. As in this case she offers the lowest price in the market in the second round of exchange, her total quantity offered gets matched with traders of type *D*. Hence Ω_{ai}^{BST} equals Ω_{ai}^{BT}. As a consequence total wealth in this case becomes $W_{iL}^{BT} = \Omega_{ai}^{BT} p^c [p_{ai}^{BT*} / p_{ci}^{BT*} - \sigma_i^{BT}] + (b_0 - b_i^{BT})\overline{p}_b$. For $W_{iL}^{BT} < W_i^{BT*}$ to hold the following condition on the minimum size of bidding steps must be fulfilled:

$$\sigma_i^{BT} > p_{ai}^{BT*} / p_{ci}^{BT*} - (\Sigma\Omega_{cf}^{DT} + \Omega_{a\max}^{BT}\overline{p}_a / p^c) / \Sigma\Omega_{aj}^{BT}]. \qquad \text{A 7.8}$$

This inequality can be rearranged to obtain

$$\sigma_i^{BT} > (p_{ai}^{BT*} / p_{ci}^{BT*} - \overline{p}_a / p^c)\Omega_{a\max}^{BT} / \Sigma\Omega_{aj}^{BT}. \qquad \text{A 7.9}$$

Note that for large *N* the minimum step size goes towards zero and $\sigma_i^{BT} > 0$. The discrete price step in the optimization problem σ^B is obtained by calculating the minimum price step in the same way as for σ_i^{BT} for any path at stage 2a) and by taking the maximum over those minimum price steps. Thereby one price scale for all paths can be obtained which ensures the optimality of the equilibrium strategies such that indeed $W_{iL}^{BT} < W_i^{BT*}$. Hence charging a lower price than the equilibrium price cannot be optimal even for the largest trader of type *B* in the market who would enjoy the biggest positive quantity effect. Offering a lower quantity at a lower price than the equilibrium price would further reduce the advantageous quantity effect for a trader and is not optimal either. Offering an even smaller price would further increase the negative price effect and is therefore not optimal.

Finally, it is shown that under the assumptions made equilibrium prices do not hit the price constraints. Consider first one polar case where traders of type *D* have exchanged minimum amounts of their endowment at maximum unfavorable prices at stage 1b) and where traders of type *B* have acquired the maximum amount possible. Tn this case the equilibrium price $p_{ai}^{BT*} / p_{ci}^{BT*}$ is greater than the lower boundary for prices if it holds that $[\rho N d_{\min}^D \overline{p}_d / \tilde{p}_c] / [\rho(N-1)] \geq \overline{p}_a / \tilde{p}_c$. For *N* going towards infinity this condition reduces to the assumption about minimum quantities to be traded at the end of section 7.1, $d_{\min}^D \overline{p}_d \geq \overline{p}_a$. Similarly, if traders of type *B* have exchanged minimum amounts of their endowment at maximum unfavorable prices at stage 1b) and traders of type *D* have acquired the maximum amount possible, in this case the equilibrium price $p_{ai}^{BT*} / p_{ci}^{BT*}$ is below the upper boundary for prices if it holds that $\rho N / [\rho(N b_{\min}^B \overline{p}_b / \tilde{p}_a - \overline{p}_b / \overline{p}_a)] \leq \tilde{p}_a / \overline{p}_c$. For *N* going towards infinity this condition reduces to the assumption about minimum quantities to be traded at the end of section 7.1, $b_{\min}^B \overline{p}_b \geq \overline{p}_c$.

At stage 1b) at any of her information sets trader *i* of type *D* has knowledge about variables which have been determined in prior play. Hence at a specific information set she knows $\Sigma\Omega_{aj}^{BT}$ from consistently expected prior play and $\Sigma\Omega_{cf}^{DT}$ from consistently expected prior and expected future optimal play. She anticipates from backward induction that by acquiring some I.O.U.s written on good *c* now she will take part in a matching process in the second round of transactions where traders of type *B* all bid the same equilibrium price at which all traders of type *D* can profitably exchange their I.O.U.s of type *c* to acquire I.O.U.s of type *a*. Just as at stage 2b) in the appendix to chapter 6 also here an argument can be made that because of the logic of the smart random matching process a trader of type *D* always finds it optimal to acquire as much as possible if she gets an offer which increases her expected total wealth and she also never finds it optimal to delay the acquisition of some required amount because future offers are less favorable for the buyer. Hence also at any information set at stage 1b) trader *i* of type *D* solves a simple static optimization problem which is part of the dynamic strategic solution:

$$\begin{aligned}&\max\ d_i^{DT}[p^a(p_{ci}^{DT}/p_{ai}^{DT})(p_{di}^{DT}/p_{ci}^{DT})-\bar{p}_d]+d_0\bar{p}_d+\\&+d_i^{DT\leftarrow}[p^a(p_{ci}^{DT}/p_{ai}^{DT})(p_{di}^{DT\leftarrow}/p_{ci}^{DT\leftarrow})-\bar{p}_d]\\&\text{s.t. }\max[0,\min[d_{\min}^{DT}-d_i^{DT\leftarrow},d_j^{CT}]]\le d_i^{DT}\le\min[d_0-d_i^{DT\leftarrow},d_j^{CT}].\end{aligned} \qquad \text{A 7.10}$$

The variable d_j^{CT} is the maximum amount of good *d* that the seller *j* of type *C* with whom the buyer is matched offers to buy at the price she bids. The variable $d_i^{CT\leftarrow}$ is the total expected amount of good *d* securitized as I.O.U.s which the buyer has already acquired at stage 1b) at prior information sets and $p_{di}^{DT\leftarrow}/p_{ci}^{DT\leftarrow}$ is the corresponding average price weighted by the quantities of her goods exchanged. Again the sign of the coefficient on the decision variable d_i^{DT} is key.[24] It is greater than zero if $p^a/\bar{p}_d\ge(p_{ai}^{DT}/p_{ci}^{DT})(p_{ci}^{DT}/p_{di}^{DT})$. If this inequality holds, trader *i* of type *D* chooses the maximum amount possible. Otherwise she chooses the minimum amount possible. Inserting for the relative prices on the equilibrium path and letting *N* go towards infinity yields the condition in Proposition 2: $p^a/\bar{p}_d\ge1/\Omega^{A*}$. Note that in the objective function above also p_{ci}^{DT}/p_{ai}^{DT} depends upon d_i^{DT}. The impact is weak, however, and goes towards zero as *N* goes towards infinity. Hence this impact is ignored in the analysis.

At stage 1b) at any of her information sets trader *i* of type *B* has knowledge about variables which have been determined in prior play. Hence at a specific information set she knows the price of the deal offered to her p_{ai}^{DT}/p_{bi}^{DT}. She anticipates that by acquiring some I.O.U.s written on good *c* now she will take part in a matching process in the second round of transactions where traders of type *B* all bid the same equilibrium price at which all traders of type *D* can profitably exchange their I.O.U.s written on goods of type *c* to acquire I.O.U.s on goods of type *a*. Just as for a trader of type *D* also here an argument can be made that because of the logic of the smart random matching process a trader of type *B* always finds it optimal to acquire as much as possible if she gets an offer which increases her expected total wealth and she never finds it optimal to delay the acquisition of some required minimum amount because future offers are less favorable for the buyer. Hence at any information set at stage 1b) trader *i* of type *B* solves a simple static optimization problem which is part of the dynamic strategic solution:

$$\begin{aligned}&\max\ b_i^{BT}[(p_{bi}^{BT}/p_{ai}^{BT})(p^c\Sigma\Omega_{cq}^{DT}+\bar{p}_a\Omega_{a\max}^{BT})/\Sigma\Omega_{aj}^{BT})-\bar{p}_b]+b_0\bar{p}_b+\\&+b_i^{BT\leftarrow}[(p_{bi}^{BT\leftarrow}/p_{ai}^{BT\leftarrow})(p^c\Sigma\Omega_{cq}^{DT}+\bar{p}_a\Omega_{a\max}^{BT})/\Sigma\Omega_{aj}^{BT})-\bar{p}_b]\\&\text{s.t. }\max[0,\min[b_{\min}^{BT}-b_i^{BT\leftarrow},b_j^{AT}]]\le b_i^{BT}\le\min[b_0-b_i^{BT\leftarrow},b_j^{AT}].\end{aligned} \qquad \text{A 7.11}$$

The variable b_j^{AT} is the amount of good *b* that the seller of type *A* with whom the buyer is matched offers to buy at the price she bids.[25] The variable $b_i^{BT\leftarrow}$ is the amount of good *b* which the buyer has already acquired at stage 1b) at prior information sets and $p_{bi}^{BT\leftarrow}/p_{ai}^{BT\leftarrow}$ is the corresponding average price weighted by the quantities of her goods exchanged. Again the sign of the coefficient on the decision variable b_i^{BT} is key. It is nonnegative if

$$p^c p_{ai}^{BT} / p_{ci}^{BT} + (\Omega_{a\max}^{BT} / \Sigma\Omega_{aj}^{BT})(\overline{p}_a - p^c p_{ai}^{BT} / p_{ci}^{BT}) \geq \overline{p}_b p_{ai}^{BT} / p_{bi}^{BT}. \qquad \text{A 7.12}$$

For $N \to \infty$ the condition reduces to $p^c / \overline{p}_b \geq (p_{ai}^{BT} / p_{bi}^{BT})(p_{ci}^{BT} / p_{ai}^{BT})$. If this inequality holds, trader *i* of type *B* chooses the maximum possible amount for b_i^{BT}. Otherwise she chooses the minimum amount possible. On the equilibrium path the condition becomes $p^c / \overline{p}_b \geq 1/\Omega^{C*}$ which is the same condition as in Proposition 2. It should be noted that b_i^{BT} also may have an impact on prices in the second round of trading via $\Sigma\Omega_{aj}^{B}$. This impact is small, however, and it approaches zero as *N* goes towards infinity. Hence it is ignored in this analysis.

At stage 1a) for traders of type *A* neither bidding a higher price than the equilibrium price nor bidding a lower price than the equilibrium price yields a higher total wealth. To see this point it should be noted first that $h_i^A(\Omega_{ai}^A)$ is a convex function[26] on the interval [0,2]. Consider the inverse function $\Omega_{ai}^A(h_i^A)$ and denote the density function of $\tilde{\psi}_i^A$ as $f(h_i^A)$ and the distribution function as $F(h_i^A)$. It can be written as

$$\Omega_{ai}^A(h_i^A) = h_i^A(1 - F(h_i^A)) + \int_{x=0}^{h_i^A} xf(x)dx. \qquad \text{A 7.13}$$

From this expression the first derivative $d\Omega_{ai}^A / dh_i^A$ can be calculated as follows: $d\Omega_{ai}^A / dh_i^A = 1 - F(h_i^A) + h_i^A(-f(h_i^A)) + h_i^A f(h_i^A) = 1 - F(h_i^A)$. The second derivative can be expressed as $d^2\Omega_{ai}^A / d(h_i^A)^2 = -f(h_i^A)$. Hence $\Omega_{ai}^A(h_i^A)$ is concave on [0,2] from which follows that $h_i^A(\Omega_{ai}^A)$ is convex.

The expected wealth maximizing quantity of I.O.U.s written on good *a* Ω^A depending upon price $p_{ai}^{AT} / p_{bi}^{AT}$ can be derived from the equation $dh_i^A / d\Omega^A = (p^b / \overline{p}_a) p_{ai}^{AT} / p_{bi}^{AT}$ which results from taking the derivative of the objective function of the trader and setting it equal to zero. Furthermore the optimal price $p_{ai}^{AT} / p_{bi}^{AT}$ players choose in equilibrium depending upon expected quantity Ω^A is $p_{ai}^{AT} / p_{bi}^{AT} = N/[(N-1)\Omega^A]$ such that *N*-1 players of type *A* find it optimal to satisfy total demand by players of type *B* at this price. This system of two equations determines Ω^{A*} and $(p_{ai}^{A*} / p_{bi}^{A*})$ where the price is the equilibrium price and $\Omega^{A*}(N-1)/N$ is the equilibrium quantity actually traded denoted by Ω_{ai}^{AS*}. Inserting for $p_{ai}^{AT} / p_{bi}^{AT}$ shows that the following condition holds for the solution of the system: $dh_i^A / d\Omega^A = (p^b / \overline{p}_a) N / [(N-1)\Omega^A]$. The expression on the left-hand side is the first derivative of h_i^A. Because of the inverse function rule it holds that $dh_i^A / d\Omega^A = 1/[1 - F(h_i^A)]$. Hence $dh_i^A / d\Omega^A$ is a monotonically rising function on the interval [0,1[for which it holds that $dh_i^A / d\Omega^A$ (0)=1, $dh_i^A / d\Omega^A$ (0.5)=2, $dh_i^A / d\Omega^A$ (1)= ∞. The expression on the right-hand side is part of a hyperbola which is convex on [0,1] and monotonically falling. Note that for $\Omega^A = 1$ the functional value of the hyperbola is $(p^b / \overline{p}_a) N / [(N-1)$ whereas it is greater than 2 for $\Omega^A = 0.5$. Hence at the point $\Omega^A = 0.5$ the falling part of the hyperbola lies above the rising first derivative function whereas at the point $\Omega^A = 1$ the reverse holds true. Because both functions are also continuous on the interval [0.5,1[they must have an intersection point for some value of Ω^A between 0.5 and 1. Hence $0.5 < \Omega^{A*} < 1$. For $N \to \infty$ also Ω_{ai}^{AS*} lies in this interval. Below it is shown that $\Omega_{ai}^{A*} = a_0$ leading to Ω_{ai}^{AS*} and $p_{ai}^{A*} / p_{bi}^{A*} = N/[(N-1)\Omega^{A*}]$ are indeed best responses for player *i* of type *A* to other players' optimal strategies.

(i) *Wealth of trader i of type A from playing the equilibrium strategy*: W_i^{A*}. In this case $\Omega_{ai}^{AS*} = \Omega^{A*}(N-1)/N$ Hence expected total wealth from playing the equilibrium strategy, W_i^{A*}, equals $W_i^{A*} = p^b[p_{ai}^{A*} / p_{bi}^{A*}][(N-1)/N]\Omega^{A*} + \overline{p}_a a_0(1+r) - \overline{p}_a h_i^A(\Omega_{ai}^{AS*})$ which can be expressed as $p^b + \overline{p}_a a_0(1+r) - \overline{p}_a h_i^A(\Omega_{ai}^{AS*})$. Note that choosing a lower quantity than the equilibrium quantity at the equilibrium price would reduce the actually traded quantity in the matching procedure further below the theoretically optimal value of Ω^{A*} and therefore is not optimal.

(ii) *Wealth of trader i of type A from charging a higher price than the equilibrium price*: W_{iH}^{A}. In this case trader i of type A places the most expensive offer and hence Ω_{ai}^{AS} equals zero. Total wealth of trader i of type A in this second case is therefore $W_{iH}^{A} = \overline{p}_a a_0(1+r)$. It holds that $W_i^{A*} > W_{iH}^{A}$ if $p^b > \overline{p}_a h_i^A(\Omega_{ai}^{AS*})$. In the case of certainty $h_i^A \leq 1$ such that the condition is always fulfilled. In the case of uncertainty it holds that due to convexity $h_i^A(0.5) < 1$. As $p^b / \overline{p}_a > 1$ the condition $p^b > \overline{p}_a h_i^A(\Omega_{ai}^{AS*})$ is therefore fulfilled if Ω_{ai}^{AS*} is sufficiently close to 0.5. This is obtained if in the intersection condition $dh_i^A / d\Omega^A = (p^b / \overline{p}_a)N / [(N-1)\Omega^A]$ the first derivative of h_i^A on the left-hand side intersects the hyperbola function on the right-hand side at some Ω^A sufficiently close to 0.5. If one random shock variable is less risky than some other shock variable in the sense of second order stochastic dominance the corresponding function $dh_i^A / d\Omega^A$ lies above the other first derivative function because $d\Omega_{ai}^A / dh_i^A = 1 - F(h_i^A)$. Hence the intersection point lies further to the left. For sufficiently low risk in the sense of second order stochastic dominance as required in Proposition 2 always an intersection point sufficiently close to 0.5 can be obtained such that the condition $p^b > \overline{p}_a h_i^A(\Omega_{ai}^{AS*})$ holds. If this condition is fulfilled, charging a price higher than the equilibrium price is not a best response to other traders' strategies. Offering a lower quantity of good a at a price lower than the equilibrium price also leads to a wealth of W_{iH}^{A} and cannot be optimal either.

(iii) *Wealth of trader i of type A from charging a lower price than the equilibrium price:* W_{iL}^{A}. Consider the case in which trader i of type A offers some quantity Ω_{aiL}^{A} at a price of $p_{ai}^{A*} / p_{bi}^{A*} - \sigma^A$. As in this case she offers the lowest price in the market, her total quantity offered gets matched with traders of type B. Hence Ω_{ai}^{AS} equals Ω_{aiL}^{A}. The quantity offered by the trader will be such that the trader maximizes total wealth. Hence Ω_{aiL}^{A} is derived from the equation $\partial h_i^A / \partial \Omega_{ai}^A = p^b (p_{ai}^{A*} / p_{bi}^{A*} - \sigma^A)$. Ω_{aiL}^{A} is expressed as $\Omega_{aiL}^{A} = \Omega_{ai}^{AS*} + \varepsilon_{\Omega}^{A}$ where ε_{Ω}^{A} is the amount by which Ω_{aiL}^{A} exceeds the quantity actually traded in equilibrium Ω_{ai}^{AS*}. Inserting into total wealth for trader i of type A in case (iii) yields the following expression: $W_{iL}^{A} = p^b[p_{ai}^{A*} / p_{bi}^{A*} - \sigma^A](\Omega_{ai}^{AS*} + \varepsilon_{\Omega}^{A}) + \overline{p}_a a_0(1+r) - \overline{p}_a h_i^A(\Omega_{ai}^{AS*} + \varepsilon_{\Omega}^{A})$ which is equal to $p^b + p^b \varepsilon_{\Omega}^{A} p_{ai}^{A*} / p_{bi}^{A*} - \sigma^A(\Omega_{ai}^{AS*} + \varepsilon_{\Omega}^{A}) + \overline{p}_a a_0(1+r) - \overline{p}_a h_i^A(\Omega_{ai}^{AS*} + \varepsilon_{\Omega}^{A})$. $W_i^{A*} > W_{iL}^{A}$ holds if $\sigma^A > (\overline{p}_a / p^b)[h_i^A(\Omega_{ai}^{A*}) - h_i^A(\Omega_{ai}^{AS*} + \varepsilon_{\Omega}^{A})] / [(\Omega_{ai}^{AS*} + \varepsilon_{\Omega}^{A})] + (\varepsilon_{\Omega}^{A} p_{ai}^{A*} / p_{bi}^{A*}) / (\Omega_{ai}^{AS*} + \varepsilon_{\Omega}^{A})$. Note that as N goes towards infinity ε_{Ω}^{A} goes towards zero and hence the discrete minimum price step goes towards zero. For Ω_{ai}^{AS*} sufficiently close to 0.5 which corresponds to the case of low risk considered in the analysis σ^A is indeed positive. The condition for a positive σ^A is $\varepsilon_{\Omega}^{A} p_{ai}^{A*} / p_{bi}^{A*} > (\overline{p}_a / p^b)[h_i^A(\Omega_{ai}^{AS*} + \varepsilon_{\Omega}^{A}) - h_i^A(\Omega_{ai}^{AS*})]$. Finally note that if choosing the optimized amount Ω_{aiL}^{A} does not yield a higher expected total wealth than wealth in equilibrium, any other quantity with any lower price will not yield a higher expected total wealth either.

At stage 1a) for traders of type C the optimal decision is derived in an analogous fashion as for traders of type A. It should be noted though that traders of type C do not choose the same prices and quantities as traders of type A because due to the fact that traders of type B and D do not exchange the same quantity of I.O.U.s but traders of type B actually exchange less due to the necessity for a small strategic excess supply traders of type C anticipate (slightly) different prices than traders of type A. Still, the formal derivation of the optimal choices has the same structure as above. The difference between the optimal decisions vanishes as N goes towards infinity.

Appendix 2 to Chapter 7

The optimal debt contract in the model of Diamond (1984) is characterized as the solution to the following problem (see Proposition 1 in Diamond, 1984):

$$\begin{aligned} &\max_{\phi(\bullet)} && E_{\tilde{y}}[\max_{z\in[0,\tilde{y}]} \tilde{y} - z - \phi(z)] \\ &\text{s.t.} && z \in \arg\max_{z\in[0,y]} y - z - \phi(z) \\ &&& E_{\tilde{y}}[\arg\max_{z\in[0,\tilde{y}]} \tilde{y} - z - \phi(z)] \geq R \end{aligned} \qquad \text{A 7.14}$$

where $\tilde{y}$ is the random variable describing the stochastic return of an investment project undertaken by an entrepreneur, y is some realization of this random variable, z is the payment made by the entrepreneur, $\phi(z)$ is the nonpecuniary penalty to be paid by the entrepreneur in need of financing, and R is some alternative return that can be obtained from the capital market. The optimal nonpecuniary penalty $\phi^{*}(z)$ is $\phi^{*}(z) = \max(h - z,\ 0)$ where h is the smallest solution to

$$P(\tilde{y} < h)E_{\tilde{y}}[\tilde{y} \mid y < h] + P(\tilde{y} \geq h)h = R. \qquad \text{A 7.15}$$

Hence the optimal solution is a debt contract with face value h and a non-pecuniary bankruptcy penalty equal to the shortfall from face value h, where h is the smallest face value which provides lenders with an expected return of R. Note that in Diamond (1984) the probability distribution for $\tilde{y}$ is kept more general than in this chapter. Diamond simply assumes i.i.d. random variables which are bounded below by zero and which have some finite upper boundary. In this monograph the distribution of the shock variable is more specific. It has a bell-shaped and symmetric distribution function which is defined on the interval [0, 2].

Given some optimal choice of Ω_{ai}^{A*} leading to some value Ω_{ai}^{AS*} determining the size of the debt contract, variables from the model in chapter 7 exactly correspond to the variables in the problem analyzed by Diamond (1984):

$\tilde{y} \approx \dot{\tilde{\psi}}_i^A[p^b b_i^A + \overline{p}_a a_0(1+r)]$,
$z \approx \overline{p}_a a_i^{AY}$,
$R \approx \overline{p}_a \Omega_{ai}^{AS*}(h_i^{A*})$,
$\phi \approx \overline{p}_a \phi_i^A(\Omega_{ai}^{AS})$.

Because all variables in the original contract design problem of Diamond (1984) correspond to analogously defined variables in the model considered in this chapter and the basic setup with ex post asymmetric information about debt repayment is the same, the two contract design problems are equivalent. Hence the proof of Diamond for the optimality of debt contracts is also applicable here.

8

Money as Central Bank Debt

In chapter 6 it was argued that trade with intermediate exchange of goods is a costly and burdensome way of conducting transactions. Chapter 7 introduced privately issued I.O.U.s as a rudimentary financial transaction technology. Rather than exchanging goods themselves, debt claims written on those goods could be exchanged and the cost of intermediate exchange could be saved. One key problem with privately issued I.O.U.s was asymmetric information about the ability of a debtor to repay her debt. To rule out moral hazard it was necessary to establish an incentive structure relying on penalties which had to be imposed even if agents were truly unable to repay their debt. Because these incentive costs were sharply rising in the share of the endowment which an agent decided to securitize as an I.O.U., trading volumes got depressed. Traders decided to issue I.O.U.s only on part of their endowment. Hence a private decentralized creation of I.O.U.s as a medium of exchange led to an underprovision of this medium. Benefits from trade between agents could not be fully exhausted. Once these I.O.U.s had been issued, however, they performed well the function of a medium of exchange. In the secondary market between traders of type *B* and *D* the I.O.U.s issued by traders of type *A* and *C* were easily tradable due to their credible, incentive compatible structure. Hence the major problem to be addressed is how to reduce the cost of credibly issuing I.O.U.s.

The cost of issuing I.O.U.s is related to the stochastic wealth shock by which the issuer of the I.O.U. is affected. In the previous section identical agents were considered such that no trader had an advantage over others in issuing I.O.U.s. If the severity of shocks by which agents are affected differs, one way of reducing the cost of issuing I.O.U.s serving as a medium of exchange is to delegate this activity to those agents who can issue at the lowest cost. Traders with a high cost of issuing I.O.U.s could exchange their endowments against I.O.U.s created by agents with lower issuing costs. These I.O.U.s could function then as a medium of exchange in further transactions.

Issuing I.O.U.s for the mere purpose of creating a medium of exchange is different from issuing I.O.U.s backed by the endowment of a trader as in the preceding chapter because the leverage is much higher. Consider the case of creating an I.O.U. with one unit of a good of type *a*. An agent with low issuing costs accepts this good and credibly issues an I.O.U. promising to deliver this one unit. Suppose that before delivery the wealth of this agent is affected by a multiplicative stochastic shock with expectation one defined on the interval [0,2] just as in the preceding chapter. From the analysis there it is clear that the agent would have to issue an I.O.U. with a face value of 2 units of good *a* such that the acquirer of the I.O.U. could expect the delivery of one unit of the good. To make the I.O.U. credible, nonpecuniary penalties would have to be imposed on the agent such that she always has an incentive to deliver. Suppose that the price of good *a* is p_a. The expected value for the trader from issuing the I.O.U. would be $p_a - 2p_a < 0$ where p_a is the expected value of the good accepted and $2p_a$ is the cost for the trader from delivering the good and from undergoing nonpecuniary punishment in the case of nondelivery. Clearly, no trader would want to engage in this activity.[27] Even if she earned returns on the goods during the issuing of the I.O.U. and the delivery of the goods, these returns would have to be very high for the trader to break even. Hence accepting goods and issuing credible I.O.U.s on them is viable only if these I.O.U.s are issued at a lower face value. In the example above an issuer would be indifferent between issuing and not issuing if the face value of the debt were p_a rather than $2p_a$. Such a debt contract would imply that for exchanging one unit of good *a* worth p_a the trader would receive an I.O.U. as a medium of exchange with an expected value below p_a. A trader may still be willing to acquire a medium of exchange of this kind if alternative transaction technologies are more costly. For less risky issuers (in the sense of second order stochastic dominance) the expected value of the I.O.U. gets closer to p_a. Under certainty the good to be exchanged would have the same value as the I.O.U. issued on the good.

Typically, the agent which gets least affected by random shocks in an economy is the government. Provided a sufficiently stable political system and adequate incentives to repay, the government is able to issue debt having the lowest degree of risk. Because agents can be almost sure to receive value back in return when accepting government debt in exchange, government debt fulfils a major requirement for issuing a medium of exchange at low incentive costs. Holding I.O.U.s issued by the government written on specific goods will be almost equivalent to holding the goods backing the I.O.U.s themselves. Hence looking at the question of creating a credible medium of exchange from a cost perspective suggests to centralize the task of issuing this medium of exchange in the hands of the government. Central banks typically take over this role. The I.O.U.s issued by the central bank serving as a medium of exchange can be considered as money. The central bank acts like a trusted warehouse issuing notes. Hence the currency is backed by real goods. The case of unbacked fiat money will be discussed at the end of this chapter.

The analysis above suggests that agents who require a medium of exchange for trading can approach the central bank and exchange their goods against a special I.O.U. issued by the central bank. Thereby they acquire a claim which is fully trusted by the other agents in the economy. In this way the introduction of money circumvents the problem of asymmetric information about ex post shocks affecting individual traders. An agent accepting the special I.O.U. issued by the central bank can be sure to receive value in return. Traders requiring a medium of exchange need not support the value of the I.O.U. with their own willingness to undergo punishment to make it an acceptable medium of exchange as in the case of privately issued I.O.U.s. The problem of trust between traders due to asymmetric information about their ability to fulfil their obligations as introduced in the preceding chapter is solved in the monetary economy. Traders "borrow" the credibility of the central bank by using debt issued by this trustworthy institution as a medium of exchange.

One implication of this structure is that the ex post informational asymmetry about the ability of an agent to repay will not explicitly appear in the following model. The limiting case of zero risk borne by the central bank will be considered. Still it is important to see that the analytical origin of the central bank and money as central bank debt goes back to the discussion of incentive problems related to private debt contracts in chapter 7 which were introduced to avoid burdensome barter. It is not just imposed ad hoc.

An incentive structure with nonpecuniary penalties has to remain in place to make the repayment of the debt credible even if there is zero risk. In the current context the nonpecuniary penalties for the central bank provide these incentives. In other contexts the literature on central banking has developed a variety of approaches to provide incentives ensuring sound behavior of central banks (e.g., conservative central bankers; see Rogoff, 1985; central bank independence; see Alesina and Summers, 1993; incentive contracts determining the monetary compensation of central bankers; see Walsh, 1995).

The price to be paid for acquiring a widely trusted medium of exchange is the need to physically exchange goods at the central bank before making purchases. By abandoning control over the endowments early in the transaction process returns earned from keeping the endowments until they are actually exchanged with other traders are lost. In the economy with privately issued I.O.U.s analyzed in the preceding chapter traders could retain control over their goods until the goods were actually handed over to buyers. The traders could generate additional returns on their endowments. These returns get lost in the monetary economy because the central bank does not pay interest on money. Private solutions to reduce these losses such as the introduction of commercial banks will be analyzed in the next chapter.

The basic structure of the model of exchange will again be the shopper's paradise model. The model introduced in this chapter mainly differs in the transaction technology used. Because the basic economic setup is the same across all models, it will be straightforward to compare the welfare implications of the various transaction technologies in later chapters.

8.1 The formal structure of the model of exchange with money as central bank debt

There are four types of agents denoted by *A, B, C, D* and four types of goods, *a, b, c, d*. A total number of *N* traders exist in each group, i.e. there is a total of 4*N* traders in the model. *N* is supposed to be a large number. The analysis focuses on the case in which *N* goes towards infinity. Each agent of type *A* is endowed with quantity a_0 of good *a*, each agent of type *B, C*, and *D* is endowed with quantities $b_0 + \varepsilon^B$, c_0, and $d_0 + \varepsilon^D$ of goods *b, c*, and *d*, respectively (it holds that $a_0 = b_0 = c_0 = d_0 = 1$). The basic goal of traders is to exchange their endowments among each other in order to acquire goods which they can profitably resell in an external resale market. Thereby their expected wealth can be increased compared to just keeping their endowment.

Agents can deal in three different types of markets and they can exchange goods with the central bank. The three markets are the market of traders, the external market, and the resale market. Transporting goods between markets incurs a transportation cost. This cost creates some scope for autonomous price formation as will be explained below. The analysis focuses on the market of traders. Conclusions about transaction technologies will be drawn by comparing the outcomes in this market. All prices are expressed in monetary terms.

The market of traders: In the market of traders agents of type *A* and *C* exchange money against goods from traders of type *B* and *D* in a shopper's paradise market. The money is obtained from the central bank in exchange for their endowment goods. Prices and quantities are derived endogenously from the strategic interactions between traders.

The external market: The market of traders can be considered as a segment in a bigger market in which the same goods are traded against money as in the market of traders. This market is called the external market. Trading in this market is costly for the agents from the market of traders because of transportation costs. These costs are reflected in the prices for selling and buying goods as viewed by the agents in the market of traders. The structure of the market is similar to the market of traders in the sense that money is exchanged against goods of type *b* and *d*. However, unlike in the market of traders no strategic interactions are considered in the external market. It is just assumed that agents can buy and sell there at the exogenously given prices. Hence the market of traders is supposed to be small relative to the external market.

In the external market goods of type *b* can be sold at a price $\overline{p}_b$ and can be acquired at a price $\widetilde{p}_b$ by agents from the market of traders. These prices include the transportation cost as viewed by agents in the market of traders. Hence it holds that $\widetilde{p}_b > 1 > \overline{p}_b$. Similarly, goods of type *d* can be sold externally at a price $\overline{p}_d$ whereas they can be acquired at a price $\widetilde{p}_d$. Again it holds that $\widetilde{p}_d > 1 > \overline{p}_d$. Further it is assumed that $\widetilde{p}_b = \widetilde{p}_d$ and $\overline{p}_b = \overline{p}_d$. These prices in the external market narrow down the range of prices that can be agreed upon in the market of traders. An agent is willing to accept a deal in the market of traders only if she cannot get a better deal in the external market.

The resale market: Traders of the same type in the market of traders have special access to a third market where they can profitably sell goods of a type which is different from the type of their endowment good. Hence they have to acquire goods of the required type to resell them. This explains why the third market is called resale market. Traders of type *A* have a special advantage at selling goods of type *b* in the resale market. Traders of type *B*, *C*, and *D* have a special advantage at selling goods of type *c*, *d*, and *a*, respectively. The advantage is due to the ability of traders to transport these goods from the market of traders to the resale market at zero cost.

The resale market is supposed to import goods of type *a*, *b*, *c*, and *d* from the external market and from the market of traders. The prices of these goods include a substantial cost for transporting goods from the external market to the resale market. As the market of traders is small relative to the external market, agents from the market of traders potentially have the benefit of selling goods in the resale market at the high price reflecting the transportation costs between the external market and the resale market without actually having to pay this cost. The resale price of good *a* for a trader of type *D* is denoted as p^a. In an analogous way agents of type *A*, *B*, and *C* can trade at prices p^b, p^c, and p^d, respectively. It holds that $p^a = p^b = p^c = p^d$ and $p^b > \widetilde{p}_b$, and $p^d > \widetilde{p}_d$. Although in the resale market goods are exchanged against money, the central bank does not offer there an opportunity to exchange money directly against goods of type *a* and *c*. It has offices only in the external market and in the market of traders. Hence when importing goods to the resale market the same transportation cost incurs for goods of type *a* and *c* as for goods of type *b* and *d*. If the central bank offered an opportunity to exchange goods of type *a* and *c* directly in the resale market, their prices would also have to be one rather than $p^a > 1$ and $p^c > 1$.

Arbitrage between the external market and the market of traders performed by agents in the market of traders is limited because the benefit from exploiting price differences is supposed to be too small relative to the transaction costs stemming from transporting goods from the external market to the market of traders and from the cost of writing incentive compatible debt contracts. Hence borrowing and trading on price differences between the external market and the resale market is not profitable due to transaction costs. Still an incentive may exist for agents in the market of traders to exchange endowments among each other to resell them, thereby enjoying the transportation cost advantage. If this exchange takes place at sufficiently attractive prices, agents can profit by reselling those goods which they can transport costlessly. If all traders want to trade, a lack of double coincidence of needs and wants exists in the market of traders which is a classical problem in monetary theory.

Effectively, agents from the market of traders deal only in their own market and in the resale market. The external market has the function of restricting the admissible range of prices at which agents in the market of traders are willing to exchange goods. First, traders of type *A* and *C* approach the central bank to acquire a medium of exchange. The central bank is assumed to exchange $p_a = 1$ units of money against one unit of good *a* and $p_c = 1$ units of money against one unit of good *c*. Then the traders of type *A* and *C* deal with traders of type *B* and *D*, respectively, in order to acquire their actually desired goods in exchange for money. Trading takes place within the framework of the shopper's paradise model. Traders of type *B* and *D* are willing to accept money in return for abandoning control over their goods because they know that money is a safe I.O.U. issued by a trustworthy central bank. They can exchange the money at the central bank against goods of type *a* or *c*. The central bank takes back the money and exchanges the goods it had received in the beginning from the traders of type *A* and *C*. The central bank is not supposed to be affected by a random shock. Hence the incentive costs of issuing the I.O.U.s are zero.

Transactions involving the central bank occur in a noncompetitive environment. The central bank simply fixes the ratio between money and goods to be exchanged at the bank and is willing to buy and sell money at this ratio. Hence those transactions do not take place within the framework of the shopper's paradise model which also simplifies the analysis of the game.

Formally, the model of trade with money as central bank debt corresponds to a game in extensive form. The simplification of transactions achieved by the introduction of money is also reflected in the structure of the model. Compared to the models in the preceding two chapters exchange with money as a transaction technology is simpler. Whereas the notation here describes only the general structure of the decision problems at the various stages of the game without referring to specific information sets of a trader, the notation will be analogous in the following sections. Only superscript *T* will be added when complete strategies for all the information sets of a trader at a certain stage of the game are discussed. The exact sequence of trades and events is described in the following paragraphs:

1) Acquisition of money from the central bank
   - Each trader of type *A* acquires money from the central bank. Trader *i* of type *A* exchanges a_i^A units of her endowment a_0 against a certain amount of money denoted as m_i^A where one unit of good *a* buys $p_a = 1$ units of money.
   - Each trader of type *C* acquires money from the central bank. Trader *i* of type *C* exchanges c_i^C units of her endowment c_0 against a certain amount of money denoted as m_i^C where one unit of good *c* buys $p_c = 1$ units of money.
2) Monetary exchange between agents in the market of traders

2a) Supply
   - Each trader of type *B* strategically offers a certain quantity b_i^B from her endowment $b_0 + \varepsilon^B$ at a price p_{bi}^B. She receives an amount of money denoted by m_i^B.
   - Each trader of type *D* offers a certain quantity d_i^D from her endowment $d_0 + \varepsilon^D$ at a price p_{di}^D. She receives an amount of money denoted by m_i^D.

2b) Smart random matching and demand:
   - Traders of type *A* get randomly matched with the cheapest offers submitted by traders of type *B*.
   - Traders of type *C* get randomly matched with the cheapest offers submitted by traders of type *D*.
   - Given some average price $\dddot{p}_{bi}^A$ (weighted by the quantities of her own goods exchanged) which she gets offered in the random matching process trader *i* of type *A* optimally chooses to spend a total amount of money m_{2i}^A to buy a certain amount of goods of type *b* denoted as b_i^A.
   - Given some average price $\dddot{p}_{di}^C$ (weighted by the quantities of her own goods exchanged) which she gets offered in the random matching process trader *i* of type *C* optimally chooses to spend a total amount of money m_{2i}^C to buy a certain amount of goods of type *d* denoted as d_i^C.

3) Acquisition of goods from the central bank
   - Traders of type *B* and *D* exchange their money against goods at the central bank.
   - Trader *i* of type *B* acquires c_i^B units of good *c* at the central bank in exchange for money at the price p_c set by the central bank.
   - Trader *i* of type *D* acquires a_i^D units of good *a* at the central bank in exchange for money at the price p_a set by the central bank.
   - All traders sell the goods acquired for reselling in the resale market.

A sketch of the game in extensive form is shown in figure 8.1. As argued in chapter 5 the shopper's paradise model is designed to capture behavior in markets with many participants. But off the equilibrium path small numbers of active traders could exist (i.e., agents trading nonzero quantities) in markets with low trading volumes. Restrictions on quantities and prices ensure some minimum trading activity also off the equilibrium path of the game. Minimum prices and maximum prices are pinned down by alternative trading opportunities in the external market.

In their decision problems agents have to decide how much to sell of the goods they own. If they are sellers, they also have to determine the price at which they sell. The goal of all traders is to maximize total expected wealth. Again the notation here describes only the general structure of the decision problems of traders at the various stages of the game without referring to specific information sets of a trader. The notation will be analogous in the following sections. Only superscript T will be added when complete strategies for determining play at all the information sets of a trader at a certain stage of the game will be discussed because it will suffice to consider just one representative path through the game to show the equilibrium. Hence given a specific information set in the game considered variables with hats refer to i) variables determined or consistently expected in prior play on the path leading to the information set, (ii) variables determined at the information set considered, and (iii) optimally anticipated variables in future play following the information set.

The decision problems of traders are described in the following paragraphs. At the end of the game total wealth for trader i of type A can be represented as in 8.1 below:

$$p^b b_i^A + (a_0 - a_i^A) p_a + m_i^A - m_{2i}^A. \qquad 8.1$$

At stage 1) trader i of type A decides how many units a_i^A of her endowment a_0 of good a she exchanges at the central bank against money denoted as m_i^A where one unit of good a buys $p_a = 1$ units of money. Hence at this stage the trader decides about the amount of transaction funds to be raised which can be used for making purchases later in the game.

$$m_i^A = p_a a_i^A. \qquad 8.2$$

She cannot spend more than her endowment but must exchange at least some minimum quantity $a_{\min}^A$. Thereby also an upper limit is imposed upon the amount of transaction funds the trader can raise.

$$a_{\min}^A \leq a_i^A \leq a_0, \qquad 8.3$$

Goods which trader i of type A cannot sell are valued at the price set by the central bank as can be seen from 8.1.

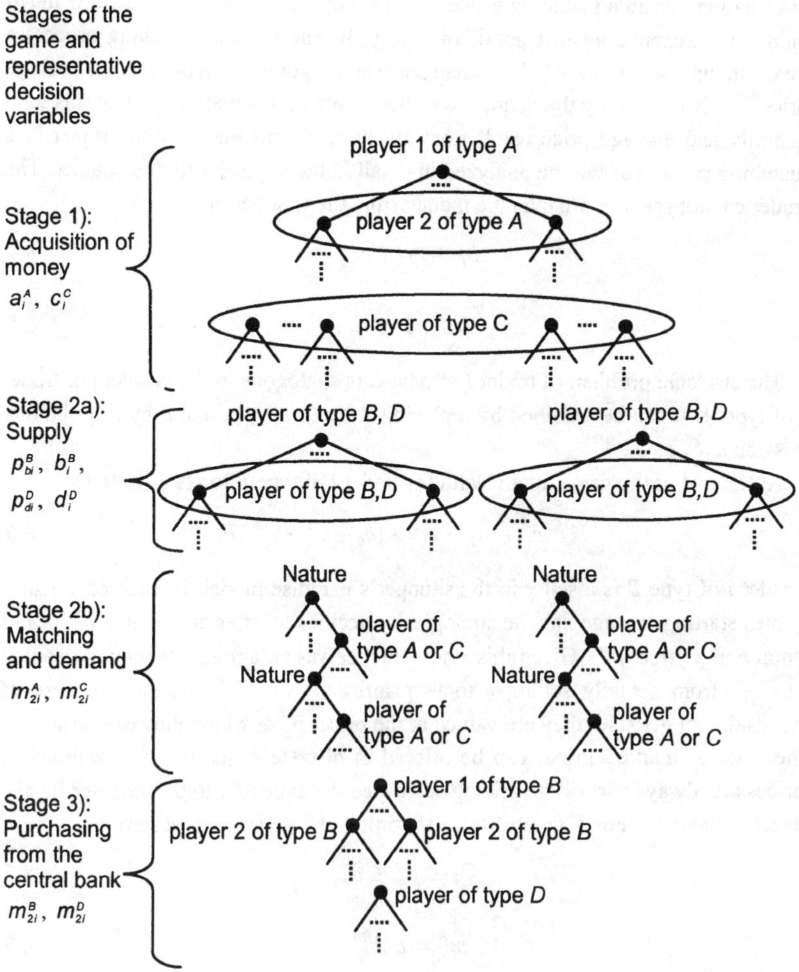

Figure 8.1 The sketch of a game tree for the model of money as central bank debt

Note: The dots indicate a reduplication of the structure of the tree to which the dots refer.

In each of the random matching processes starting at stage 2b) at each of her information sets in a matching process trader i of type A has to decide how much money to exchange against goods of type b. In one random matching process a total amount of money m_{2i}^A is exchanged against goods of type b at an average price $\ddot{p}_{bi}^A$ (weighted by the quantities of her goods exchanged). Note that this total quantity and average price result from all the decisions taken by the trader in a matching process as will be analyzed in detail in the appendix to this chapter. The trader cannot spend more than the money from the first period:

$$b_i^A = m_{2i}^A / \ddot{p}_{bi}^A, \qquad 8.4$$

$$0 \le m_{2i}^A \le m_i^A. \qquad 8.5$$

The strategic problem of trader i of type C is analogous to the problem of trader i of type A. It can be obtained by replacing A by C, a by c, and b by d in the discussion above.

At the end of the game total wealth for trader i of type B looks as follows:

$$p^c c_i^B - m_{2i}^B + m_i^B + (b_0 + \varepsilon^B - b_i^{BS})\overline{p}_b. \qquad 8.6$$

Trader i of type B is a seller in the shopper's paradise model. In each of the subgames starting at stage 2a) she strategically decides to offer an amount b_i^B of her good b at a price p_{bi}^B. Given this offer she receives an amount of money denoted by m_i^B from actually selling a total quantity b_i^{BS} in the matching process. If goods do not get sold, they are valued at the price $\overline{p}_b$ at which they can be sold in the external market. Prices can be offered in discrete steps of σ^B. Equilibrium prices are always part of the pricing scale (see the appendix to this chapter for the exact derivation). For N going towards infinity, σ^B goes towards zero.

$$\overline{p}_b \le p_{bi}^B \le \widetilde{p}_b, \qquad 8.7$$

$$m_i^B = p_{bi}^B b_i^{BS}, \qquad 8.9$$

$$\varepsilon^B = 1/(N-1). \qquad 8.10$$

The price p_{bi}^B a trader of type B can offer in the market of traders is restricted by the alternative trading opportunities in the external market. If $\overline{p}_b > p_{bi}^B$ the seller would prefer to trade in the external market. If $\widetilde{p}_b < p_{bi}^B$ the buyer would prefer to acquire goods in the external market. Hence any prices on which agents in the market of traders can agree have to lie between $\overline{p}_b$ and $\widetilde{p}_b$.

The rules in one smart random matching process starting at the beginning of stage 2b) as viewed by a seller of type B can be described by the following restrictions. It should be noted that the randomization in the smart random matching processes occurs only across individual buyers. For sellers the amount b_i^{BS} which can be sold depending upon their strategy is known with certainty. Σb_j^A is the total market demand of traders of type *A* which can be optimally anticipated by trader *i* of type *B* and which is independent from her own actions. In the expression below indices are defined as follows: *j*=1...*N* across all traders of type *A*; *s*: all traders of type *B* for whom $p_{bs}^B \leq p_{bi}^B$; *k*: all traders of type *B* for whom $p_{bk}^B < p_{bi}^B$; *g*: all traders of type *B* for whom $p_{bg}^B = p_{bi}^B$.

$$b_i^{BS} = \begin{Bmatrix} b_i^B \text{ if } \sum_j b_j^A \geq \sum_s b_s^B, \\ 0 \text{ if } \sum_j b_j^A \leq \sum_k b_k^B, \\ (b_i^B / \sum_g b_g^B)(\sum_j b_j^A - \sum_k b_k^B) \text{ if } \sum_j b_j^A > \sum_k b_k^B \text{ and } \sum_j b_j^A \leq \sum_s b_s^B \end{Bmatrix} \quad 8.11$$

At stage 3) trader *i* of type *B* chooses to exchange m_{2i}^B units of money to acquire c_i^B units of good *c* at the central bank in exchange for money at the price p_c set by the central bank to resell them at price p^c.

$$0 \leq m_{2i}^B \leq m_i^B, \quad 8.12$$

$$c_i^B = m_{2i}^B / p_c. \quad 8.13$$

The strategic problem of trader *i* of type *D* is exactly analogous to the problem of trader *i* of type *B*. It is obtained by replacing *b* by *d*, *B* by *D*, *a* by *c*, *A* by *C*, and *c* by *a* in the discussion above.

Minimum quantities to be exchanged by traders are chosen to ensure a certain aggregate volume of trading on any path in the game. In particular, the trading volume must be large enough such that the impact which at the first stage of the game traders have on the equilibrium price at stage 2) goes towards zero as *N* approaches infinity. Also, minimum amounts are chosen such as to simplify play off the equilibrium path of the game. If the conditions below are fulfilled, the equilibrium prices later analyzed in the game never hit the pricing constraints imposed by the prices in the external market. Even if all traders of type *A* or *C* exchange only the minimum amounts of their endowments against money, the equilibrium prices derived in the next section will not fall below $\overline{p}_b$ or $\overline{p}_d$, respectively. Thereby the analysis can be concentrated on the market of traders which is of primary interest because transaction technologies are studied in this market.

$$a_{\min}^A \geq \overline{p}_b, \quad 8.14$$

$$c_{\min}^C \geq \overline{p}_d. \quad 8.15$$

Just as in chapters 6 and 7 discrete quantities for goods and for money are introduced as a final technical assumption. Hence quantities, money, and prices in the model are all discrete. This feature allows to apply sequential equilibrium which will be used as an equilibrium concept in the next section (see e.g., Fudenberg and Tirole, 1991, p. 345). However, several problems result from the introduction of discrete prices, money, and quantities. As will be seen in the next section, equilibrium prices at stage 2) are derived from the total amount of money acquired in the first round. The scales for prices and money need not be compatible, however. To avoid these problems it is assumed that just like for prices the size of the discrete steps of monetary units goes towards zero as N goes towards infinity. Because the analysis focuses on this case, in the limit the problem of the incompatibility of the monetary scales and quantity scales "disappears". Hence for specifying expectations in sequential equilibrium the model is analyzed from the point of view of discrete strategies. For analyzing money, prices and quantities the model is analyzed as if strategies became continuous in the limiting case of N going towards infinity. A more refined mathematical analysis of these technical problems is not undertaken at this point.

8.2 The equilibrium in the model of exchange with money as central bank debt

In Proposition 3 a symmetric sequential equilibrium in the model with money as central bank debt is described. As in the preceding chapters the concept of sequential equilibrium is used because in extensive form the simultaneous move game between sellers becomes a game of imperfect information such that an equilibrium concept with expectation formation is required which restricts beliefs on all paths of the game.

Proposition 3: There exists a symmetric sequential equilibrium with maximum trading volume such that all endowments get traded on the equilibrium path in the market of traders (except for one strategic unit of good b and d necessary to discipline sellers). Traders of type A and C convert their entire endowments into cash at the central bank. All traders of type B and D offer their entire endowments at a price such that (N-1) traders of their type can satisfy total market demand at this price. All traders of type A and C accept these offers. Traders of type B and D exchange all their money against goods at the central bank.

Proof: See appendix to chapter 8.

Traders of type A and C realize the full potential for exchange that money issued by the central bank creates. Under the equilibrium prices in the market they have an incentive to trade as large a volume as possible because this yields the maximum quantity for profitable reselling. Unlike in the preceding two chapters where severe market imperfections could hinder trade, money allows to conduct transactions smoothly. The I.O.U.s of the central bank serving as money are perfectly credible. The incentive costs of dealing with the ex post informational asymmetry are zero because of the assumption that debt issued by the central bank is riskless. The problem of underissuing I.O.U.s as in the case of individual traders analyzed in the preceding chapter disappears by delegating the task of issuing I.O.U.s as a medium of exchange to the central bank. By reducing transaction costs money promotes trade.

Still there is a cost incurred by using money. By exchanging their endowments at the beginning against money traders lose the return $1+r$ they could earn on their endowments in the case of privately issued I.O.U.s when credit was extended to agents.[28] As will be argued in the next chapter, this feature of money issued by the central bank creates a role for commercial banks to provide transaction services.

In the paragraphs below the equilibrium in Proposition 3 is described in full detail. Because a symmetric equilibrium is considered, it suffices to describe the equilibrium strategy for one representative trader of each type. The following strategies of players form a symmetric sequential equilibrium in the model of exchange with money as central bank debt:

- Trader i of type A optimally chooses $a_i^{A*} = a_0 = 1$, expecting other traders of type A before her to choose also a_0 at stage 1) of the game. At stage 2b) trader i of type A accepts any offer made at any of her information sets to the fullest extent possible. On the equilibrium path trader i of type A chooses $a_i^{A*} = 1$ and $m_{2i}^{A*} = 1$.
- Trader i of type C pursues an optimal strategy which is analogous to the one chosen by trader i of type A. It can be obtained by replacing A with C, and a with c in the description of the optimal strategy above.
- Trader i of type B optimally chooses $b_i^{B*} = 1 + \varepsilon^B$ and $p_{bi}^{BT*} = \Sigma m_f^{AT} / N$ at stage 2a) at each of her information sets where for one specific subgame starting at the beginning of stage 2a) p_{bi}^{BT*} is the optimal price chosen there and Σm_f^{AT} is the sum over all monetary balances of traders of type A resulting from prior play on the path leading to the subgame. Trader i of type B expects other traders of her own type choosing before her to take the same decision as her own equilibrium decision in each of the subgames starting at stage 2a). At stage 3) trader i of type B optimally chooses $m_{2i}^{BT*} = m_i^{BT*}$ at any information set at which she draws where m_{2i}^{BT*} is the amount optimally chosen at one such information set and m_i^{BT*} denotes the monetary balances held by the trader resulting from prior play on the path leading to this information set. On the equilibrium path trader i of type B chooses $b_i^{B*} = 1 + \varepsilon^B$, $p_{bi}^{B*} = 1$ and $m_{2i}^{B*} = 1$.
- Trader i of type D pursues an optimal strategy which is analogous to the one chosen by trader i of type B. It can be obtained by replacing B by D, b by d, and A by C in the description of the optimal strategy above. She expects traders of type B to take their equilibrium decisions at stage 2a) and she expects traders of

her own type choosing before her at stage 2a) to take the same decision as her own equilibrium decision.

The equilibrium decisions follow from the basic incentive to trade due to the differences of traders in endowments and reselling opportunities. The market environment of the shopper's paradise model and money as a transaction technology determine how these basic incentives to trade can be translated into specific economic interactions between traders.

At stage 3) players of type *B* and *D* find it profitable to spend all their transaction funds on buying goods of type *c* and *a* because resale prices are higher than the price of acquiring the goods from the central bank. Because the prices for these goods are fixed by the central bank these transactions do not take place within the strategic framework of the shopper's paradise model.

Traders of type *B* and *D* are sellers in the shopper's paradise model at stage 2a). At the equilibrium price *N*-1 traders of type *B* offer exactly the total quantity demanded by traders of type *A*. Thereby individual sellers get disciplined as they realize that by charging a higher price than the equilibrium price they would have no match for their offer and hence could not engage in profitable reselling. Bidding a lower price than the equilibrium price would not be attractive either because this would lead to lower total wealth. Hence all traders of type *B* offer the equilibrium price and demand gets split equally among them. The same logic holds true also for the relationship between traders of type *C* and *D*. Buyers of type *A* and *C* in the smart random matching process realize at any information set at which they choose that they get offered the best deal yet available in the market Hence they agree to any offer they get.

The subgames starting at the beginning of stage 2) differ with respect to the amounts of funds for transactions that traders of type *A* and *C* have raised at stage 1). The equilibrium prices reflect differences in the total amounts raised. On the equilibrium path traders acquire the maximum amount of transaction funds possible.

Transactions along the equilibrium path have a simple structure which can be described as follows. First, traders raise as much money as possible. Then sellers offer all their endowments at a price of one. Smart random matching takes place as a straightforward process because all traders offer the same price. Hence according to the rules of the smart random matching procedure exactly one seller gets matched with exactly one buyer and they exchange one unit of their endowments as prices on the equilibrium path equal one. Eventually the sellers at stage 3) acquire one unit of their actually desired good from the central bank to sell them in the resale market.

8.3 Conclusions from the model of exchange with money as central bank debt

The analysis of money as central bank debt was motivated by inefficiencies associated with the transaction technologies analyzed in the preceding chapters. It was shown that by creating secure debt which agents can safely accept in exchange, the central bank alleviates market frictions such as a lack of trust in the ability of a transaction partner to repay or the costly inconvenience of intermediate exchange of goods.

Traders exhaust the full potential for beneficial trade when money can be used. The key difference compared to privately issued I.O.U.s is to delegate the creation of a medium of exchange to a central institution which is better equipped to deal with the incentive problems associated with this activity. Thereby the incentive cost of issuing a medium of exchange could be significantly reduced. When private agents themselves created I.O.U.s as analyzed in the preceding chapter, an underprovision of this medium of exchange occurred due to the high incentive costs necessary to make the I.O.U.s credible in the presence of lack of trust in transaction partners to repay. Money provided by a trustworthy central bank eliminates this underprovision of the medium of exchange and thereby promotes trade.

It is key for the interpretation of the model of exchange with money as central bank debt that the ex post informational asymmetry about traders' wealth remains implicit in the model although this form of market friction does not explicitly appear in the monetary model. The friction is important to motivate the introduction of money because the major benefit provided by money is exactly to avoid the appearance of the friction in the transactions between traders. Hence, the feature that there is no friction explicitly appearing in the monetary model does not mean per se that there is no role for money. It rather shows how efficiently money addresses ex post informational asymmetries about the ability of transaction partners to repay which otherwise would pose a major obstacle in the transactions between traders.

Clearly money cannot do magic in the sense of creating a world without frictions from a world with frictions. Generally speaking, the efficiency of addressing the informational friction between traders varies among different transaction technologies. It is possible that under a certain technology the friction gets shifted to a different level. Still, the problem will get conserved in some form and some cost of resolving it will exist. In the model of exchange with money as central bank debt the incentive problem gets all concentrated at one institution, the central bank. Ignoring the incentive cost of the central bank – which may be justified if the cost of providing sound incentives to a central bank is relatively small – leads then to the impression that a world of perfect markets without any frictions or role for money is considered. Note that if money were eliminated from the model the informational friction would reappear. Agents would have to use privately issued I.O.U.s again as a transaction technology. In this sense the informational friction remains implicit in the monetary model.

This insight about ex post informational frictions concerning the ability of an agent to repay which are implicit in the monetary model but do not appear explicitly is likely to hold also in more general contexts. Hence this result suggests an interpretation of the role of money in the large number of economic models in which money exists but no explicit monetary friction creating a role for money is introduced. The argument put forward in this chapter may justify why frictions giving rise to a role for money are not explicit in those models. The presence of money indicates an efficient solution for dealing with the informational friction that implicitly still exists. Of course, there are several caveats with this interpretation. First, it has to be checked for a specific model whether indeed the basic ideas about the role of money in this chapter can be transferred to this other context. Second, as will be seen in the next chapter there are even more efficient solutions for dealing with ex post informational asymmetries about the ability of an agent to repay than the introduction of cash. Hence additional explanations would be needed why cash is used in the model rather than money provided by private banks.

Money is not neutral in the model of exchange with money as central bank debt because it reduces the amount of resources required for overcoming frictions in exchange. In this sense it lubricates economic transactions, thereby promoting economic activity and increasing the welfare of economic agents. This role of money was often stressed by earlier writers on monetary economics (e.g., Mill, 1929). Changes in the quantity of money at the start of the sequence of trades do not have an impact on the economic transactions which agents perform. Because in equilibrium all traders correctly anticipate the exchange ratio for money set by the central bank, only the price level would change if the central bank altered the exchange ratio and thereby the quantity of money in the economy. In this sense money is neutral. These considerations illustrate a key point. To see one of the major impacts of money on the economy it is necessary to compare the outcome of the monetary economy with the outcome from other transaction technologies. Hence comparisons across various transaction technologies show real benefits of money. Looking only at money itself does not show any welfare benefits because changes in the quantity of money affect only the price level, but no real variables. Of course, this result hinges upon the specific assumptions made in the model. E.g., nothing can be said about behavior of the system out of equilibrium. Imperfections in information, price setting, etc. can lead to other results. Still, within the framework of the monetary model considered in this chapter changes in the quantity of money have no impact on real variables. The interaction of money with other features in the economy such as sticky prices may be required to produce real effects.

Price determination is an interesting feature in the monetary model. For a specific good the central bank fixes the ratio at which it exchanges money against the good and vice versa. Relative prices get determined in the economy according to economic forces shaping the transactions which agents conduct. If the absolute price of one good in terms of money is determined and if relative prices for all goods are known, absolute prices also follow directly. Strictly speaking, in the model considered here the central bank fixes prices for two goods, namely goods of type a and c. In this case the central bank determines the relative prices between these two goods.

An important institutional feature of the model is the property that money is debt issued by the central bank. Debt contracts were given a deeper economic interpretation in chapter 7 by linking them endogenously to the specific informational friction considered. Money as publicly issued debt was motivated from the analysis of shortcomings of individual, privately issued debt. Hence also the results of this chapter underline the role of debt in facilitating exchange. However, interpreting money as debt requires considering the case of a backed currency rather than fiat money. Hence the case of money backed by real goods was considered in this chapter. To analyze the relationship between money as central bank debt backed by real goods and fiat currency, one approach might be to introduce longer chains of transactions, such that very long or infinite time horizons can be analyzed. Typically, money is not returned to the central bank and exchanged against some good as in the model of this chapter but is used for further transactions. Hence if the date of exchanging money back into goods is postponed further and further into the future and agents discount future trades, in the limit the backing of the currency should play no role. Rather it matters that agents anticipate that they can exchange goods against money and that the other agents in the economy have the same anticipation. Of course, these ideas have to be explored in formal detail before more definite conclusions can be drawn. Still, it seems that the concept of money as central bank debt backed by real goods need not necessarily be completely detached from the concept of fiat money. The analysis in the other chapters does not critically hinge upon the question whether money is fiat money. Hence comparing barter, I.O.U.s, and private banks does not depend upon the concept of fiat money versus a backed currency.

One important question is why there should be just one central banking institution and not several banks issuing bank notes. There exists a long controversy in the literature on free banking discussing this question. The incentive cost argument put forward in this chapter suggests a centralization of the task of issuing money in the hands of the government. However, also other aspects have been discussed in the literature (e.g., see White, 1993 and 1999). Here this discussion cannot be resolved within the model and is therefore not the focus of the analysis.

Because in the model no financial assets exist before the introduction of money, the central bank has to accept real assets. If traders were able to credibly issue I.O.U.s, it would be possible to denominate them in money and exchange them against money issued by the central bank. After completing their trades agents could fulfil their obligations from the I.O.U.s vis à vis the central bank by paying back in money. In this way a real exchange of goods with the central bank could be avoided. Such an exchange of I.O.U.s issued by private agents against money somewhat mimics the discount policy performed by central banks in which privately issued bills of exchange are accepted against money. Still, the problem of a lack of trust in private agents about whether they honor their debt would remain. Unless the central bank has (by assumption) the power to ensure the enforcement of contracts, the issue of how to deal with the moral hazard problem in transactions based upon credit remains. In the next section it will be shown how some rudimentary form of a commercial bank can have a role in dealing efficiently with this problem of trust. Clearly, if central banks conduct their policy by buying and selling secure government securities, the issue of trust will not arise. Some argument may be constructed relating this widely observable feature of central banking to the basic ideas about money, debt, and trust put forward here.

One feature which seems to be missing in the simple model of the central bank is a rate of interest that is influenced by the central bank. It should be noted, however, that by exchanging money for goods and keeping the goods for some time under its control the central bank enjoys the benefits from returns earned on these goods. Clearly, if the bank exchanged goods against some financial assets, the central bank would earn income on these assets in the interim period. Hence there is an opportunity cost of holding money for traders because agents have to exchange their goods at the central bank to get money and therefore do not enjoy returns earned from the goods that accrue during the time the central bank holds those goods. This interest rate is a simple real interest rate determined by the increase of endowments. No interest rate set by the central bank exists in the model which could be different from this real interest rate. A richer model with financial assets would allow to analyze further these questions and to address such important issues as interest rate policy conducted by the central bank. Still, the opportunity cost of holding money already present in this simple model will play an important role in the next chapter.

To sum up this chapter and to compare money with the other transaction technologies analyzed so far the following points are worth noting:

- Money does not require inefficient intermediate exchange of goods between private agents which would lead to losses of resources and welfare.

- Money does not require the high incentive costs necessary to support a system of privately issued I.O.U.s. Thereby the problem of the underprovision of a medium of exchange which existed in the preceding chapter when private individuals issued I.O.U.s can be addressed efficiently.
- Money promotes trade and reduces the resource costs which arise in the transaction process, thereby lubricating economic transactions.
- Money circumvents the problem of a lack of trust in exchange by providing a safe and liquid medium of exchange which is generally accepted.
- Money has an opportunity cost because potentially productive resources have to be exchanged prematurely to acquire money as a medium of exchange.

One age-old question in monetary economics arises also in the context of this simple model: If the security of an I.O.U. is what matters for agents to be acceptable in exchange, would they still want to use cash if other secure but interest-bearing assets such as government bonds existed? This question will be the starting point for the introduction of commercial banks in the next chapter.

Appendix to Chapter 8: Proof of Proposition 3

For the sequential equilibrium considered in Proposition 3 beliefs are derived which are consistent with the strategies of players. Because a symmetric equilibrium in pure strategies is considered in a game which is a simultaneous move game represented in extensive form, agents expect other traders deciding "before" them to choose the their equilibrium strategies. This result can also be obtained by considering a sequence of completely mixed strategies which approach the equilibrium strategies in the limit such that beliefs consistent with strategies can be derived everywhere in the game by applying Bayes' rule. Given this system of beliefs the sequential rationality of the strategies of players is analyzed in the following paragraphs. Note that any indices in summation signs run from 1 to N in the derivations below (e.g., index k for some good of type y in Σy_k).

At stage 3) the optimal choice of player i of type B is strategically independent from the choices of other players at this stage because everybody can exchange money against goods at the central bank at the same ratio. Hence at any information set at stage 3) player i of type B solves the same decision problem. Consider one representative information set of player i of type B at stage 3) and denote variables pertaining to this information set with superscript T. On the path to the information set player i of type B has offered some quantity of her endowment b_i^{BT} at price p_{bi}^{BT} in previous play and has actually sold a quantity of b_i^{BST} in a matching process. The revenue of this transaction is kept as cash being equal to m_{2i}^{BT}. Hence total wealth for trader i of type B at the information set in the specific subgame is $(p^c/p_c-1)m_{2i}^{BT}+m_i^{BT}+(b_0+\varepsilon^B-b_i^{BST})\overline{p}_b$. Because $p^c>p_c$ the coefficient on m_{2i}^{BT} is positive. Hence the trader optimally chooses $m_{2i}^{BT*}=m_i^{BT}$. The same kind of reasoning also holds true for traders of type D.

At stage 2b) the optimal choice of player i of type A has the same general structure in any of the subgames starting at this stage at any information set at which she has to choose. Consider one representative subgame starting at stage 2b) and denote variables belonging to the subgame with superindex T (i.e. prior variables determined or consistently expected on the path leading to the information set where the subgame starts, variables determined at the information set). On the game path to the subgame player i of type A has acquired some monetary balances m_i^{AT} resulting from exchanging a certain amount a_i^{AT} of her endowment at the central bank against money and she has already acquired a total amount of money $m_i^{AT\leftarrow}$ at an average price $p_{bi}^{AT\leftarrow}$ (weighted by the quantities of her goods exchanged) in the random matching process leading to the information set at which she decides. Just as in the preceding chapters a buyer of type A always finds it optimal to acquire as much as possible if she gets an offer which increases her expected total wealth because the terms of future offers are less favorable for the buyer (see chapter 6, stage 2b for a formal presentation of this argument). Hence at any information set at stage 2b) trader i of type A solves a simple static optimization problem which is also part of the dynamic strategic solution:

$$\begin{aligned}&\max\ (p^b/p_{bi}^{AT}-1)m_{2i}^{AT}+m_i^{AT}+(a_0-a_i^{AT})p_a+(p^b/p_{bi}^{AT\leftarrow}-1)m_{2i}^{AT\leftarrow}\\&\text{s.t. } 0\le m_{2i}^{AT}\le\min[m_i^{AT}-m_{2i}^{AT\leftarrow},m_j^{BT}].\end{aligned}\qquad \text{A 8.1}$$

The variable m_j^{BT} is the maximum amount of money the trader of type B with whom trader i of type A is matched at the information set is willing to exchange given her offer. The sign of the coefficient on the decision variable m_{2i}^{AT} is key.[29] Because it holds that

$p^b \geq \tilde{p}_b \geq p_{bi}^{AT}$ the coefficient is positive and the agent chooses the maximum amount possible at the information set. The same basic argument about the optimal decision at stage 2b) holds true also for players of type *C*.

At stage 2a) subgames start in which players of type *B* strategically offer prices and quantities in the respective shopper's paradise games. In any one of these subgames player *i* of type *B* is faced with one information set. Consider one specific subgame starting at the beginning of stage 2a) and denote variables pertaining to the information set of the trader with superindex *T* (i.e., variables determined or consistently expected on the path to the information set and at the information set as well as anticipated future optimal variables determined after play at the information set). The subgame is characterized by a certain sum Σm_f^{AT} being the total amount of money held by traders of type *A* resulting from prior play on the path leading to the subgame. Player *i* of type *B* expects other players in the subgame to play their equilibrium strategies. When playing herself also the equilibrium strategy which is $b_i^{BT*} = 1 + \varepsilon^B$ and $p_{bi}^{BT*} = \Sigma m_f^{AT} / N$, the matching procedure leads to a quantity actually sold which is equal to $b_i^{BST*} = \Sigma m_f^{AT} /N / \Sigma m_f^{AT} /N = 1$. Hence total wealth from playing the equilibrium strategy, W_i^{BT*}, equals $W_i^{BT*} = p^c + \varepsilon^B \overline{p}_b$. Selling a lower quantity than the equilibrium quantity at the equilibrium price would reduce the volume of goods for profitable resale and is not optimal therefore.

If player *i* of type *B* charges a higher price than the equilibrium price the quantity actually sold after matching, b_i^{BST} equals zero. Hence expected wealth from charging a higher price than the equilibrium price, W_{iH}^{BT}, equals $W_{iH}^{BT} = (1 + \varepsilon^B)\overline{p}_b$. Clearly, $W_{iH}^{BT} < W_i^{BT*}$ because $p^c > \overline{p}_b$ and therefore bidding a lower price than the equilibrium price is not optimal. Because bidding a higher price and a lower quantity than in equilibrium would also lead to W_{iH}^{BT*}, such a deviation from the equilibrium cannot be optimal either.

When offering less than the equilibrium price player *i* of type *B* bids some price $p_{bi}^{BT*} - \sigma_i^{BT}$ where σ_i^{BT} is the minimum step size of the price on the game path considered which is necessary for the equilibrium to obtain. Because player *i*'s offer is the cheapest in the market, she can actually sell all her quantity offered such that $b_i^{BST*} = 1 + \varepsilon^B$. The player's wealth in the case of undercutting, W_{iL}^{BT}, equals $W_{iL}^{BT} = p^c (p_{bi}^{BT*} - \sigma_i^{BT})(1 + \varepsilon^B)$. Comparing W_{iL}^{BT} with W_i^{BT*} shows that the equilibrium wealth for the trader is higher if the following inequality is fulfilled: $\sigma_i^{BT} > \Sigma m_f^{AT} / N - (p^c + \varepsilon^B p_b)/(p^c + \varepsilon^B)$. Note that the following relationships also hold: $\Sigma m_f^{AT} / N \leq 1$ and $(p^c + \varepsilon^B \overline{p}_b)/(p^c + \varepsilon^B p^c) < 1$ Hence the maximum across all σ_i^{BT} is denoted as σ^B is positive, and goes towards zero for $N \to \infty$. Thereby it is ensured that no trader of type *B* finds it optimal to offer the equilibrium quantity at a lower price than the equilibrium price. Clearly, offering a lower quantity than the equilibrium quantity at a lower price than the equilibrium price is not optimal either because this would reduce the positive quantity effect. The analysis of the incentives for deviating from the equilibrium strategy is the same in any of the subgames starting at the beginning of stage 2a). Only Σm_i^{AT} differs but the argument above was kept general and not restricted to any specific value of Σm_i^{AT}. The proof for the optimality of the strategies of players of type *D* is analogous to the proof for the optimality of the strategies of players of type *B*.

At stage 1) player *i* of type *A* expects to be at the node in her information set corresponding to the equilibrium path of the game. Hence she maximizes max $(p^b - 1)a_i^{AT} + 1$ obeying the constraint that she cannot exchange more than her endowment.[30] Because $(p^b - 1) > 0$ it is optimal to exchange the entire endowment such that $a_i^{A*} = 1$. The same argument holds for players of type *C*.

9

The Transactions Bank – On the Missing Link Between Monetary Theory and Banking Theory

'A central quandary in modern economics in general, and monetary theory in particular, is this: today, in advanced industrial economies, most money – certainly money at the margin – is interest bearing, and the difference between the interest paid on money in, say, a cash management account and a T-bill is determined not by monetary policy, but by transactions costs. In effect, with modern technology, individuals can use T-bills for transactions. There is no opportunity cost, at the margin, in holding "money".'
Stiglitz, Joseph E., Greenwald, Bruce, 2003. *Towards a New Paradigm in Monetary Economics*, p. 12.

'Moreover, most transactions do not require money, but can be mediated through credit; and this is increasingly the case. Indeed, the reason that credit could not previously be used as a basis of exchange was the informational problem of ascertaining whether or not a credit guarantor (a credit card company or a bank) had "certified" an individual as credit worthy. The decentralized nature of information in the market economy made the transfer of such information costly.'
Stiglitz, Joseph E., Greenwald, Bruce, 2003. *Towards a New Paradigm in Monetary Economics*, p. 16.

In chapter 2 it was argued that monetary theory and banking theory have developed separately although money and banking are closely related. It was suggested that much potential exists for cross-fertilization between these two research fields. In this chapter one key link between money and banking is analyzed: a rudimentary form of a bank focusing on transaction services. These services include the efficient creation of deposits which can be transferred between agents as a means of payment, the extension of trade credit, and monitoring services to deal with problems of asymmetric information. The institutional structure of the bank created to perform these services shares key features with the Diamond model of banking theory (see section 3.2.1) although the Diamond model ignores transaction services and focuses on financing and investment in an informationally opaque capital market. In this sense an analytical link between monetary theory and banking theory is established which has not been considered yet in existing formal research. This "missing link" is called "T-bank" (transactions bank). It bridges the gap between the transactions role of money and the store of value function. Most research in monetary economics explains only one of these functions.

The model of the T-bank starts from the simple exchange problem introduced in chapter 6. The key question is whether the efficiency of conducting transactions can be further improved compared to the monetary economy. Any alternative transaction technology has to provide a solution to the same sort of frictions in exchange analyzed there. In particular, the lack of trust in the ability of a transaction partner to repay needs to be addressed. The potential for further efficiency increases is clear. Because traders can privately issue I.O.U.s only at a cost to avoid burdensome intermediate exchange of physical goods, in the economy with money as central bank debt they had to exchange their goods against the I.O.U.s of a trustworthy institution. Thereby a trader could use the good credit of the central bank to obtain a medium of exchange acceptable to other traders. The central bank could substantially reduce the incentive cost of issuing credible I.O.U.s serving as a medium of exchange. But because the trader had to exchange her goods to obtain money, she could not enjoy all the benefits that would have accrued to her if she had kept her goods until they were actually passed on to other traders. These benefits can be considered as constituting the real interest rate on holding goods across the trading period. Hence holding money has an opportunity cost for traders in terms of the real interest forgone that would have accrued from keeping the endowment longer.

Monetary research has put much effort into the question of why agents hold money if there are other equally safe and liquid assets such as government bills or bonds which dominate money in return (e.g., see Hellwig, 1993). In accordance with the opening citation by Stiglitz and Greenwald it is argued here that agents will search for transaction technologies which reduce this opportunity cost. Banks play an important role in this context because they offer interest-bearing deposits that are transferable between agents and hence function also as a medium of exchange. Credit and an efficient solution for the problem of trust are essential features of the solution.

The model in this chapter shows how the institutional structure of a bank emerges from the search for an efficient transaction technology. This analysis sheds some light on the historical development of banking from the provision of monetary services (see section 3.1). The model developed in the subsequent sections is not meant to be historically accurate. Still it captures a similar logic of development in the sense that the efficient private provision of transaction services leads to an institutional structure which can provide also financing and investment services.

9.1 A formal model of the transactions bank

There are four types of agents denoted by *A, B, C, D* and four types of goods, *a, b, c, d.* A total number of *N* traders exist in each group, i.e. there is a total of 4*N* traders in the model. *N* is supposed to be a large even number. The analysis focuses on the case in which *N* goes towards infinity. Each agent of type *A* is endowed with quantity a_0 of good *a*, each agent of type *B, C,* and *D* is endowed with quantities $b_0 + \varepsilon^B$, c_0, and $d_0 + \varepsilon^D$ of goods *b, c,* and *d*, respectively ($a_0 = b_0 = c_0 = d_0 = 1$). Traders of type *A* and *C* are split up into two subgroups as described below. The basic goal of all traders is to exchange their endowments among each other in order to acquire goods which they can profitably resell in an external resale market. Thereby their expected wealth can be increased compared to just keeping their endowment.

Agents can deal in three different types of markets and they can exchange goods with the central bank. The three markets are the market of traders, the external market, and the resale market. Transporting goods between markets incurs a transportation cost. This cost creates some scope for autonomous price formation as will be explained below. The analysis focuses on the market of traders. Conclusions about transaction technologies will be drawn by comparing the outcomes in this market. All prices are expressed in monetary terms.

The market of traders: In the market of traders agents of type *A* and *C* exchange money obtained from the central bank and from the T-bank against goods of traders of type *B* and *D.* The market is set up as a shopper's paradise market. Prices and quantities are derived endogenously from the strategic interactions between traders. The T-bank is assumed to take deposits and make loans only in the market of traders.

The external market: The market of traders can be considered as a segment in a bigger market in which the same goods are traded against money as in the market of traders. This market is called the external market. Trading in the external market is costly for the agents from the market of traders because of transportation costs. These costs are reflected in the prices for selling and buying goods as viewed by the agents in the market of traders. The structure of the market is similar to the market of traders in the sense that goods of type *b* and *d* are traded. However, unlike in the market of traders no strategic interactions are considered in the external market. It is just assumed that agents can buy and sell there at the exogenously given prices. Hence the market of traders is supposed to be small relative to the external market. All goods are traded against money provided by the central bank

In the external market goods of type *b* can be sold at price $\overline{p}_b$ and can be acquired at price $\widetilde{p}_b$ by agents from the market of traders. These prices reflect already the transportation cost as viewed by agents in the market of traders. Hence it holds that $\widetilde{p}_b > 1 > \overline{p}_b$. Similarly, goods of type *d* can be sold externally at price $\overline{p}_d$ and can be acquired at price $\widetilde{p}_d$. Again it holds that $\widetilde{p}_d > 1 > \overline{p}_d$. Further it is assumed that $\widetilde{p}_b = \widetilde{p}_d$ and $\overline{p}_b = \overline{p}_d$. These prices in the external market narrow down the range of prices that can be agreed upon in the market of traders. An agent is willing to accept a deal in the market of traders only if she cannot get a better deal in the external market.

The resale market: Traders of one type in the market of traders have special access to a third market where they can profitably sell goods of a type which is different from the type of their endowment good. They have to acquire goods of the required type to resell them in the resale market. Traders of type *A* have a special advantage at selling goods of type *b* in the resale market. Traders of type *B*, *C*, and *D* have a special advantage at selling goods of type *c*, *d*, and *a*, respectively. The advantage is due to the ability of traders to transport these goods from the market of traders to the resale market at zero cost.

The resale market is supposed to import goods of type *a*, *b*, *c*, and *d* from the external market and from the market of traders. The prices of these goods include a substantial cost for transporting goods from the external market to the resale market. As the market of traders is small relative to the external market, agents from the market of traders potentially have the benefit of selling goods in the resale market at the high price reflecting the transportation costs between the external market and the resale market without actually having to pay this cost. The resale price of good *a* for a trader of type *D* is denoted as p^a. In an analogous way agents of type *A*, *B*, and *C* can trade at prices p^b, p^c, and p^d, respectively. It holds that $p^a = p^b = p^c = p^d$ and $p^b > \widetilde{p}_b$, and $p^d > \widetilde{p}_d$. Although in the resale market goods are exchanged against money, the central bank does not offer there an opportunity to exchange money directly against goods of type *a* and *c*. It has offices only in the external market and in the market of traders. Hence when importing goods to the resale market the same transportation cost incurs for goods of type *a* and *c* as for goods of type *b* and *d*. If the central bank offered an opportunity to exchange goods of type *a* and *c* directly in the resale market, their prices would also have to be one rather than $p^a > 1$ and $p^c > 1$.

Arbitrage between the external market and the market of traders performed by agents in the market of traders is limited because the benefit from exploiting price differences is supposed to be too small relative to the transaction costs stemming from transporting goods from the external market to the market of traders and from the cost of borrowing funds in the external market. Hence borrowing and trading on price differences between the external market and the resale market is not profitable due to transaction costs. Still an incentive may exist for agents in the market of traders to exchange endowments among each other to resell them, thereby enjoying the transportation cost advantage. If this exchange takes place at sufficiently attractive prices, agents profit by reselling those goods which they can transport at zero cost. If all traders want to trade, a lack of double coincidence of needs and wants exists in the market of traders. Effectively, in the equilibrium considered in the next section agents from the market of traders deal only in their own market and in the resale market. The external market has the function of restricting the admissible range of prices at which agents in the market of traders are willing to exchange goods.

A central bank and a private T-bank exist to provide transactions services to traders. Half of the traders of type *A* and *C* (denoted as type *A*1 and type *C*1, respectively) exchange their endowments at the central bank to acquire money. They deposit the money in an account at the T-bank. The depository contract is a debt contract endogenously derived from a contract design problem analogous to the one studied in chapter 7. In the depository debt contract depositors get promised a certain rate of interest.

The T-bank uses the funds raised from deposits to make loans to the second half of traders of type *A* and *C* (denoted as type *A*2 and type *C*2) who take out those loans for transaction purposes against promising to pay a certain rate of interest. In the following shopper's paradise game traders of type *A*1 and *A*2 buy goods sold by traders of type *B* in the market of traders, traders of type *C*1 and *C*2 buy goods sold by traders of type *D*. Traders of type *A*1 and *C*1 pay by transferring their depository claims against the bank to the sellers. Traders of type *A*2 and *C*2 pay by transferring the funds from their loans to the sellers. Then the wealth of traders of type *A*2 and *C*2 is affected by individual random shocks unobservable to other traders. The T-bank can infer the shock from the change in the accounts held by traders of type *A*2 and *C*2 at the bank. Hence transaction accounts are informative for assessing the ability of loan customers to repay their loans and allow costless monitoring of loan customers. Finally, traders of type *B* and *D* buy the actually desired goods of type *a* and *c* from traders of type *A*2 and *C*2 as well as from the central bank. Traders of type *B* and *D* pay for goods acquired from traders of type *A*2 and *C*2 by transferring money deposited in their bank accounts. Those who buy from the central bank withdraw cash[31] from their bank accounts and use it for payment. If the bank goes bankrupt its assets get liquidated and any available funds are paid out in cash to depositors. In this case also any further transactions take place in cash.

Several points are noteworthy about the transaction technology in this model setup. Traders of type *A*1 and *C*1 as well as traders of type *B* and *D* have full trust in the depository debt contracts issued by the T-bank although they cannot observe the quality of the bank's loan portfolio because project outcomes are unobservable to traders. One major feature creating trust is the debt contract with non-pecuniary punishment which the bank concludes with its depositors. The contractual form is endogenously derived from the ex post asymmetric information problem between the bank and its depositors just as in chapter 7. The other key feature for creating trust is the high degree of diversification the T-bank can achieve in its loan portfolio.

A key feature of the model is the specific stochastic structure of shocks. Because the individual shocks to the wealth of traders are identically, independently distributed, the weak law of large numbers can be applied in a symmetric equilibrium in which all loan customers play the same strategies. Hence the average value of the shock variable converges to its expected value of one as the number of traders goes towards infinity. As a consequence, the average endowment per trader of type $A2$ or $C2$ which is also affected by the same shocks converges to one.

The T-bank credibly creates a medium of exchange for traders in the form of deposits such that transactions rely less on non-interest bearing money issued by the central bank. This medium of exchange is provided in part by extending credit which increases the total amount of deposits available as a medium of exchange. Because less money issued by the central bank is required, additional returns accrue from the goods formerly handed over to the central bank in exchange for money. These gains get distributed among traders through interest rate payments which the T-bank administers.

In the following description of the game the notation represents only the general structure of the decisions at the various stages of the game without referring to specific information sets of a trader. A similar notation will be used in the subsequent sections. Only superindex T will be added when complete strategies for determining play at all the information sets of a trader at a certain stage of the game will be discussed because it will suffice to consider just one representative path through the game to show the equilibrium. Hence given a specific information set in the game considered variables with superindex T refer to i) variables determined or consistently expected in prior play on the path leading to the information set, (ii) variables determined at the information set considered, and (iii) optimally anticipated variables in future play following the information set.The sequence of decisions and events in the model of the T-bank is as follows:

1) Exchanging money
   - The first half of the group of traders of type A and C (denoted as type $A1$ and $C1$, respectively) exchange a certain quantity of their endowments against money at the central bank. Trader i of type $A1$ exchanges a_i^{A1} of her endowment against m_i^{A1} units of money, trader i of type $C1$ exchanges c_i^{C1} of her endowment against m_i^{C1} units of money. The central bank

fixes the ratio for exchange between goods and money such that one unit of good a is exchanged against one unit of money (exchange ratio $p_a = 1$) and also one unit of good c is exchanged against one unit of money (exchange ratio $p_c = 1$).

2) Depositing money
   - All these traders convert their money into deposits at the T-bank. Trader i of type $A1$ holds an amount of deposits δ_i^{A1}, trader i of type $C1$ holds an amount of deposits δ_i^{C1}. The T-bank promises to pay back deposits plus interest at the end of the sequence of transactions. The interest rate on deposits is r_1.
3) Loans
   - Agents in the second group of traders of type A and C (denoted as type $A2$ and type $C2$, respectively) get a loan from the bank to pay for trading at stage 4b). They retain their initial endowments because they need not convert them into money at the central bank. This allows them to earn additional returns on the endowment before passing it on to other traders.
4) Shopper' paradise game in the market of traders

4a) Supply
   - Each trader of type B strategically offers a certain quantity from her endowment at a certain price. Trader i of type B strategically offers an amount b_i^B of her endowment $b_0 + \varepsilon^B$ at a price p_{bi}^B. In exchange she receives an amount of deposits denoted as δ_i^B.
   - Each trader of type D strategically offers a certain quantity from her endowment at a certain price. Trader i of type D strategically offers an amount d_i^D of her endowment $d_0 + \varepsilon^D$ at a price p_{di}^D. In exchange she receives an amount of deposits denoted as δ_i^D.

4b) Smart random matching and demand
   - Traders of type $A1$ and $A2$ get randomly matched with the cheapest offers submitted by traders of type B.
   - Traders of type $C1$ and $C2$ get randomly matched with the cheapest offers submitted by traders of type D.
   - Trader i of type $A1$ optimally chooses an amount m_{2i}^{A1} of her money deposited at the bank to acquire a total quantity b_i^{A1} of goods of type b at an average price $\dddot{p}_{bi}^{A1}$ she gets offered in the matching process (prices entering into this average price are weighted by the quantities of her goods exchanged). Trader i of type $A2$ optimally chooses a loan of λ_i^{A2} to acquire a total quantity b_i^{A2} of goods of type b at some quantity weighted average price $\dddot{p}_{bi}^{A2}$ she gets offered in a matching process.
   - Trader i of type $C1$ optimally chooses an amount m_{2i}^{C1} of her money deposited at the bank to acquire a total quantity d_i^{C1} of goods of type d at an average price $\dddot{p}_{di}^{C1}$ she gets offered in a matching process (prices entering

into this average price are weighted by the quantities of her goods exchanged). Trader i of type $C2$ optimally chooses a loan of λ_i^{C2} to acquire a total quantity d_i^{C2} of goods of type d at some quantity weighted average price $\ddot{p}_{di}^{C2}$ she gets offered in the matching process.
- Traders of type $A2$ and $C2$ sell the goods acquired in the resale market. They receive cash in those transactions which they put into their bank accounts at the T-bank.

5) Returns on the endowment
   - Traders of type $A2$ and $C2$ earn a real return r per unit on their endowments which they exchange against money at the central bank and deposit at the T-bank. They do not earn interest on these deposits.[32]
6) Random shocks
   - Individual random shocks affect the wealth of each trader of type $A2$ and $C2$ (including their endowment plus the return earned on it and the revenue from reselling goods). Trader i of type $A2$ is affected by the random variable $\tilde{\psi}_i^{A2}$, trader j of type $C2$ is affected by the random variable $\tilde{\psi}_j^{C2}$. Any possible realizations lie between zero and two. All random shock variables are identically, independently distributed with expectation one.
7) Monitoring
   - The T-bank monitors the individual wealth shocks to traders of type $A2$ and $C2$. Assuming that the bank can observe account balances without a cost, she can infer the size of the shock from the changes in the accounts.
8) Bank Failure
   - If many traders are adversely hit by shocks and are unable to fully repay their loans, as a consequence the bank may go bankrupt. Hence after having observed traders' returns an insolvent bank declares bankruptcy. It collects early repayments from her loan customers who have funds from the revenues of reselling goods. They also can exchange their endowments at the central bank in order to raise the money for repaying loans. Assets get distributed to depositors as cash payouts proportional to the share of their funds in total deposits. The bank has to undergo nonpecuniary punishment equal to the shortfall between total promised and actual repayments to depositors.
9) Purchasing goods
   - Traders of type B and D buy goods of type c and a from traders of type $A2$ and $C2$ as well as from the central bank at the price set for these goods by the central bank. Trader i of type B optimally chooses quantity δ_{2i}^{B} to be exchanged against goods of type c. If trader i of type B buys from a trader of type $C2$ she pays by transferring money from her bank account to the other trader's account. Hence trader i of type $C2$ receives δ_i^{C2} in deposits. If she buys from the central bank she withdraws cash from the bank ac-

count and exchanges it at the central bank against the goods of type c which traders of type $C1$ had sold to the central bank at stage 1). Similarly trader i of type D optimally chooses quantity δ_{2i}^{D} to be exchanged against goods of type a. She buys goods either from traders of type $A2$ or from the central bank. In the first case trader i of type $A2$ receives δ_i^{A2} in deposits. The central bank acts as a buffer, sticking to fixed exchange ratios between money and goods even though the total quantity of goods in the market of traders can vary depending upon the stochastic shocks.

10) Reselling
    - Traders of type $A1$ resell their acquired goods at prices p^b, traders of type $C1$ resell at p^d, traders of type B resell at p^c, traders of type D resell at p^a. They all receive cash in these transactions.

11) Loan repayments
    - If the T-bank has not gone bankrupt at stage 8) traders of type $A2$ and $C2$ repay their loans plus interest. Because their wealth is totally transparent to the bank due to the monitoring, traders of type $A2$ and $C2$ cannot escape repayment. Hence repayment is not modeled as a decision variable of traders but the amount due gets simply subtracted from the total wealth of a trader. If traders get hit by an adverse shock such that they are unable to fully repay, they do not get punished because the bank knows that they are unable to pay.

12) Interest payment
    - The bank pays out the interest accrued on deposits to depositors of type $A1, C1, B$ and D.

A sketch of the game in extensive form is shown in figure 9.1. As argued in chapter 5 the shopper's paradise model is designed to capture behavior in markets with many participants. But off the equilibrium path there could exist small numbers of active traders (i.e., agents trading nonzero quantities) in markets with low trading volumes. Restrictions on quantities and prices ensure some minimum trading activity also off the equilibrium path. As in the preceding chapter minimum prices and maximum prices are pinned down by alternative trading opportunities in the external market. Minimum quantities to be exchanged are chosen to ensure a certain aggregate volume of trading on any path in the game. In particular, trading volume must be large enough such that the impact which at the first stage of the game traders have on the equilibrium price at stage 4) goes towards zero as N approaches infinity. Also, minimum amounts are chosen such as to simplify play off the equilibrium path of the game. If the conditions below are fulfilled, the equilibrium prices analyzed later in the game never hit the pricing constraints imposed by the prices in the external market even if minimum quantities are traded at maximum prices. Thereby the analysis can be concentrated on

Stages of the
game and
representative
decision
variables

Stage 1):
Exchanging
and deposit-
ing money
a_i^{A1}, c_i^{C1}

Stage 4a):
Supply
p_{bi}^B, b_i^B,
p_{di}^D, d_i^D

Stage 4b):
Matching
and demand
m_{2i}^{A1}, m_{2i}^{C1},
λ_i^{A2}, λ_i^{C2}

Stage 6):
Stochastic
shock
$\tilde{\psi}_i^{A2}$, $\tilde{\psi}_i^{C2}$

Stage 9):
Purchasing
from the
central bank
δ_{2i}^B, δ_{2i}^D

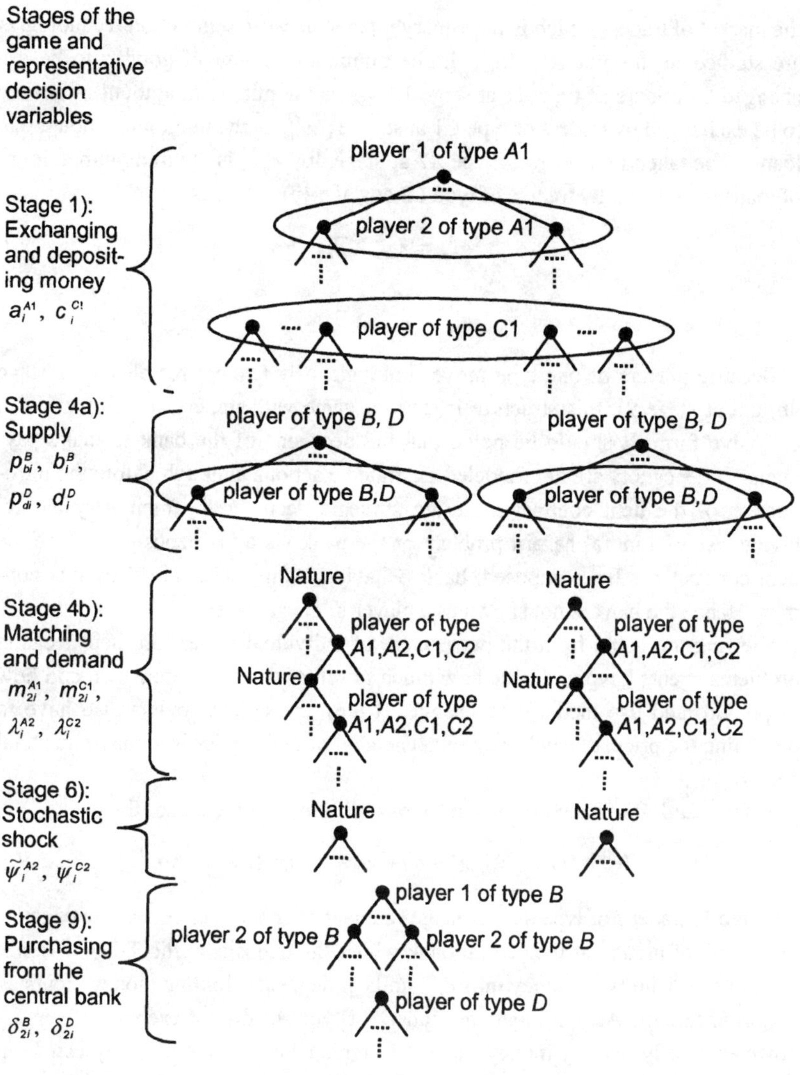

Figure 9.1 The sketch of a game tree for the model of the transactions bank

Note: The dots indicate a reduplication of the structure of the tree to which the dots refer.

the market of traders which is of primary interest because transaction technologies are studied in this market ($a^{A1}_{\min}$ is the minimum amount of good a to be exchanged by traders of type $A1$ at stage 1; $c^{C1}_{\min}$ is the minimum amount of good c to be exchanged by traders of type $C1$ at stage 1; $\lambda^{A2}_{\min}$ is the minimum amount of loans to be taken by traders of type $A2$ at stage 4b; $\lambda^{C2}_{\min}$ is the minimum amount of loans to be taken by traders of type $C2$ at stage 4b):

$$a^{A1}_{\min} = \lambda^{A2}_{\min} \geq \overline{p}_b, \qquad 9.1$$

$$c^{C1}_{\min} = \lambda^{C2}_{\min} \geq \overline{p}_d. \qquad 9.2$$

Because players of one type move simultaneously (except for players at stage 4b and at stage 9), this structure leads to a game with imperfect information in extensive form. It should be noted that the decisions of the bank to make payments to depositors are not modeled as strategic actions although before the introduction of the debt contract these are strategic decisions by their very nature, giving rise to a moral hazard problem of the bank vis á vis depositors. Once the debt contract has been imposed, bank behavior is fully determined by this contract. Hence the bank is not shown as a player in the game tree.[33]

Viewing the game from the perspective of individual traders, in their decision problems agents have to decide how much to sell of the goods they own and how to procure and use media of exchange. If they are sellers, traders also have to determine the price at which they sell. The goal of each trader is to maximize total wealth.

Total wealth for trader i of type $A1$ looks as follows at the end of the game:

$$p^b b^{A1}_i + (m^{A1}_i - m^{A1}_{2i})(1+r_1) + (a_0 - a^{A1}_i) p_a (1+r) + r_1 \delta^{A1}_i. \qquad 9.3$$

At stage 1) trader i of type $A1$ exchanges a quantity a^{A1}_i of her endowment against m^{A1}_i units of money at the central bank which she deposits at the T-bank. Hence she turns m^{A1}_i units of money into δ^{A1}_i units of deposits. Holding money incurs an opportunity cost. As a comparison traders of type $A2$ do not exchange their endowments early against money but get a trading loan. Therefore they can keep their endowment longer and earn an additional return at rate r per unit of their endowment. Traders of type $A1$ lose these returns when they exchange their endowments against money. Any part of their endowment which traders of type $A1$ do not turn into money also earns a rate of r per unit of endowment.

At stage 1) the trader has to obey the following restrictions which ensure that the trader does not exchange more than her endowment but at least the minimum amount $a^{A1}_{\min}$ and which determine how goods can be exchanged against money and money can be turned into deposits:

$$a_{\min}^{A1} \leq a_i^{A1} \leq a_0, \tag{9.4}$$

$$m_i^{A1} = p_a a_i^{A1}, \tag{9.5}$$

$$\delta_i^{A1} = m_i^{A1}. \tag{9.6}$$

At stage 4b) she decides how much of her money m_{2i}^{A1} deposited at the bank she is going to spend on acquiring goods of type *b*. She acquires a total amount b_i^{A1} of goods of type *b* at an average price of $\dddot{p}_{bi}^{A1}$ (weighted by the quantities of her goods exchanged). Note that this total quantity and average price result from all the decisions taken by the trader in a matching process as will be analyzed in detail in the appendix to this chapter. She pays by transferring funds from her bank account as a means of payment to her transaction partner(s). She cannot spend more than her bank deposits where it is assumed that the trader cannot purchase goods also from the interest she earns on her deposits because interest rates are paid only at stage 12):

$$0 \leq m_{2i}^{A1} \leq \delta_i^{A1}, \tag{9.7}$$

$$b_i^{A1} = m_{2i}^{A1} / \dddot{p}_{bi}^{A1}. \tag{9.8}$$

Eventually, at stage 12) trader *i* of type *A*1 receives an interest payment from the bank which is equal to $r_1\delta_i^{A1}$. This payment stems from depositing money between stage 1) and 4) at the T-bank. If the trader does not transfer all her deposits for purchasing goods but leaves her money in the bank till to the end of the game, she earns $(-m_{2i}^{A1} + m_i^{A1})(1 + r_1)$. The deposit rate on these holdings is again r_1. Note that for simplicity compounding interest is ignored.

The decision problem of trader *i* of type *C*1 is analogous to the decision problem above. Total wealth and the restrictions to be obeyed at the various stages of the game can be obtained by replacing *A* with *C*, *a* with *c*, and *b* with *d*.

Total wealth for trader *i* of type *A*2 at the end of the game looks as follows:

$$\max[\psi_i^{A2}[p^b b_i^{A2} + p_a a_0(1 + r)] - \lambda_i^{A2}(1 + r_{2i}^{A2}), 0]. \tag{9.9}$$

Total wealth reflects how starting from the initial endowment a_0 valued at the price set by the central bank p_a trades of real goods and financial transactions change the wealth position of the trader at the various stages of the game. At stage 4b) trader *i* of type *A*2 takes out a trading loan from the T-bank equal to λ_i^{A2} providing her with a medium of exchange to acquire a total amount b_i^{A2} of goods of type *b* at an average price $\dddot{p}_{bi}^{A2}$ (weighted by the quantities of her goods exchanged) in a matching process starting at the beginning of stage 4b). Note that this total quantity and average price result from all the decisions taken by the trader in a matching process as will be analyzed in detail in the appendix to this chapter. Any funds raised from the loan are directly turned into purchases. The goods acquired get resold at price p^b. The cash obtained in the resale transactions is deposited at the T-bank in a noninterest-bearing account. The trader is limited to receive a maximum amount of loans equal to λ^M which is the total sum of deposits made by all traders of type $A1$ and $C1$ divided by N.

$$b_i^{A2} = \lambda_i^{A2} / \dddot{p}_{bi}^{A2}. \tag{9.10}$$

$$\lambda_{\min}^{A2} \leq \lambda_i^{A2} \leq \lambda^M. \tag{9.11}$$

In the model of Diamond (1984) the loan size is taken as given whereas loan interest rates are determined by the condition that in expectation they have to be equal to the exogenously given interest rate on the capital market. Hence the loan market is kept simple. In the same spirit it is assumed here that interest rates are determined relative to some exogenously given capital market rate as described further below. Neither banks nor loan customers have an influence on rates. Because all loan customers are identical and take the same decisions in the symmetric equilibria considered, this implies that one trader cannot get a higher loan than a proportionate share in the pool of total deposits. This share equals the sum of deposits made by traders of type $A1$ and $C1$ divided by N. The corresponding amount of loans is λ^M.

At stage 5) trader i of type $A2$ earns a return on her endowment which is equal to $rp_a a_0$ and put into the bank account. This return is the benefit of holding the endowment longer than traders of type $A1$ during stage 1) and stage 9) before the endowment goods are exchanged with traders of type D. These returns are the major benefit for the trader from getting a trading loan for acquiring goods of type b at stage 4b).

After having acquired and resold the actually desired goods of type b the wealth of trader i of type $A2$ is affected by the stochastic shock variable $\tilde{\psi}_i^{A2}$ at stage 6) (note that the random variable is denoted as $\tilde{\psi}_i^{A2}$ whereas a realization of the random variable is denoted as ψ_i^{A2}). This shock gets monitored by the bank. Vis à vis other traders a moral hazard problem would arise due to the unobservability of the shock to outsiders. Traders who have taken out a loan might claim a low value of their shock variable such that they do not have to repay the loan even if the true realization of the shock is positive for them, thereby exploiting their informational advantage vis à vis other traders. But for the bank the shock is observable. Because both financial wealth from trading and real wealth in the form of the unsold endowment of these traders are subject to the same shock, the transaction account is informative for the bank if the traders of type $A2$ and $C2$ leave all their financial wealth in the bank. Assuming that the bank can observe account balances without a cost, she can infer the size of the shock from the changes in the account. If traders withdrew their trading revenues and returns from the bank, she would have to engage in costly monitoring to observe the shock.[34] But the traders of type *A*2 and *C*2 know that the bank will make inquiries about their wealth if they do not keep their financial funds in the transaction accounts. Hence they have no incentive to withdraw because there is no way of cheating on the bank. They are indifferent between withdrawing or not withdrawing their financial wealth from their accounts. For society it is clearly better if the bank does not have to spend additional resources on monitoring. Hence it is assumed that the traders leave their trading revenues and returns on endowments in the transactions accounts, thereby making the shock observable to the bank.

At stage 9) in the matching process trader *i* of type *A*2 sells her endowment to traders of type *D* at the price p_a set by the central bank and receives deposits δ_i^{A2} in return. Because these goods are valued at the price set by the central bank p_a and because traders of type *B* and *D* also buy at this price, trader *i* of type *A*2 is indifferent between selling or not selling her endowment. It is assumed that she sells her goods to other traders because she may need the proceeds from the sale to pay back the loan plus interest at stage 10). Loan repayment equals $\lambda_i^{A2}(1+r_{2i}^{A2})$ if the trader has enough total wealth in the end to fully repay the loan plus interest where the interest rate to be paid equals r_2. Otherwise any wealth the trader owns gets seized by the bank and the trader is left with zero wealth. Because the bank has full information about the true ability of a trader of type *A*2 to repay the loan, no moral hazard problems exist and the repayment is not explicitly modeled as a strategic problem.

Traders of type *C*2 solve a decision problem which is analogous to the decision problem of traders of type *A*2. It can be obtained by replacing *A* by *C*, *a* by *c*, and *b* by *d*.

Total wealth for trader *i* of type *B* at the end of the game looks as follows:

$$p^c c_i^B - \delta_{2i}^B + \delta_i^B + (b_0 + \varepsilon^B - b_i^{BS})\overline{p}_b + r_1 \delta_i^B . \qquad 9.12$$

Total wealth reflects how starting from the initial endowment b_0 trades of real goods and financial transactions change the wealth position of the trader at the various stages of the game. First, at stage 4a) trader *i* of type *B* strategically offers a price of p_{bi}^B for a maximum quantity of goods to be sold b_i^B in the shopper's paradise game. She cannot offer more than her endowment:

$$0 \le b_i^B \le b_0 + \varepsilon^B , \qquad 9.13$$

$$\varepsilon^B = 1/(N-1). \qquad 9.14$$

If goods from the endowment remain unsold, they are valued at the price $\overline{p}_b$ at which they can be sold in the external market. Note that ε^B is chosen such that *N*-1 traders of type *B* can supply one unit of the good by delivering ε^B which matters for the strategic logic of the shoppers' paradise game. Price bids can be made only in discrete steps of σ^B. Equilibrium prices are supposed to be always part of the scale of admissible prices (for the derivation of σ^B see the appendix to this chapter, stage 4a). If the number of traders goes towards infinity, σ^B goes towards zero. The price range within which goods can be traded in the market of traders is determined by external prices:

$$\overline{p}_b \leq p^B_{bi} \leq \widetilde{p}_b. \qquad 9.15$$

The smart random matching procedure determines how much of good *b* the trader can sell in the market at the price offered. The quantity actually sold after matching is denoted as b_i^{BS}. It is determined according to the following rules as perceived by a seller. It should be noted that this quantity is not random for the seller (definition of indices: *e*=1…*N*/2 across all traders of type *A*1; *f*=1…*N*/2 across all traders of type *A*2; *s*: all traders of type *B* for whom $p^B_{bs} \leq p^B_{bi}$; *k*: all traders of type *B* for whom $p^B_{bk} < p^B_{bi}$; *g*: all traders of type *B* for whom $p^B_{bg} = p^B_{bi}$).

$$b_i^{BS} = \begin{cases} b_i^B \text{ if } \sum_e b_e^{A1} + \sum_f b_f^{A2} \geq \sum_s b_s^B, \\ 0 \text{ if } \sum_e b_e^{A1} + \sum_f b_f^{A2} \leq \sum_k b_k^B, \\ (b_i^B / \sum_g b_g^B)(\sum_e b_e^{A1} + \sum_f b_f^{A2} - \sum_k b_k^B) \text{ if } \sum_e b_e^{A1} + \sum_f b_f^{A2} > \sum_k b_k^B \text{ and } \sum_e b_e^{A1} + \sum_f b_f^{A2} \leq \sum_s b_s^B \end{cases} \qquad 9.16$$

$\sum b_e^{A1} + \sum b_f^{A2}$ is the total market demand by traders of type *A*1 and *A*2 for good *b* can be optimally anticipated by her. A trader does not get matched with buyers if total market demand can be satisfied at prices lower than her own offer. She will be able to sell all the quantity offered if her offer is sufficiently cheap. If a trader bids a price at which market demand is positive but smaller than the total quantity of goods offered at this price, total demand at this price gets split up among sellers according to the quantities offered relative to the total quantity offered. Because trader *i* of type *B* gets paid by a transfer of deposits, she receives deposits denoted as δ_i^B equal to the value of the goods sold:

$$\delta_i^B = p^B_{bi} b_i^{BS}. \qquad 9.17$$

Eventually, at stage 9) trader *i* of type *B* uses the funds deposited in her account to purchase goods of type *c* at price p_c either from the central bank or from traders of type *C*2 in order to resell them at price p^c. She cannot spend more than the funds in her deposit account:

$$0 \le \delta_{2i}^{B} \le \delta_{i}^{B}. \qquad 9.18$$

If the bank goes bankrupt, it distributes any funds available among depositors. The amount trader i of type B receives is denoted as δ_i^{BL}. In this case the constraint becomes

$$0 \le \delta_{2i}^{B} \le \delta_{i}^{BL}. \qquad 9.19$$

Note that if the trader acquires goods at the central bank, she has to convert the funds in her account into cash. It will be seen below that the T- bank has exactly the cash reserves required for satisfying this liquidity demand. Eventually, at stage 11) trader i of type B gets paid the interest she has earned from holding deposits at the T-bank which is equal to $r_1\delta_i^{B}$.

The decision problem for traders of type D is analogous to the decision problem for traders of type B. It can be obtained by replacing B by D, b by d, c by a, and A by C in the description above.

There are two interest rates in the model: The deposit rate r_1 and the loan rate r_2. They are determined as follows. The expected rate of return on deposits r_1 should be equal to the rate of return denoted by R which depositors could earn elsewhere on the capital market between stages 1) and 12): E(2 r_1)=R. Note that depositors earn a rate of r_1 on interest-bearing deposits between stage 1) and 4) and between stage 5) and 12). The condition above implies that simple interest on deposits is considered (i.e., compounding between the two subperiods is ignored). For the relationship between the real rate on the endowment r and financial rate R equality is assumed such that R=r.

The bank must charge loan customers a sufficiently large rate r_{2i}^{A2} and r_{2j}^{C2}, respectively, such that in expectation she is able to pay back deposits plus interest on deposits. Note that the bank has raised all deposits and has made all loans at stage 4b). Hence also loan rates are set at this stage. At this point the bank anticipates further optimal play of traders and sets loan rates accordingly. Therefore the optimal loan rate depends upon the equilibrium strategies of the players. The equilibrium strategies of players described in the next section imply that a bank setting loan rates at stage 4b) takes the total amount of deposits $\Sigma\delta_i^{A1T} + \Sigma\delta_j^{C1T}$ determined in prior play as given. The bank anticipates that players of type $A2$ and $C2$ optimally raise this amount as loans. The amount chosen is denoted by $(\lambda_i^{A2T}N/2 + \lambda_i^{C2T}N/2)$. As on all anticipated optimal paths all loan customers choose the same strategies, loan repayments are i.i.d. random variables. For $N \to \infty$ the probability for the bank to go bankrupt goes towards zero which implies that 2 r_1 =R. From these considerations follows that the loan interest rate must be set according to the following condition such that in expectation the bank is able to pay back deposits plus interest on deposits (denote the loan interest rate by r_2 because in a symmetric equilibrium it is the same for all loan customers):

$$E[(1+r_2)(\lambda_i^{A2T}N/2+\lambda_i^{C2T}N/2)]= \\ 2r_1(\Sigma\delta_i^{A1T}+\Sigma\delta_j^{C1T})+(1+r_1)(\lambda_i^{A2T}N/2+\lambda_i^{C2T}N/2). \quad 9.20$$

Note that the total interest the bank has to pay on deposits at stage 12) equals $3r_1(\Sigma\delta_i^{A1T}+\Sigma\delta_j^{C1T})$.[35] The condition above can be simplified to

$$E[(1+r_2)]=1+3r_1. \quad 9.21$$

Hence the loan rate r_2 must be set such that in expectation the bank earns a rate of $3r_1$ per dollar lent.

The T-bank is the key financial institution providing transaction services. At stage 1) the bank collects deposits from traders of type $A1$ and $C1$. At stage 4b) the T-bank turns deposits into loans by extending credit to traders of type $A2$ and $C2$. Traders of type $A2$ and $C2$ hold the funds from the loans they have received also in (non-interest bearing) transaction accounts at the T-bank. Because funds from loans get turned into deposits again the bank increases the amount of total deposits beyond the amount of money issued by the central bank. Thereby the bank creates additional deposits equal to the amount of loans extended. Transfers of deposits are used for making payments in transactions. The deposits can be considered as a kind of "near money" functioning as a medium of exchange.

The depository contracts are debt contracts with a nonpecuniary penalty in the case of default of the bank. The specific contractual form is endogenously derived from the same contract design problem as in the appendix to chapter 7. Note that an ex post informational asymmetry exists also between the bank and depositors. Depositors cannot observe the bank's income ex post because they cannot observe the stochastic shocks to individual traders' wealth which determine loan repayments. Debt contracts with a nonpecuniary penalty equal to the shortfall are the optimal contractual form to solve the incentive problem between the bank and depositors. Because wealth shocks and hence loan repayments are i.i.d. random variables, for a large bank the law of large numbers can be applied. As will be seen in the next section, on the equilibrium path the likelihood for the bank to go bankrupt and get punished approaches zero as the bank size goes towards infinity (see Diamond, 1984).

Off the equilibrium path loan repayments need not be i.i.d. because traders can choose different loan sizes, leading to different distributions for loan repayments. Hence the convergence of the average repayment towards some fixed value is not ensured and even a large bank can go bankrupt. In this case, at stage 8) once the bank has observed the shocks to its loan customers, the bank knows whether it will be unable to fully pay depositors and hence whether it is bankrupt. In the case of bankruptcy the bank gets liquidated. It requests loan customers to repay their loans in cash prematurely (which can be done without a loss at this stage of the game because traders can simply exchange their endowments against cash at the central bank). Eventually, the bank distributes its assets (which are all in the form of cash) among depositors. Each depositor receives cash in proportion to the share of her deposits in total deposits. Because of the bankruptcy the bank has to undergo nonpecuniary punishment according to the rules of the depository debt contract.

At stage 7) the bank monitors the wealth of its loan customers. As already explained in the description of this stage, the bank can monitor the realizations of stochastic shocks to the wealth of her loan customers at zero cost because the bank accounts which these loan customers hold reveal the size of the shock. This specific feature of the model shows synergies between transaction services and financing services: The transaction accounts are informative for assessing the solvency of loan customers. Note that in the model of Diamond (1984) a bank similar to the T-bank has to incur some positive monitoring cost because informative transaction accounts are ignored.

Traders use bank accounts to make payments for their transactions at stages 4) and 9). By transferring the claims against the bank to their trading partners traders can pay just as if they were holding cash. The debt claims against the T-bank have a high degree of transferability because due to the incentive compatible debt contracts and due to the large size of the bank funds deposited there are as credible and safe just as if they were issued by the central bank. However, the advantage of the T-bank over cash is that deposits are interest bearing. The bank can pay interest at a rate of r_1 because it creates money by extending loans such that the loan customers do not have to use their resources to acquire a medium of exchange. They can earn additional returns at a rate of r on the value of their endowments. Part of these additional returns flow back to the bank in the form of loan interest payments (at an expected rate of $3\,r_1$ per dollar borrowed) and get distributed among deposit holders at deposit rate r_1.

The central bank has a supplementary role in the model of the T-bank. It provides money as a medium of exchange which can be deposited at the T-bank. In principle the T-bank could also accept goods directly in exchange for opening a deposit account and make real loans by lending out those goods. For this purpose the T-bank would have to credibly stick to a fixed ratio according to which it exchanges a certain quantity of a good against a certain amount of deposits. The formal structure of such a model would be very similar to the structure of the model developed here. Still, following existing institutional rules the creation of deposits by banks has to start with initial injections of money provided by the central bank. Hence a model incorporating this rule is considered.

One other important role of the central bank is to provide an efficient transaction technology if the bank collapses. Money issued by the central bank also provides a standard of value because even bank deposits are denominated in money and wealth is denominated in monetary terms after the bank ceases to operate. Finally, note that the central bank acts as a buffer because off the equilibrium path the total amounts of goods of type a and c to be exchanged against money vary with the random shocks. By fixing the ratio at which those goods can be exchanged against money the bank has to buy any excess amounts in the market and it has to supply goods in the case of adverse shocks.

Just as in chapters 6 and 7 as a final technical assumption discrete quantities for goods and for money (including deposits which are denominated in monetary terms) are introduced. Hence quantities, money, and prices in the model are all discrete. This feature allows to apply sequential equilibrium which will be used as an equilibrium concept in the next section (see, e.g., Fudenberg and Tirole, 1991, p. 345). However, several problems result from the introduction of discrete prices, money, and quantities. As will be seen in the next section, equilibrium prices are derived from the total quantities of money acquired earlier. The scales for prices and money need not be compatible, however. To avoid these problems it is assumed that just like for prices the size of the discrete steps for monetary units goes towards zero as N goes towards infinity. Because the analysis focuses on this case, in the limit the problem of the incompatibility of the monetary scales and quantity scales "disappears". Hence for specifying expectations in sequential equilibrium the model is analyzed from the point of view of discrete strategies. For analyzing money, prices, and quantities the model is analyzed as if strategies became continuous in the limiting case of N going towards infinity. A more refined mathematical analysis of these technical problems is not undertaken at this point.

9.2 The equilibrium in the model of the transactions bank

In Proposition 4 a symmetric sequential equilibrium in the model of the transactions bank is described. The concept of sequential equilibrium is used because in extensive form the simultaneous move game between sellers becomes a game of imperfect information such that an equilibrium concept with expectation formation is required which restricts beliefs everywhere in the game.

Proposition 4: There exists a symmetric sequential equilibrium with maximum trading volume in which traders of type $A1$ and $C1$ exchange their entire endowments against money and deposit it at the T-bank and in which traders of type $A2$ and $C2$ take out the maximum possible amount of loans. Traders of type B and D offer all their endowments in the shopper's paradise game at a price at which N-1 traders of type B and D can satisfy total market demand. Traders of type $A1$, $A2$, $C1$, and $C2$ accept all these offers. On the equilibrium path a large T-bank pays interest on deposits almost with certainty. For the equilibrium to obtain the benefit of resale relative to the maximum possible acquisition costs of goods to be resold must be higher than the expected financing cost such that $p^b / \widetilde{p}_b > 1 + 3r_1$.

Proof: See appendix to chapter 9.

The trading outcomes in the equilibrium with the T-bank are similar to the equilibrium with money as central bank debt. However, the institutional setup is quite different. The T-bank combines the provision of a credible medium of exchange with the private productive investment of resources such that interest can be paid on deposits. The cost of issuing deposits functioning as a medium of exchange is kept low because of the high degree of diversification in the loan portfolio of a bank which reduces the incentive cost of issuing a credible medium of exchange to almost zero just as in the case of the central bank.

The equilibrium in Proposition 4 is described in full detail in the following paragraphs. Because a symmetric equilibrium is considered, it suffices to describe the equilibrium strategy for one representative trader of each type.

- Trader i of type $A1$ optimally chooses $a_i^{A1*} = a_0 = 1$, expecting other traders of type $A1$ deciding before her also to choose a_0 at stage 1) of the game. At stage 4b) trader i of type $A1$ accepts any offer made at any information set. Hence in any one smart random matching process at stage 4b) she optimally chooses the maximum amount of deposits possible to exchange. On the equilibrium path trader i of type $A1$ chooses $a_i^{A1*} = 1$ and $m_{2i}^{A1*} = 1$.
- Trader i of type $C1$ pursues an optimal strategy which is analogous to the one chosen by trader i of type $A1$. It can be obtained by replacing A with C, and a with c in the description of the optimal strategy above. She expects traders of type $A1$ to choose $a_i^{A1*} = a_0 = 1$ at stage 1).
- Trader i of type $A2$ optimally chooses the maximum amount of loans possible at any information set at stage 4b). On the equilibrium path trader i of type $A2$ chooses $\lambda_i^{A2*} = 1$.
- Trader i of type $C2$ pursues an optimal strategy which is analogous to the one chosen by trader i of type $A2$. It can be obtained by replacing A with C in the description of the optimal strategy above.
- At stage 4a) at each of her information sets trader i of type B optimally chooses $b_i^{B*} = 1 + \varepsilon^B$ and $p_{bi}^{BT*} = (\Sigma \delta_i^{A1T} + \Sigma \lambda_j^{A2T}) / N$. The variable p_{bi}^{BT*} is the optimal price chosen in one of the subgames starting at the beginning of stage 4). $\Sigma \delta_i^{A1T}$ is the sum over all deposits held by traders of type $A1$ on the path leading to the information set in this specific subgame at which trader i of type B decides and $\Sigma \lambda_j^{A2T}$ is the sum across all loans taken out by traders of type $A2$ on the anticipated optimal path following the information set. Trader i of type B expects other traders of her own type choosing before her to take the same decision as her own equilibrium decision in each of the subgames starting at stage 4a) and she expects traders of type D to play also their equilibrium strategies. At stage 9) trader i of type B optimally chooses $\delta_{2i}^{BT*} = \delta_i^{BT}$ at any information set at which she draws where δ_i^{BT} denotes the deposits held by the trader resulting from the path leading to the information set and δ_{2i}^{BT*} is the optimal amount of deposits chosen at the information set. If the bank goes

bankrupt, $\delta_{2i}^{BT*} = \delta_i^{BLT}$ where δ_i^{BLT} is the amount of money the trader obtains in the bankruptcy proceedings of a bank which failed on the path leading to δ_i^{BLT}. On the equilibrium path trader i of type B chooses $b_i^{B*} = 1 + \varepsilon^B$, $p_{bi}^{B*} = 1$, and $\delta_{2i}^{B*} = 1$ and the bank never becomes bankrupt as N goes towards infinity.

- Trader i of type D pursues an optimal strategy which is analogous to the one chosen by trader i of type B. It can be obtained by replacing B by D, b by d, and A by C in the description of the optimal strategy above.

The equilibrium decisions follow from the basic incentive to trade due to the differences of traders in endowments and reselling opportunities. The market environment of the shopper's paradise model and the transaction technology provided by the T-bank determine how these basic incentives to trade can be translated into specific economic interactions between traders.

Traders in the model of the T-bank can realize the full potential for exchange. Under the equilibrium prices in the market they have an incentive to trade as large a volume as possible because this yields the maximum quantity for profitable reselling and hence maximizes expected wealth. The T-bank provides a highly efficient transaction technology for conducting transactions. Unlike in the models with intermediate exchange of goods and privately issued I.O.U.s where severe market imperfections could hinder trade, transferable deposits provided by the T-bank allow transactions to be conducted as smoothly as in the model with money issued by the central bank. A credible structure of incentives supports the bank deposits functioning as a medium of exchange. Just as in the case of the central bank the potentially costly creation of a medium of exchange is delegated to an agent who is particularly well suited to deal with this cost. Unlike the central bank, however, the T-bank keeps the risk of bankruptcy low by making diversified investments into loans. Due to this reinvestment of funds the T-bank can offer the additional benefit of paying interest on deposits. The bank also has the advantage of observing wealth shocks to traders without a cost due to information provided by transaction accounts and it can credibly promise funds to be paid back at a much lower incentive cost than individual traders because of its large size and its diversification benefits.

At stage 9) players of type B and D find it profitable to spend all their transaction funds on buying goods of type c and a because resale prices are higher than the price of acquiring the goods from traders of type $A2$ and $C2$ or from the central bank. Because the prices for these goods are fixed by the central bank and because the central bank acts as a buffer satisfying any excess demand from its own stock (and absorbing any excess supply if traders of type B and D cannot buy all the goods available in the economy at the price set by the central bank), these transactions do not take place in the strategic context of a shopper's paradise model.

Traders of type B and D are sellers in the shopper's paradise model at stage 4). At the equilibrium price N-1 traders of type B offer exactly the total quantity demanded by traders of type A. Thereby sellers of type B get disciplined as they realize that by charging a higher price than the equilibrium price they would have no match for their offer and hence could not engage in profitable reselling. Bidding a lower price than the equilibrium price would not be attractive either because due to the constraint on the discrete bidding steps the total quantity sold would go up but total expected wealth would go down. Hence all traders of type B offer the equilibrium price and demand gets split up among them. The same logic holds true also for the relationship between traders of type C and D. Buyers in the smart random matching process realize that any bid to make a deal offers the best terms available to them in the market because any other future offers will be at best at the same price, but possibly at a lower quantity or at a higher price. Hence they do not postpone purchases.

The subgames starting at the beginning of stage 4) differ with respect to the amount of funds for transactions that traders of type $A1$ and $C1$ have raised. The equilibrium prices reflect differences in the total amounts. On the equilibrium path traders acquire the maximum amount of transaction funds possible. Transactions along the equilibrium path have a simple structure. First, traders raise as much transaction funds as possible. Then sellers offer all their endowments at a price of one. Smart random matching is simple in this case because everyone offers the same price. Eventually the sellers acquire one unit of the good for resale. Because on the equilibrium path loan repayments are i.i.d. random variables, the law of large numbers can be applied. The more loans a bank takes, the lower is the probability of going bankrupt.

On the equilibrium path and on all paths it optimally anticipates after stage 4a) a large bank always keeps financial balance and breaks even in the end almost with certainty.[36] The financial balance of the T-bank on these paths can be traced back step by step. At stage 1) the T-bank raises a total amount $\sum m_i^{A1} + \sum m_i^{C1}$ of cash which is turned into deposits. Till to stage 4) depositors of type $A1$ and $C1$ are promised a rate of r_1 on these deposits (note that interest gets paid out only at stage 12). At stage 4) the bank turns the $\sum m_i^{A1} + \sum m_i^{C1}$ units of cash into $\sum m_i^{A1} + \sum m_i^{C1}$ units of loans. Because loan customers put the funds acquired also into deposit accounts, at the end of stage 4) the T-bank has $\sum m_i^{A1} + \sum m_i^{C1}$ units of cash, $\sum m_i^{A1} + \sum m_i^{C1}$ units of loans with an expected return of $(\sum m_i^{A1} + \sum m_i^{C1})(1+3r_1)$ and $2(\sum m_i^{A1} + \sum m_i^{C1})$ units of deposits. Because depository funds raised from loans are immediately used for paying in transactions they do not earn any interest. Hence total interest promised up to this point to traders of type $A1$ and $C1$ equals $r_1(\sum m_i^{A1} + \sum m_i^{C1})$. In the shopper's paradise game at stage 4) deposits get transferred as a medium of exchange between agents which leaves the balance sheet of the T-bank unaffected. Traders of type B and D

get promised interest payments of $2\,r_1 N$ in total which accrue at stage 12). Hence total interest promised up to this point by the bank equals $3Nr_1$. At stage 5) traders of type $A2$ and $C2$ put their trading revenues and cash returns into noninterest-bearing accounts. Hence total assets in the bank increase to $(\Sigma m_i^{A1} + \Sigma m_i^{C1})(1 + p^b) + rN$ units of cash plus $\Sigma m_i^{A1} + \Sigma m_i^{C1}$ units of loans with an expected return of $(\Sigma m_i^{A1} + \Sigma m_i^{C1})(1 + 3r_1)$. Total deposits equal $(\Sigma m_i^{A1} + \Sigma m_i^{C1})(2 + p^b) + rN$.

After having observed the individual wealth shocks affecting the wealth of her loan customers the T-bank can assess its solvency. Bankruptcy occurs if the total value of loan repayments plus interest that can be made by loan customers after having been hit by the shock is less than the total amount owed by the bank to depositors plus any remaining noninterest-bearing deposits of nondefaulting traders of types $A2$ and $C2$. If assets do not cover liabilities the bank gets liquidated. If the bank does not go bankrupt, it collects loans and repays deposits plus interest at the end of the game. It should be noted, however, that the bank charges loan interest rates at stage 4b) such that anticipating future optimal play of traders it breaks even on average. Because all loan customers play the same strategies on the anticipated optimal path following stage 4a) such that loan repayments are i.i.d. random variables and because the case of $N \to \infty$ is considered in the limit the probability for the bank of going bankrupt along these paths goes towards zero. Therefore aggregate assets and liabilities on the balance sheet of the bank remain unaffected by the stochastic shocks on the optimally anticipated paths following stage 4a).

At stage 9) on the paths considered where financial balance is always maintained the bank pays out cash to those traders of type B and D who buy goods from the central bank. Assuming that first goods of traders of type $A2$ and $C2$ get sold and assuming further that traders of type B and D have enough funds to buy those goods,[37] N units of deposits from traders of type B and D get transferred to traders of type $A2$ and $C2$. The rest is paid out in cash to traders of type B and D such that they can acquire goods from the central bank. Hence after those transactions the T-bank has $(\Sigma m_i^{A1} + \Sigma m_i^{C1})(1 + p^b) + rN - (2(\Sigma m_i^{A1} + \Sigma m_i^{C1}) - N) = (1 + r)N + (p^b - 1)(\Sigma m_i^{A1} + \Sigma m_i^{C1})$ units of cash plus $\Sigma m_i^{A1} + \Sigma m_i^{C1}$ units of loans with an expected return of $(\Sigma m_i^{A1} + \Sigma m_i^{C1})(1 + 3r_1)$. Its depository liabilities equal $(\Sigma m_i^{A1} + \Sigma m_i^{C1})(2 + p^b) + rN - (2(\Sigma m_i^{A1} + \Sigma m_i^{C1}) - N)$ which can be simplified to $(1 + r)N + p^b(\Sigma m_i^{A1} + \Sigma m_i^{C1})$.

Eventually, traders of type $A2$ and $C2$ pay back their loans. Note that in the scenario considered they have sold all their endowments in exchange for deposits. Due to the condition on loan rates and the large number of agents traders of type $A2$ and $C2$ pay back a total amount of $(\Sigma m_i^{A1} + \Sigma m_i^{C1})(1 + 3r_1)$ which gets subtracted both from the bank's assets and liabilities. Therefore after loan repayments the bank has total assets of $(1 + r)N + (p^b - 1)(\Sigma m_i^{A1} + \Sigma m_i^{C1})$ in cash and total deposits outstanding equal to $(1+r)N+(p^b-1-3r_1)(\Sigma m_i^{A1}+\Sigma m_i^{C1})$. Because $r>r_1$ the bank has enough cash to pay out all deposits to traders of type *A*2 and *C*2 and to pay at stage 12) all the interest promised on deposits which is equal to $3r_1(\Sigma m_i^{A1}+\Sigma m_i^{C1})$. Hence indeed a T-bank having a structure as described in this chapter is economically viable and breaks even exactly on all the paths it optimally anticipates after stage 4a). Off these paths following stage 4b) the bank can go bankrupt and may have to undergo nonpecuniary punishment.

9.3 Conclusions from the model of the transactions bank

This chapter shows how a transactions-oriented private bank with a similar institutional structure as the bank in Diamond (1984) provides efficient solutions to transactions problems between agents. Just as the other debt-based financial solutions (privately issued I.O.U.s and money provided by the central bank) transferable bank deposits eliminate the need to conduct burdensome barter. However, the T-bank is also highly efficient at dealing with the frictions arising in those debt relationships. Ex post informational asymmetries about the ability of transaction partners to repay debt was considered as the main friction as suggested by contemporary banking theory. This friction allowed to derive endogenously bank debt as an institutional design optimally responding to this friction.

The incentive cost of issuing debt serving as a medium of exchange was shown to be a key problem in chapter 7 for private agents individually issuing I.O.U.s serving as a medium of exchange because an underprovision of this medium occurred. In chapter 8 this underprovision could be eliminated by delegating the issuing of debt serving as a medium of exchange to the central bank. In the absence of wealth shocks affecting the central bank the incentive costs of providing money could be significantly reduced to practically zero. However, the central bank did not invest the funds raised in the process such that interest could be paid. Hence, eventually the T-bank turned out to be an even more efficient institutional form for providing transaction services. Just like the central bank it could provide credible debt in the form of deposits at almost zero incentive costs due to highly diversified investments into trading loans which reduced the probability of bankruptcy for the T-bank to almost zero. Hence also the T-bank could provide transferable deposits as a medium of exchange and thereby eliminate the problem of underprovision by individual private agents just like the central bank. It was equally effective at promoting beneficial trade. Because the loans paid interest the T-bank could also pay interest on the deposits serving as a medium of exchange whereas money provided by the central bank did not pay interest.

As will be seen in the next chapter, the institutional structure of the T-bank efficiently addressing transaction problems is also useful for providing financing and investment services in a capital market with frictions. Essentially, because credit problems arise both in transactions contexts and in financing and investments contexts and because commercial banks are efficient at addressing such credit problems, they can provide useful services for both purposes.

The old question in monetary economics why individuals use money if it is dominated in return by other equally safe assets is addressed in a straightforward way: Transferable deposit contracts acting as "near money" *are* interest-bearing and the interest paid is one of the main reasons why transactions are conducted through banks rather than with cash. This does not explain the coexistence of cash and money provided by banks, however. More elaborated theories analyzing differences between these two economically close but still distinct financial assets are necessary to explain coexistence. In the model of this chapter money issued by the central bank has the role of providing a standard of value and an efficient alternative transaction technology if the T-bank goes bankrupt (which only happens off the equilibrium path, however). Thereby the relationship between the central bank and the T-bank is captured only in a rudimentary form. Many other important issues arise in this relationship such as the lender of last resort function of the central bank or the role of the central bank in the payments system.

Monetary theory has not settled on "the" friction providing the "best" explanation for the role of money and probably this question is futile because money is likely to address several frictions simultaneously which cannot be ranked in importance. In conjunction with a barter friction that gets efficiently addressed by the introduction of money, lack of trust in the ability of transaction partners to repay is a friction which provides internally consistent explanations for key institutional features of monetary economies. It leads to a characterization of money as debt. This specific contractual form is endogenously derived from the problem of trust. Hence lack of trust and money as debt are internally consistent. Also, the problem of trust leads to banks as financial institutions addressing this friction effectively.

Comparing the model of the transactions bank to the other transaction technologies leads to the following assessment:

- The deposit contracts created by the T-bank help avoid burdensome barter by providing a system of transferable debt which allows conducting transactions smoothly.
- Transferable deposit contracts created by the T-bank effectively address the problem of a lack of trust in exchange by providing a safe and liquid transactions medium which is generally accepted. The trust in deposits provided by the T-bank is supported by the diversification of assets and by incentive compatible debt contracts.
- Transferable deposit contracts functioning as a medium of exchange do not require the high incentive costs necessary to support a system of privately issued I.O.U.s. For large, well diversified banks the incentive cost captured by

the expected nonpecuniary punishment a debtor (in this case the bank) has to undergo even if she is really unable to pay approaches zero.

- Due to the reduction of the incentive cost of issuing credible deposits the problem of the underprovision of a medium of exchange which existed in the case of privately issued I.O.U.s gets solved.
- Transferable deposit contracts serving as a medium of exchange promote trade just like money provided by the central bank and reduce the loss of resources in the transactions process.
- Unlike cash transferable bank deposits serving as a medium of exchange have the additional benefit of paying interest because the bank creates deposits partly by extending loans which enable traders and the bank to make interest payments.
- The T-bank has an insitutional structure which is closely related to the banking model by Diamond (1984).

Further conclusions from the model of the transactions bank will be drawn in the next chapter. In particular it will be interesting to investigate the question whether other transaction technologies exist which are even more efficient than the T-bank. Also the results of this chapter and of the other preceding chapters will be discussed in the broader context of monetary theory and banking theory.

Appendix to Chapter 9: Proof of Proposition 4

For the sequential equilibrium considered in Proposition 4 beliefs are derived which are consistent with the strategies of players. Because a symmetric equilibrium in pure strategies is considered in a game which is a simultaneous move game represented in extensive form, agents expect other traders deciding "before" them to choose the same equilibrium strategies as their own equilibrium strategies. This result can also be obtained by considering a sequence of completely mixed strategies which approach the equilibrium strategies in the limit such that beliefs consistent with strategies can be derived everywhere in the game by applying Bayes' rule. Given this system of beliefs the sequential rationality of the strategies of players is analyzed in the following paragraphs. Note that any indices in summation signs run from 1 to N in the derivations below (e.g., index k for some good of type y in Σy_k). If sums are calculated over groups of traders of type $A1$, $A2$, $C1$, or $C2$, the summation index runs from 1 to $N/2$.

At stage 9) consider one information set in any of the subgames starting at this stage where player i of type B has offered some quantity b_i^{BT} of her endowment at price p_{bi}^{BT} in previous play and has actually sold a quantity of b_i^{BST} in the matching process leading to the information set. The revenue of this transaction is kept as a deposit equal to δ_i^{BT}. Hence at this specific information set in this specific subgame trader i of type B solves the following decision problem:

$$\begin{aligned} &\max\,(p^c / p_c - 1)\delta_{2i}^{BT} + \delta_i^{BT} + (b_0 + \varepsilon^B - b_i^{BST})\overline{p}_b + r_1\delta_i^{BT} \\ &\text{s.t.}\, 0 \le \delta_{2i}^{BT} \le \delta_i^{BT} \end{aligned} \qquad \text{A 9.1}$$

The maximum amount the trader can spend on buying goods of type c is δ_i^{BT} If the bank goes bankrupt, the constraint becomes $0 \le \delta_{2i}^{BT} \le \delta_i^{BLT}$. δ_i^{BLT} is the amount of deposits the trader gets paid in the liquidation of the bank during the bankruptcy proceedings. Because $p^c > p_c$ the coefficient on the decision variable δ_{2i}^{BT} is positive and the trader optimally chooses the maximum amount possible $\delta_{2i}^{BT*} = \delta_i^{BT}$ or $\delta_{2i}^{BT*} = \delta_i^{BLT}$, respectively. The same reasoning also holds true for traders of type D.

At stage 4b) the optimal choice of player i of type $A1$ has the same general structure in any of the subgames starting at this stage at any information set at which she has to choose. Consider one representative subgame starting at stage 4b) and denote variables belonging to the subgame with superindex T. On the game path to the subgame player i of type $A1$ has acquired monetary balances m_i^{A1T} resulting from exchanging a certain amount a_i^{A1T} of her endowment at the central bank into money in previous play and she has already spent a total amount of $m_{2i}^{A1T\leftarrow}$ at an average price $p_{bi}^{A1T\leftarrow}$ (weighted by the quantities of her funds exchanged) in the random matching process leading to the information set at which she decides. Just as in the preceding chapters where buyers in the smart random matching process had to decide also here an argument can be made that because of the logic of the smart random matching process a trader of type $A1$ always finds it optimal to acquire as much as possible if she gets an offer which increases her expected total wealth and she never finds it optimal to delay dropping out of the market by buying a zero quantity because the terms of future offers are less favorable for the buyer. Hence at any information set at stage 4b) trader i of type $A1$ solves a simple static optimization problem whose solution is also part of the dynamic strategic solution (see the appendix to chapter 6, stage 2b for an analogous formal argument):

$$\begin{aligned}\max\ & (p^b / p_{bi}^{A1T} - 1 - r_1)m_{2i}^{A1T} + m_i^{A1T}(1+r_1) + (a_0 - a_i^{A1T})p_a(1+r) + \\ & + (p^b / p_{bi}^{A1T\leftarrow} - 1 - r_1)m_{2i}^{A1T\leftarrow} + r_1\delta_i^{A1T} \\ \text{s.t.}\ & 0 \le m_{2i}^{A1T} \le \min[m_i^{A1T} - m_{2i}^{A1T\leftarrow}, m_j^{BT}]\end{aligned} \qquad \text{A 9.2}$$

m_j^{BT} is the maximum amount of money that trader j of type B with whom trader i of type $A1$ got matched at the information set considered is ready to exchange according to her offer. The sign of the coefficient on m_{2i}^{A1T} is key.[38] If $p^b / p_{bi}^{A1T} > 1 + r_1$ the agent chooses the maximum amount possible at the information set. Because according to the condition in Proposition 4 it holds that $p^b / \tilde{p}_b > 1 + 3r_1$ the condition is indeed fulfilled. The same basic argument about the optimal decision at stage 4b) holds true also for players of type $C1$.

At stage 4b) the optimal choice of player i of type $A2$ has the same general structure in any of the subgames starting at this stage at any information set at which she has to choose. Consider one specific information set at stage 4b) and denote variables pertaining to the information set with superindex T. Just as for buyers in chapter 6), stage 2b) it also holds for trader i of type $A2$ that postponing trades is never optimal because she does not get better terms in future offers. Hence the solution to the problem below is also part of the general dynamic solution for the optimal decision of trader i of type $A2$:

$$\begin{aligned}&\max \mathrm{E}\{\max[\tilde{\psi}_i^{A2}(\lambda_i^{A2T} p^b / p_{bi}^{A2T} + \lambda_i^{A2T\leftarrow} p^b / p_{bi}^{A2T\leftarrow} + 1 + r) - (\lambda_i^{A2T} + \lambda_i^{A2T\leftarrow})(1 + r_{2i}^{A2T}), 0]\} \\ &\text{s.t. } \lambda_{\min}^{A2} \le \lambda_i^{A2T} \le \min[\lambda^{MT} - \lambda_i^{A2T\leftarrow}, b_j^{BT\leftarrow} p_{bi}^{A2T}].\end{aligned} \qquad \text{A 9.3}$$

The decision variable in the decision problem is λ_i^{A2T}. The variable $\lambda_i^{A2T\leftarrow}$ is the total amount of loans already taken out earlier in the matching process at prior information sets and $p_{bi}^{A1T\leftarrow}$ is the average price of those deals weighted by the quantities of her funds exchanged.[39] $b_j^{BT\leftarrow}$ is the remaining amount of her offer which trader j of type B with whom trader i of type $A2$ has been matched at the information set has not yet exchanged in prior matches. Denote $\tilde{\psi}_i^{A2}(\lambda_i^{A2T} p^b / p_{bi}^{A2T} + \lambda_i^{A2T\leftarrow} p^b / p_{bi}^{A2T\leftarrow} + 1 + r) - (\lambda_i^{A2T} + \lambda_i^{A2T\leftarrow})(1 + r_{2i}^{A2T})$ by x and the expression $2(\lambda_i^{A2T} p^b / p_{bi}^{A2T} + \lambda_i^{A2T\leftarrow} p^b / p_{bi}^{A2T\leftarrow} + 1 + r) - (\lambda_i^{A2T} + \lambda_i^{A2T\leftarrow})(1 + r_{2i}^{A2T})$ by z. The density function pertaining to x is denoted as $f_x(x)$. With this notation the expected return for the trader in the optimization problem above can be rewritten as

$$\int_0^z x f_x(x) dx \,. \qquad \text{A 9.4}$$

Denoting $\tilde{\psi}_i^{A2}(\lambda_i^{A2T} p^b / p_{bi}^{A2T} + \lambda_i^{A2T\leftarrow} p^b / p_{bi}^{A2T\leftarrow} + 1 + r)$ as y and denoting the corresponding density function as $f_y(y)$, one can rewrite the integral above as follows:

$$\begin{aligned}\int_0^z x f_x(x) dx = & \int_{(\lambda_i^{A2T} + \lambda_i^{A2T\leftarrow})(1 + r_{2i}^{A2T})}^{2[\lambda_i^{A2T} p^b / p_{bi}^{A2T} + \lambda_i^{A2T\leftarrow} p^b / p_{bi}^{A2T\leftarrow} + 1 + r]} y f_y(y) dy - \\ & - \int_{(\lambda_i^{A2T} + \lambda_i^{A2T\leftarrow})(1 + r_{2i}^{A2T})}^{2[\lambda_i^{A2T} p^b / p_{bi}^{A2T} + \lambda_i^{A2T\leftarrow} p^b / p_{bi}^{A2T\leftarrow} + 1 + r]} (\lambda_i^{A2T} + \lambda_i^{A2T\leftarrow})(1 + r_{2i}^{A2T}) f_y(y) dy\end{aligned} \qquad \text{A 9.5}$$

Note further that the expected loan repayment of the trader to the bank is as follows:

$$\int_{0}^{(\lambda_i^{A2T}+\lambda_i^{A2T\leftarrow})(1+r_{2i}^{A2T})} yf_y(y)dy + \int_{(\lambda_i^{A2T}+\lambda_i^{A2T\leftarrow})(1+r_{2i}^{A2T})}^{2[\lambda_i^{A2T}p^b/p_{bi}^{A2T}+\lambda_i^{A2T\leftarrow}p^b/p_{bi}^{A2T\leftarrow}+1+r]} (\lambda_i^{A2T}+\lambda_i^{A2T\leftarrow})(1+r_{2i}^{A2T})f_y(y)dy. \qquad \text{A 9.6}$$

By assumption this expected loan repayment is equal to $(\lambda_i^{A2T}+\lambda_i^{A2T\leftarrow})(1+3r_1)$. It further holds that the expected return for the trader plus the expected loan repayment equal

$$\int_{0}^{2[\lambda_i^{A2T}p^b/p_{bi}^{A2T}+\lambda_i^{A2T\leftarrow}p^b/p_{bi}^{A2T\leftarrow}+1+r]} yf_y(y)dy. \qquad \text{A 9.7}$$

This expression can be considered as the gross return of the trader before financing costs. From the relationship between the expected return for the trader, expected loan repayments, and the expected gross return follows that the expected return for the trader is equal to the expected gross return minus expected loan repayments. Because the expected gross return equals $(\lambda_i^{A2T}p^b/p_{bi}^{A2T}+\lambda_i^{A2T\leftarrow}p^b/p_{bi}^{A2T\leftarrow}+1+r)$ and because the expected loan repayment equals $(\lambda_i^{A2T}+\lambda_i^{A2T\leftarrow})(1+3r_1)$, the expected return for the trader can be written as the difference between these two expressions which is linear in the decision variable λ_i^{A2T}. Hence for maximizing the expected return of the trader with respect to λ_i^{A2T} it matters whether the slope on this variable in $(\lambda_i^{A2T}p^b/p_{bi}^{A2T}+\lambda_i^{A2T\leftarrow}p^b/p_{bi}^{A2T\leftarrow}+1+r)-(\lambda_i^{A2T}+\lambda_i^{A2T\leftarrow})(1+3r_1)$ is positive or negative. The trader chooses the maximum amount possible of loans if $p^b/p_{bi}^{A2T}>1+3r_1$. The condition in Proposition 4 ensures that this inequality is fulfilled.

At stage 4a) subgames start in which players of type B strategically offer prices and quantities in the respective shopper's paradise games. In any one of these subgames player i of type B is faced with one information set. Each subgame is characterized by a certain sum $\Sigma\delta_f^{A1T}$ being the total amount of deposits held by traders of type $A1$ resulting from prior play leading to the subgame and by a certain sum $\Sigma\lambda_j^{A2T}$ being the total amount of loans taken by traders of type $A2$ as optimally anticipated on the path following the subgame. This sum of total deposits and total loans is the total amount of transactions media in any one of the subgames starting at the beginning of stage 4a). The optimal decision for player i of type B can be characterized in general terms for all her information sets at stage 4a) depending upon $\Sigma\delta_f^{A1T}+\Sigma\lambda_j^{A2T}$. Consider one of the subgames starting at the beginning of stage 4a) and denote variables pertaining to this subgame with superindex T. Player i of type B expects other players in the subgame to play their equilibrium strategies. When playing herself also the equilibrium strategy which is $b_i^{BT*}=1+\varepsilon^B$ and $p_{bi}^{BT*}=(\Sigma\delta_f^{A1T}+\Sigma\lambda_j^{A2T})/N$ the matching procedure leads to a quantity actually sold by the trader which is equal to $b_i^{BST*}=1$. Hence total expected wealth from playing the equilibrium strategy, W_i^{BT*}, equals $W_i^{BT*}=(r_1+p^e)p_{bi}^{BT*}+\overline{p}^B\varepsilon^B$. Selling a lower quantity than the equilibrium quantity at the equilibrium price would reduce the volume of goods for profitable resale and is therefore not optimal.

If player i of type B charges a higher price than the equilibrium price the quantity actually sold after matching b_i^{BST} equals zero. Hence wealth from charging a price higher than the equilibrium price W_{iH}^{BT} equals $W_{iH}^{BT}=(1+\varepsilon^B)\overline{p}_b$. It holds that $W_{iH}^{BT}<W_i^{BT*}$ because $r_1+p^e>\overline{p}^B/p_{bi}^{BT*}$ and therefore bidding a lower price than the equilibrium price is not optimal. Because bidding a higher price than the equilibrium price and a lower quantity than the equilibrium quantity would also lead to W_{iH}^{BT}, such a deviation from equilibrium cannot be optimal either. When bidding less than the equilibrium price player i of type B offers some price $(\Sigma\delta_f^{A1T}+\Sigma\lambda_j^{A2T})/N-S\sigma^B$ where S is some positive integer indicating by how many discrete price steps the player underbids the equilibrium price. Because player i's offer is the cheapest now in the market, she can actually sell all her quantity offered such that $b_i^{BST*} = 1+\varepsilon^B$. To derive σ^B in the following σ_i^{BT} is considered which is the minimum price step necessary on the path considered for the equilibrium to obtain. The player's wealth in this case of undercutting W_{iL}^{BT} equals $W_{iL}^{BT} = (p^c + r_1)(1+\varepsilon^B)(p_{bi}^{BT*} - S\sigma_i^{BT})$. Comparing W_{iL}^{BT} with W_i^{BT*} shows that the equilibrium wealth is higher if $S\sigma_i^{BT} > 1/N[p_{bi}^{BT*} - \overline{p}_b/(p^c + r_1)]$. Hence σ_i^{BT} must fulfil the following condition for the equilibrium decision to obtain on the path considered: $\sigma_i^{BT} > 1/N[p_{bi}^{BT*} - \overline{p}_b/(p^c + r_1)]$ such that it follows that $W_i^{BT*} > W_{iL}^{BT}$ even if S=1. The parameter σ^B referred to in the description of the decision problems of players in section 9.2 refers to the maximum over the sigma values as derived above taken over all off equilibrium paths. Hence the optimality of the equilibrium strategy is ensured. In any case σ^B is positive and for $N \to \infty$ it holds that $\sigma^B \to 0$. Offering a lower quantity than the equilibrium quantity at a lower price than the equilibrium quantity is not optimal either because this would reduce the positive quantity effect from being able to sell a higher quantity of goods by undercutting. The proof for the optimality of the strategies of players of type D is analogous to the proof for the optimality of the strategies of players of type B.

At stage 1) player i of type $A1$ expects to be at the point in her information set corresponding to the equilibrium path of the game. Hence she has to solve the decision problem $\max(p^b + r_1 - 1 - r)a_i^{A1} + 1 + r$ by choosing a_i^{A1} and obeying the constraint that she cannot exchange more than her endowment. If $(p^b + r_1 - 1 - r) > 0$ it is optimal to exchange the entire endowment such that $a_i^{A1*} = 1$. This analysis leads to the condition that $p^b > 1 + r - r_1$ under which indeed $a_i^{A1*} = 1$ is optimal. Because $r = R = 2r_1$ the condition in Proposition 4 implies this inequality to hold. Note that in the objective function above $p_{bi}^{BT*} = (\Sigma\delta_i^{A1T} + \Sigma\lambda_j^{A2T})/N$ depends upon a_i^{A1} through $\Sigma\delta_i^{A1T}$. The impact is weak, however, and goes towards zero as N goes towards infinity. Hence this impact is ignored in the analysis. The same argument holds true for traders of type $C1$.

10
Efficient Transactions and Synergies in Banking

Transaction technologies are not intrinsically useful by themselves. Their main purpose is to lower transaction barriers to facilitate trade such that individuals can exchange goods more easily which provide them utility. The efficiency of a transaction technology is key for the degree to which transaction barriers get effectively lowered. Hence the efficiency of the various transaction technologies analyzed in the preceding chapters is compared in section 10.1.

When analyzing efficiency it is not only interesting to look at the comparison of the T-bank with other transaction technologies in solving transaction problems. In section 10.2 it is argued that the same institutional structure of the T-bank which provides an efficient solution to the problem of trust in exchange can be useful also for other activities of banks.

Transactions are typically short-term. But if one lengthens the time horizons considered in the model of the T-bank, interest paying accounts become attractive forms of safe, highly liquid investments whereas loans can be used not only for financing transactions short-term but also for financing longer-term, information sensitive projects just as in the banking model of Diamond (1984). In this sense an integrated theory of money and banking starting from the problem of trust in exchange provides an analytical foundation for contemporary banking theory. It should be noted that in the preceding chapters the institutional form of a bank emerged quite naturally from a discussion of efficient ways of creating transaction technologies dealing with the problem of trust in exchange. A monetary analysis gave rise to this institutional form rather than the usual analysis of financial intermediation.

The provision of transaction services, liquidity insurance services, and financing and investment services under the roof of one banking institution is likely to exhibit economies of scope. Synergies between these different activities presumably exist. Hence it is not only the flexibility of the institutional structure stemming from the monetary origins of banks but also the associated cost advantages which explain what banks do and why they exist.

10.1 Comparing the efficiency of transaction technologies

The four different transaction technologies in the models of chapters 6 to 9 lead to different outcomes for traders. Because endowments, externally given prices, and basic trading patterns within the framework of the shopper's paradise model are very similar in all four models, the differences in outcomes are mainly due to the differences in transaction technologies.

As a proper benchmark case the first-best solution in the model of trade with privately issued I.O.U.s is considered. In this model the asymmetric information problem is manifest in its most direct form. Hence if traders had the ability to observe the wealth of their trading partners ex post and therefore were willing to use I.O.U.s as a medium of exchange, (almost) all endowments would be exchanged (except for one strategic unit of the goods of suppliers which can be neglected for a large group of traders) at prices of one. In addition buyers in the first round of exchange could fully profit from not having to exchange their endowments prematurely and would therefore earn additional returns on them. No resources would get lost in the trading process. The maximum potential for advantageous trade at market clearing prices could be fully exhausted. Total wealth for traders would be $N(4p^a + 2r\overline{p}_a)$ which serves as a basic benchmark.[40]

The efficiency of transaction technologies can be viewed from different angles. From a welfare perspective one transaction technology may be considered as being more efficient than some other if it is Pareto-better, i.e. if it increases the wealth of some traders without decreasing the wealth of other traders. Pareto efficiency is an important concept in economics and will therefore be used also for the comparison of transaction technologies. However, not all technologies can be ranked according to the Pareto-criterion. Other problems exist with this approach in the current context. E.g., arbitrary factors such as the sequence of moves may matter. In some models traders of a group moving first do not have to bear the burden of the trading friction whereas traders of some other group have to bear it. However, assigning traders to groups and determining the sequence of moves is arbitrary. Furthermore, the incidence of the burden from trading frictions may be different depending upon the specific market context such that generalizations of results may be problematic. A measure of aggregate welfare such as total wealth in the society of traders can deal better with those problems. It captures the overall impact of the trading technology on society.

Total social wealth may be regarded as a social welfare function weighing equally the wealth of each individual trader. Relative price effects favoring one group of traders at the expense of some other group cancel out in such an aggregate measure. First-mover advantages matter less because both advantages and disadvantages are captured. For the efficiency comparisons made in this section both measures of welfare are used to rank the transaction technologies in terms of efficiency. Clearly, if two technologies can be ranked according to the Pareto criterion, total social wealth will also be higher for the alternative which is better according to the Pareto-criterion. If a ranking according to the Pareto-criterion is difficult or impossible, total social wealth can provide additional insights.

Table 10.1 Individual expected wealth of traders and total social wealth under various transaction technologies.

Type of trader	Intermediate Exchange	I.O.U.s	Cash	T-Bank
A	p^b	$p^b + \overline{p}_a[1+r-h_i^A(\Omega_{ai}^{AS*})]$	p^b	
B		$\Omega_{ci}^{B*} p^c$	p^c	$p^c + r_1$
C	p^d	$p^d + \overline{p}_c[1+r-h_i^C(\Omega_{ci}^{CS*})]$	p^d	
D	ρp^a	$\Omega_{ai}^{D*} p^d$	p^a	$p^a + r_1$
$A1, A2$				$p^b + r_1$
$C1, C2$				$p^d + r_1$
Total wealth	$N[4p^a - 2(1-\rho)p^a]$	$N[4p^a - 2(1-\Omega_{ai}^{AS*})p^a + +2\overline{p}_a(1+r-h_i^A(\Omega_{ai}^{AS*}))]$	$4Np^a$	$N[4p^a + 2r(1-1/v)$

Table 10.1 shows the individual expected wealth of traders belonging to a certain group and total social wealth of traders for the transaction technologies analyzed in chapters 6 to 9. The values on the equilibrium paths of the games are considered. The limiting values for N going towards infinity are displayed. Hence the incentive cost for the T-bank or small unsold quantities of traders are ignored. For the efficiency comparison it is also assumed that traders of type $A1$ and $A2$ have the same expected wealth in the banking model.

A Pareto ranking is possible between intermediate exchange, cash as central bank debt, and the T-bank. Cash leads to a Pareto improvement relative to intermediate exchange. The T-bank is Pareto better than cash provided by the central bank. Hence the T-bank is the most efficient transaction technology with respect to the Pareto criterion among these three transaction technologies. This result is in line with much of the literature in monetary economics. Accordingly, total social wealth leads to the same efficiency ranking.

Assessing the efficiency of privately issued I.O.U.s relative to the other transaction technologies is more difficult because it hinges upon the question how much risk is associated with the unobservable shock. Individual expected total wealth for a trader of type A in the scenario with privately issued I.O.U.s is lower than total wealth for a trader of type A in the case of the T-bank if the following condition holds:

$$\overline{p}^a(1-h_i^A(\Omega_{ai}^{AS*}))+\overline{p}^a r<r_1. \qquad 10.1$$

For this comparison it has to be taken into account that returns on the endowment are valued at $\overline{p}^a<1$ in the scenario with privately issued I.O.U.s whereas they are valued at one in the T-bank scenario. It will be assumed for the comparison that $\overline{p}^a$ lies close to one to avoid this arbitrary discrepancy between the results. Furthermore it holds that $h_i^A(\Omega_{ai}^{AS*})$ is less than one for smaller values of Ω_{ai}^{AS*} which – as argued in chapter 7 – is optimal for stochastic shock variables with lower risk. $h_i^A(\Omega_{ai}^{AS*})$ rises above one for higher values of Ω_{ai}^{AS*} that are associated with higher risk. As the riskiness of the shock variable gets too high, no trade at all is better for traders of type A than issuing I.O.U.s. From these considerations follows that for low risk (and $\overline{p}^a$ close to one) the inequality above will not be fulfilled. Hence if the stochastic shock on the trader's wealth is mild, privately issued I.O.U.s get close to the first best solution and yield higher expected wealth for the trader of type A than the T-bank. Using the T-bank would not be a Pareto improvement for the trader of type A. For shocks with higher risk the equality will be fulfilled. The trader will obtain higher wealth by using the T-bank. For traders of type B and D the T-bank is always better. Hence in this case the T-bank leads to a Pareto improvement vis à vis privately issued I.O.U.s. In the case of low risk the T-bank and I.O.U.s cannot be compared according to the Pareto-criterion. Hence looking at total social wealth can provide additional insights.

Comparing the model of the T-bank with the economy based upon I.O.U.s in terms of total social wealth shows that for a sufficiently high ratio v of deposits to cash the T-bank is always better. This ratio depends upon the velocity at which cash inflows are turned into loans which get redeposited again to make new loans etc. The transaction structure in the model of the T-bank implied a ratio of deposits to cash equal to 2, but a quicker turnover of deposits could have led to a higher ratio. A comparison of total social wealth under the T-bank and the I.O.U. scenario shows that for a sufficiently high ratio of deposits to cash the T-bank always provides higher total social wealth than exchange supported by privately issued I.O.U.s. The condition for this result to hold is

$$\overline{p}^a(1-h_i^A(\Omega_{ai}^{AS*}))-p^a(1-\Omega_{ai}^{AS*})+\overline{p}^a r<r(1-1/v). \qquad 10.2$$

Because $h_i^A(\Omega_{ai}^{AS*})\geq\Omega_{ai}^{AS*}$ and $p^a>\overline{p}^a$ this condition can always be fulfilled for sufficiently large v. Fixing v, e.g. at the value of 2 considered in chapter 9 shows that again also the riskiness of the stochastic shock variables matters. If the riskiness of the shock variable is very small both $h_i^A(\Omega_{ai}^{AS*})$ and Ω_{ai}^{AS*} lie slightly above 0.5. If also the benefits from reselling are not too big, it is possible that

I.O.U.s yield a higher total social wealth than the T-bank. If the riskiness rises, $\overline{p}^a(1-h_i^A(\Omega_{ai}^{AS*}))$ can even get negative such that the T-bank yields higher total social wealth. Hence, qualitatively also total social wealth as a welfare measure leads to similar conclusions as the Pareto-criterion.

Summarizing the results from the efficiency comparisons of the transaction technologies it was found that the T-bank Pareto dominated cash and cash Pareto dominated intermediate exchange of goods. Except for the case of stochastic wealth shocks with very low risk the T-bank Pareto dominated privately issued I.O.U.s as a transaction technology. The results on total social wealth as a welfare measure largely confirmed these findings.

In the case of very low risk privately issued I.O.U.s can dominate the T-bank in efficiency. However, the T-bank can achieve a solution which comes close to the first best. The main factor which keeps it a step apart from there is the requirement to finance initial loans from money issued by the central bank. Thereby returns on endowments get lost. If one loosens the assumption made in chapter 9, however, that one unit of money is used only once for making a loan but if longer chains of money and credit creation by the T-bank are admitted, then the T-bank can come arbitrarily close to the first best solution. One major difference between the T-bank and privately issued I.O.U.s is, however, that the T-bank can come close to the first best for *any* degree of risk of the random wealth shocks. Privately issued I.O.U.s achieve high social welfare only for very low risk shocks. In this sense the findings on the welfare achieved by using the T-bank as a transaction technology are independent from the severity of the underlying friction which underlines the superiority of this transaction technology in most economic circumstances. The same holds true for cash issued by the central bank. The efficiency of privately issued I.O.U.s and of intermediate exchange of goods critically hinges upon the severity of the frictions. More severe frictions would render these transaction technologies almost useless. By hampering trade they would reduce welfare even more than shown in table 10.1.

In the search for ever more efficient transaction technologies the analysis moved step by step and finally stopped at chapter 9 where transaction services provided by the T-bank were examined. A natural question to ask is whether even more efficient transaction technologies than the T-bank might exist. As long as such an analysis remains within the framework considered it is clear that any welfare improvement – if any such alternative transaction technology were to exist – could only be small. Because the T-bank already gets close to the first best solution, there is not much scope for further efficiency improvements.

The findings on the efficiency comparison support the hypothesis that financial solutions to transaction problems are more efficient than solutions involving the exchange of physical goods in situations characterized by a lack of double coincidence of needs and wants. Even for very mild frictions in intermediate exchange of goods cash, the T-bank, and for some cases also privately issued I.O.U.s yield a higher welfare. This result is likely to hold even if other barter scenarios are considered (e.g., with asymmetric costs of intermediate exchange or with quality uncertainty about goods). The main reason is that using potentially productive resources as a medium of exchange always implies forgoing the benefits of using these goods more productively. Furthermore, part of the resources are likely to get lost in the trading process itself. Financial solutions to transaction problems avoid these losses.

Efficiency comparisons among various transaction technologies raise the question of the coexistence of several technologies. The results derived so far suggest that T-banks and privately issued I.O.U.s can coexist to some degree. The I.O.U.s are confined, however, to issuers with low risk affecting their wealth. In chapter 9 it was argued that money issued by the central bank has a role in providing a fairly efficient transaction technology if private banks collapse (which happened there only off the equilibrium path). Several other explanations for the coexistence of banks and cash going beyond this model exist.

Zero incentive costs for commercial banks and the central bank are implied by the models considered here. Clearly, in other settings these incentive costs would not be zero. Banking regulation, the costs of distortions due to regulation, and incentive structures for central banks may incur considerable costs. Still, the underlying presumption is that these costs are substantially smaller than the benefits created by these institutions such that they do not affect the efficiency ranking of transaction technologies.

10.2 Money, trust, and synergies in banking

One of the major reasons for developing an integrated theory of money and banking is to have a unified approach which explains both the role of money and the role of banks from one source of frictions. Key institutional characteristics of monetary and banking institutions should emerge from this analysis. It can also be regarded as an attempt to provide a monetary interpretation of contemporary banking theory which typically neglects the role of money. Key building blocks of such an integrated approach have been analyzed already in chapters 6 to 9. After revisiting the main steps in that analysis, this section suggests to go even beyond these results. Other activities of banks may be interpreted within the framework established so far, suggesting the existence of ties with other key concepts in monetary theory. Some of the conclusions in this section are only tentative, just pointing at the potential for developing further an integrated approach of money and banking.

The search for an efficient transaction technology in chapters 6 to 9 proceeded step by step. First, in chapter 6 the inconvenience of barter in an economic environment characterized by a lack of double coincidence of needs and wants was shown. This classical result was derived within the framework of the shopper's paradise model serving as a strategic market setup for studying transaction technologies. A "best case" scenario was considered by looking at mild frictions in exchange and simple transaction structures. Still, the intermediate exchange of goods turned out to be an inefficient way of conducting transactions because resources get lost when goods have to be acquired that are not actually desired and because productive inputs remain idle when circulating as a medium of exchange. Financial solutions to transaction problems can avoid these losses. Hence the analysis turned to a closer examination of financial approaches.

In a second step in chapter 7 it was argued that in order to avoid burdensome intermediate exchange goods should be exchanged against transferable debt. A decentralized setup was considered in which individual agents requiring a medium of exchange issued debt securities promising the delivery of a certain amount of goods. These privately issued I.O.U.s turned out to be problematic, however, if the trader receiving the I.O.U. in exchange could not fully trust her trading partner. Even if upon issuing the I.O.U. there was no doubt about the economic soundness of the issuer, this situation could change later due to circumstances that were unobservable to the outside trading partner trader receiving the I.O.U. If unobservable shocks affect the wealth of the debtor, the issuer may exploit her informational advantage and claim that she is unable to fulfil her obligations from the I.O.U. A rational trader anticipating this behavior will not trust her trading partner and will therefore be unwilling to accept I.O.U.s in exchange unless there are some special provisions in the contract making sure that delivery occurs whenever possible. With reference to contract theory and the theory of financial intermediation it was shown that in this situation with ex post informational asymmetries the endogenously derived optimal contract is a debt contract with nonpecuniary penalties, corresponding to the I.O.U.s. Hence the consistency between contracts and frictions could be ensured by this approach.

Nonpecuniary penalties imposed upon individual traders in the case of default were a costly solution to the problem of lack of trust, however, if nonzero risk was associated with the wealth shocks. Because these costs sharply rose with the share of the endowment of a trader that got securitized, traders limited these incentive costs by issuing less I.O.U.s than the maximum possible amount, thus reducing potentially beneficial trading volume. It could also be observed that once the I.O.U.s were issued they performed well as a medium of exchange because of their credible, incentive compatible structure. Hence the key question was how to reduce the cost of issuing I.O.U.s. Public and private centralized solutions analyzed in chapters 8 and 9 turned out to lead to superior solutions.

In a third step in chapter 8 the key idea for reducing the cost of issuing credible I.O.U.s serving as a medium of exchange was to delegate this task to a special agent called central bank. Everybody had perfect trust in this institution because it was not subject to wealth shocks and because it was provided proper incentives by a debt contract. Essentially traders who themselves could not be trusted by other trading partners could avoid the high incentive costs of privately issuing I.O.U.s by acquiring the widely trusted monetary I.O.U.s issued by the central bank in exchange for their goods. The price a trader had to pay to benefit from these monetary services was the need to exchange her endowments prematurely such that they could not be used any more for productive purposes. Although delegating the solution to the problem of trust to a special institution better equipped to deal with it provided great benefits, there still remained scope to increase the efficiency of transaction technologies.

At the final stage of the search for an efficient transaction technology the challenge was to economize on money issued by the central bank such that traders would not have to divert their resources from productive uses in order to acquire a trusted medium of exchange. Hence in chapter 9 the idea of delegating the issuing of credible I.O.U.s to a special financial institution was pursued further. The debt of this institution functioning as a medium of exchange should also be as trustworthy and generally acceptable as cash. But it should allow economic agents to use their resources productively instead of having to leave them idle in order to acquire a medium of exchange. The solution for this problem was to create a transactions oriented bank. Depository debt contracts issued by this bank were credible because of the high degree of diversification in the asset portfolio of the bank and because the deposit debt contracts it concluded with its creditors were also supported by nonpecuniary penalties in the case of defaulting on its debt. Because of the high degree of trustworthiness of bank debt it was as widely acceptable as cash. Hence payments could be made by transferring bank deposits between trading partners.

A key advantage of the T-bank was that not all agents had to acquire cash from the central bank and deposit it in their bank accounts to obtain a medium of exchange. A group of them could also take out a trading loan and transfer the funds from this loan to their transaction partners as a medium of exchange. Hence by lending out depository money the bank could create additional deposits serving as a medium of exchange, thus reducing the need to rely on noninterest bearing money from the central bank. However, the loans extended had to be paid back with interest. Loan customers were on average able to pay the interest because by taking out the loan they had the benefit of acquiring a medium of exchange without having to divert their resources prematurely from productive uses. The additional return earned on the endowment allowed to pay the interest on the loan. This also enabled the bank to pay interest on deposits, thereby spreading the benefits from economizing on noninterest bearing cash to a wider group of deposit holders. As an additional feature the bank could benefit from offering both loans and transaction services because transaction accounts were informative about the economic situation of loan customers. Thereby the bank could deal with the informational problems of traders about ex post shocks in an efficient manner.

The key conclusion from this stepwise search for an efficient transaction technology is that the institutional structure of the T-bank emerged quite naturally as a solution that combined benefits from earlier transaction technologies but provided additional advantages due to its special design. However, the analysis does not stop at this point. The fundamental point to see is that the institutional structure of the T-bank is equivalent in many respects to the structure of the bank as a financial intermediary providing financing and investment services in an opaque loan market as developed by Diamond (1984). In the following the bank studied by Diamond will be called D-bank.

The main difference between the T-bank and the D-bank is the time horizon and the corresponding lower loan risk. Monetary transaction services are typically associated with shorter time horizons whereas financing and investment services require longer time horizons. The close institutional relationship between the T-bank and the D-bank can be seen from the following comparison:

- Both banks take deposits and make loans in an information sensitive market.
- Both banks hold risky assets with ex post asymmetric information vis à vis depositors about the ability to repay debt.
- The informational friction gives rise to endogenously derived depository debt contracts optimally addressing the informational friction considered in both cases.
- It is efficient to delegate the monitoring of loan customers to the banks.
- Size and diversification are key for reaping the benefits of intermediation.

The models of the T-bank and of the D-bank differ with respect to the following features:

- No transaction context and monetary interpretation is provided in the Diamond model. Hence the transferability of deposits is not considered.
- The size of debt is variable and chosen by agents requiring a medium of exchange in the model of the T-bank. The size is fixed in the model of the D-bank.
- In the model of the T-bank monitoring costs are zero due to synergies with transaction services whereas monitoring costs exist in the Diamond model.

As a key conclusion it can be seen that the same basic institutional structure which efficiently solves transaction problems also provides efficient solutions to investing and financing problems in an informationally opaque capital market. In this sense monetary theory provides a foundation for banking theory. The analysis suggests that indeed an integrated theory of money and banking can be developed based upon the problem of lack of trust in exchange.

The fundamental result about the close relationship between institutional solutions for transaction problems and financing and investment problems is due to the key role that credit plays in facilitating exchange. As argued in section 3.2.2 Wicksell was among the first to pioneer the idea of a credit economy. Credit naturally emerges if traders do not exchange physical goods on the spot as in intermediate exchange. If this debt can be made credible despite frictions typically associated with debt such as ex post asymmetric information about the ability of an agent to repay, it becomes transferable and can function as a medium of exchange. Because the Diamond-bank corresponds to an efficient institutional structure dealing with credit problems, it can solve efficiently both transaction problems and saving and investment problems.

The flexibility of the institutional structure of the T-bank and the D-bank goes even further, however. Bhattacharya, Boot, and Thakor (1998) developed a model which integrated the Diamond model of banking (i.e., the D-bank) and the Diamond-Dybvig model (see chapter 3). Hence financing and investment services and the provision of liquidity insurance in an incomplete market appear to be also mutually compatible economic functions which banks perform through one and the same channel, namely bank deposits and loans. Hence banks perform transaction services, financing and investment services, and liquidity insurance services all under one roof. When viewing these services through the lens of monetary theory, it seems that they are closely related to the transactions demand, the speculative demand, and the precautionary demand for money in the Keynesian tradition. Deeper analyses of these issues are necessary, however, before more solid conclusions can be drawn.

A focus on the joint provision of financing and investment services, liquidity services, and transaction services provided by banks through one basic institutional structure may help to interpret findings in the theoretical and empirical literature questioning the role of banks in the provision of partial functions. E.g., Jacklin (1987) argues that in some cases the optimal allocations in the Diamond-Dybvig framework are also attainable with equity rather than nontraded depository debt contracts. Deep and Schaefer (2004) empirically find that banks appear to perform only a moderate level of liquidity transformation. If it is the joint provision of various services what matters in banking, concentrating on one particular banking function may be susceptible to misinterpretations. Hence it is possible that some partial activities of banks appear to be economically redundant or empirically of moderate relevance. Still they may matter as being part of the entire bundle of services banks provide by making use of their flexible institutional structure.

From a cost perspective it is likely that banks enjoy at least some economies of scope from combining all these activities. E.g., as was argued in the model of the T-bank, transaction accounts can be informative about the ability of a loan customer to repay her debt. To give another example, holding liquidity is usually supposed to be costly (see Kashyap, Rajan, and Stein, 2002). Some liquidity reserves are required if a bank performs liquidity insurance. If, however, this liquidity can be used also in the context of transaction services, this additional use of liquidity could spread the cost of liquidity more widely across a broader set of activities supported by the liquidity holdings of the bank. A note of caution is in place at this point. There may exist also some benefits from concentrating on a smaller set of activities, representing only part of the spectrum of services offered by banks. Still, interrelationships between these various services appear to be an important feature of banking, having potentially far-reaching implications also for policy questions.[41] Eventually, the question of cost advantages in banking becomes an empirical issue which needs to be addressed with other tools than those employed in this monograph. Still, the analysis here points at the theoretical possibility of such economies of scope.

11

An Integrated Perspective on Money, Trust, and Banking

The analysis in this monograph provides a theoretical outline for an integrated theory of money and banking building upon the problem of trust in exchange. It was shown that this approach has the potential to explain a role for money and allows to integrate monetary analysis into the broader framework of contemporary banking theory. The basic question why money is used was demonstrated to have far-reaching consequences for the specific institutional structure how money is provided and managed such that a role for banks emerged in the search for efficient ways of dealing with the problem of lack of trust in exchange.

In section 10.2 a summary of the key steps in the analysis was provided. In the following paragraphs in this chapter the main results from the study are discussed and further conclusions are drawn from an integrated perspective on money, trust and banking. Ways of extending the framework developed in this monograph are indicated to analyze potentially interesting questions which currently remain underexplored.

- *A formal theoretical outline for the integration of monetary theory and contemporary banking theory was developed, thereby providing an analytical link between the function of money as a medium of exchange and as a store of value.*

One of the key insights emerging from the analysis is the finding that the institutional structure of the banking model by Diamond (1984) which is a cornerstone of contemporary banking theory also solves transaction problems. The bank in the Diamond model can be regarded as an optimally designed debt manager providing financing and investment services in a financial market with asymmetric information. However, managing debt is important also in a transactions context because debt is key in facilitating exchange. Burdensome barter can be avoided by creating a system of debt which is transferable between agents. The bank in the Diamond model provides such a system and thereby solves transaction problems, not just financing and investment problems as in the original version of the Diamond model. Thereby an analytical link between the role of money as a medium of exchange and as a store of value is established.

It should be noted that in the Diamond model no monetary analysis is conducted. Therefore the monetary interpretation of the Diamond model in this monograph had to go beyond the original analysis. For example, in a transactions context the introduction of debt serving as a medium of exchange was motivated by the goal to avoid burdensome barter rather than by financing and investment considerations. Also, in the original Diamond model the loan size is fixed. Hence for a monetary interpretation it was necessary to introduce debt of variable size being optimally chosen by agents as a medium of exchange. The transferability of the debt contracts was emphasized in the monetary analysis and the consequences of frictions for the transferability were examined whereas tradability is not considered in the original model. Finally, no synergies between transaction services and financing and investment services reducing the monitoring cost of the bank are analyzed in the Diamond model.

The results on the integration of monetary theory and banking theory in this monograph were derived for the most basic case of an economy of risk neutral traders without production or consumption. It remains to be explored further whether the results are robust with respect to the introduction of production, consumption, and risk aversion. Risk aversion creates analytical difficulties because Hellwig (2001) shows that simple debt contracts with nonpecuniary penalties as in the Diamond model are not optimal any more once risk aversion of agents is introduced. Hence more complex contractual solutions have to be considered.

- *Lack of trust in the ability of transaction partners to repay is a major monetary friction explaining monetary institutions and a role for money*

Ex post asymmetric information about the ability of a transaction partner to repay was introduced as a major friction in transactions. This friction was different from the friction existing in the barter context. Typically, the introduction of money mitigates the friction associated with barter. However, new frictions arise once a debt-based financial structure is created. Hence the focus of the analysis is shifted towards these financial frictions. Contemporary banking theory suggests to consider ex post asymmetric information about the ability of a transaction partner to repay as a major financial friction arising in debt-based transaction technologies. This friction has hardly been analyzed so far in the monetary literature. However, an analysis of this friction provides additional insights about the role of money and of monetary institutions.

The discussion of frictions analyzed in this monograph raises the general question how to deal with the large number of possible frictions in monetary economics. Monetary theory is unlikely to ever find consensus on a single friction which explains the role of money better than other frictions and will be used as the central foundation for monetary theory. Money is too flexible an instrument in exchange which helps address several important frictions simultaneously such that the emergence of such a consensus could be expected. Therefore also lack of trust in transaction partners is unlikely to be "the" friction which provides a better explanation than others for the role of money in the economy. The strength of this approach is an explicit treatment of institutional features of money and banking which are important for some questions in monetary theory and policy but can be ignored for other questions.

- *Money is debt arising endogenously from the lack of trust in transaction partners.*

Because debt has an important role in facilitating exchange by avoiding burdensome barter, the analysis of I.O.U.s and other forms of debt as a medium of exchange has a long tradition in monetary economics. But typically the contractual form of debt was taken as given rather than endogenously explained from the models. Following Diamond (1984) in this monograph debt contracts were interpreted as endogenously arising optimal responses to lack of trust in the ability of transaction partners to repay. Because this friction has not been considered so far in formal research on monetary economics, debt contracts were not provided an endogenous explanation although the concept of lack of trust in debt serving as a medium of exchange has been discussed informally in the literature (e.g., see Hicks, 1989; Goodhart, 1989; Goodfriend, 1991, Dow and Smithin, 1999). Also the analysis of monetary institutions such as central banks and commercial banks builds upon this fundamental analysis of debt, contracts, and frictions. Hence to achieve internal consistency between frictions, contracts, money, and monetary institutions lack of trust in the ability of transaction partners to repay and debt arising as an optimal response to it appear to be key elements in monetary analysis.

One implication of analyzing money as endogenously arising debt is the need to consider the case of a backed currency when analyzing money provided by central banks. Because modern money typically exists as fiat money, further exploration of the relationship between fiat money and money as debt with frictions is required in the monetary framework developed in this monograph. It should be noted that the analysis of intermediate exchange in barter and of privately issued I.O.U.s in this monograph remains unaffected by the question of fiat money. Also the results on the T-bank should not critically hinge upon the existence of fiat money as long as the central bank pays no interest on cash. Hence apart from the chapter on money provided by the central bank the analysis in other chapters, particularly the welfare comparison between privately issued I.O.U.s and the transactions bank remains practically unaffected by the introduction of fiat money. One possibility to clarify the relationship between fiat money and money as debt could be to consider debt contracts whose actual repayment is postponed further and further into the future because they are used as a medium of exchange rather than for actual delivery. In the limit, for infinitely postponed repayment the character of money as debt should vanish but the medium of exchange function should remain.

To generalize the results from the models considered it would also be necessary to generalize the conditions under which debt contracts can be endogenously derived.[42] Otherwise it becomes impossible to maintain the consistency of frictions, models and institutions at a more general level.

- *Money efficiently addresses the problem of the underprovision of a medium of exchange by individual private agents in the presence of lack of trust in transaction partners.*

In principle private individuals themselves can create a debt-based medium of exchange to avoid barter by issuing credible debt. However, it is shown in this monograph that private agents would issue only limited amounts of such debt due to the sharply rising incentive costs associated with this activity. These costs arise due to the lack of trust in transaction partners to repay their debt. Note that the contract design perspective taken in this monograph allows to adequately assess the incentive costs leading to this underprovision of a medium of exchange. By delegating the issuing of debt serving as money to central banks and private banks the incentive costs of providing a medium of exchange can be reduced because these institutions are better equipped to deal with risk giving rise to the incentive cost.

- *One major impact of money on the economy is to promote trade and save resources by efficiently addressing frictions in the transaction process.*

The real effects of money on the economy are a hotly debated issue with a long tradition in monetary economics. The models analyzed in this monograph suggest that important real effects become evident only in comparison with alternative transaction technologies. Inefficient transaction technologies are characterized by a lower trading volume and an increased use of resources absorbed in the trading process. In the barter model with intermediate exchange resources got lost because intermediate exchange reduced the volume of goods available to agents. In the scenario with privately issued I.O.U.s trading activity got depressed because private agents created only limited amounts of debt serving as a medium of exchange. Money provided by a central bank or private banks increased trading volume and reduced the use of resources in the trading process by reducing incentive costs.

Other effects of money such as those due to monetary policy, e.g., the impact of changes in the quantity of money or in the interest rate set by the central bank cannot be well studied in the simple trading models considered here. A richer framework is necessary. The introduction of production and consumption would be required to study more complex patterns of reactions to policy changes. Also richer models of financial markets and of interest rate formation are required.

- *Monetary theory building upon the problem of lack of trust in exchange provides a monetary foundation for contemporary banking theory*

A monetary foundation for contemporary banking theory is provided by showing that the institutional structure of the banking model by Diamond (1984) provides optimal solutions to transaction problems. Thereby it is demonstrated that transaction services provided by banks can be explained within the framework of existing, well established models of banking theory. This approach emphasizes the joint provision of economically distinct investment, financing, liquidity, and transaction services under one institutional roof. Such a view of banks has implications both for banking theory and banking policy. It suggests putting into perspective findings in the theoretical and empirical literature questioning the role of banks in the provision of partial banking functions. Concentrating on one particular banking function may be misleading. In the context of banking policy the potential for synergies in banking suggests that separating various banking functions as debated, e.g., in the discussion about narrow banking may lead to a less efficient provision of the various banking services.

- *A microeconomic interpretation of money is suggested for the large number of models in which money exists but an explicit friction creating a role for money is missing.*

The analysis of money in this monograph suggests an interpretation for the large number of models in economics which introduce money but lack an explicit friction explaining a role for money. If ex post asymmetric information about the ability of a transaction partner to repay creates a role for money in debt-based transaction technologies avoiding burdensome barter and if money provided by a trusted central bank eliminates this worry, the friction seems to disappear from the model. Because the incentive problem associated with issuing debt is concentrated in one institution which efficiently deals with it such that the costs can be ignored, no explicit traces of the monetary friction are visible any more. The very presence of money, however, and the willingness of agents to forgo the opportunity cost of holding money rather than trading without money indicate the lack of trust in their trading partners. If for some reason money were not available as a transaction technology, agents would have to deal again with this informational friction because the friction would explicitly reappear. Hence the friction still remains implicit in the model (see chapter 8). If this result from the analysis of the model can be generalized then, for example, the current treatment of money in macroeconomic models such as putting money as an argument into utility functions leads to erroneous conclusions. One caveat about this interpretation of monetary models is that cash issued by the central bank is not the most efficient way of addressing the implicit friction in the models considered in this monograph.

- *A model of price taking agents was developed which is amenable to monetary analysis and explains prices and quantities explicitly from the strategic interactions of agents*

A major issue which remains to be solved in monetary theory as well as in economic theory in general is the question how to model the underlying economy in which transactions and the role for money are explained. Part of the fascination but also of the challenge of monetary theory derives from the need to go beyond standard models of markets firmly established in economics to explain a role for money. Thinking about this role constantly forces to reconsider fundamental structures of the standard models (see Abele, 1970 and 1972). The approach for monetary theory proposed in this monograph is to construct models having a role for money but remaining still closely related to standard models in economics.[43] For this purpose a model of price taking agents was developed which had a well identified structure of economic transactions making it amenable to monetary analysis. The model explained key features of the contracts between agents such as prices and quantities from the strategic interactions between agents.

Still, the models developed in this monograph tackle the goal of building monetary models close to standard economic analysis only in an imperfect way. They are just one step into the direction of showing how standard economic models such as perfect competition can be provided an internally consistent monetary interpretation. If monetary theorists insist on introducing their own varieties of models whose structure is largely incompatible with standard models, then monetary theory will remain confined to esoteric circles. Applied work such as analyses of monetary policy will further have to proceed without foundation in monetary theory. The tail (i.e., monetary theory), will not wag the dog (i.e., standard economic theory). If monetary theory succeeds in sticking as closely as possible to standard models and shows which minimum changes in the standard models are required to introduce an economically meaningful role for money, then monetary theory has the potential to become both more relevant in practical applications and to contribute to a refinement of the fundamental theoretical building blocks upon which economics as a science rests today.

Notes

1 The lack of the ability to commit to some action might be considered as another concept in modern economics which also leads to a problem of lack of trust.

2 Huggett and Krasa (1996) argue that an additional source of asymmetric information has to be introduced into the Townsend model for money to be essential in the model.

3 See Winkler (1989) for a basic analysis of intermediation in a general equilibrium context.

4 Note that the Diamond model rather than the Diamond-Dybvig model was selected above as a candidate for cross-fertilization between money and banking. This is not to say, however, that the Diamond-Dybvig model is unrelated to monetary theory. It will be argued in chapter 10 that the two models are related.

5 See also Banerjee and Maskin (1996) who develop a monetary model with frictions which is closely related to general equilibrium theory. Gale (1980) analyzes game theoretical foundations for competitive markets.

6 Corbae, Temzelides, and Wright (2003) provide an analysis of matching in a monetary context which is also not purely random but where the structure of meetings is endogenously determined. For a discussion of the search and matching approach in monetary economics see also Howitt (2000).

7 Sometimes intermediate exchange of goods is called indirect barter in the literature.

8 See chapter 2.2 for asymmetric information about the quality of goods.

9 This physical cost is reminiscent of the "iceberg" models in international trade theory.

10 Note that if only one good is indicated in a relative price, this price always refers to the numeraire good. E.g., $\overline{p}_b$ indicates how many units of good b are exchanged against one unit of good a.

11 Note that c_{i2}^{DT} denotes the quantity chosen at a certain information set at stage 2b) whereas in section 6.1 c_{i2}^{D} denoted the *total* quantity exchanged by trader i at stage 2b).

12 Note that d_i^{DT} denotes the quantity chosen at a certain information set at stage 1b) whereas in section 6.1 d_i^{D} denoted the *total* quantity exchanged by trader i at stage 1b).

13 Note that b_i^{BT} denotes the quantity chosen at a certain information set at stage 1b) whereas in section 6.1 b_i^{B} denoted the *total* quantity exchanged by trader i at stage 1b).

14 This presupposes that there is not asymmetric information of agents about the quality of goods. See chapter 2 for a literature survey on this topic.

15 Relative prices without a second good always refer to the numeraire good indicating how many units of the numeraire good are exchanged against one unit of the good considered.

16 It is straightforward to introduce interest paying I.O.U.s into the model.

17 Although the penalty has to be nonpecuniary because a trader claiming she has no resources cannot be punished otherwise, for the optimization problem of a trader the nonpecuniary penalty is again expressed in pecuniary terms.

18 In the external market and the resale market the price of good a can be different from 1 as viewed by agents in the market of traders due to transportation costs.

19 See appendix 2 to this chapter.

20 Note that the derivation of convexity in the appendix holds even for more general distributions.

21 Minimum quantities to be chosen in the second round of trades are zero because there is no third round of trading for which some minimum trading volume would have to be ensured.

22 The basic results do not change if the trader is assumed to value unsold numeraire goods at a price equal to one.

23 Note that Ω_{ci2}^{DT} denotes the expected quantity chosen at a certain information set at stage 2b) whereas in section 7.1 Ω_{ci2}^{D} denoted the *total* expected endowment exchanged by trader *i* at stage 2b).

24 Note that d_{di}^{DT} denotes the quantity chosen at a certain information set at stage 2b) whereas in section 7.1 d_{di}^{D} denoted the *total* expected endowment exchanged by trader *i* at stage 2b).

25 Note that b_i^{AT} denotes the quantity chosen at a certain information set at stage 2b) whereas in section 7.1 b_i^{A} denoted the *total* expected endowment exchanged by trader *i* at stage 2b).

26 Ulrich Berger provided valuable mathematical support for the derivation of convexity.

27 This argument parallels the lack of incentives for arbitrage between the external market and the market of traders in the preceding chapter.

28 Note that throughout the monograph it is assumed that *r* accrues only if credit is explicitly extended, either by the buyers of I.O.U.s or by a bank. Simply keeping unsold goods does not increase the endowments. Hence *r* does not appear explicitly in this chapter. It would be straightforward to introduce returns on endowments without changing the main results.

29 Note that m_{2i}^{AT} denotes the amount chosen at a certain information set at stage 2b) whereas in section 8.1 m_{2i}^{A} denoted the *total* amount of money exchanged by trader *i* at stage 2b).

30 Note that the equilibrium price p_{bi}^{BT*} which is set equal to one in the derivation is also weakly dependent upon the choice of a_i^{AT} . However, this impact is small and for $N \rightarrow \infty$ it goes towards zero. Hence this impact is ignored.

31 Money as debt issued by the central bank is denoted as cash in this chapter.

32 It would be straightforward to introduce interest bearing accounts for this group of traders in a slightly more complex model.

33 Also in chapter 7 variables determined by the I.O.U. contracts were not modelled as strategic variables.

34 In Diamond (1984) it is shown for a bank performing monitoring that the deposit contract also gives banks incentives to monitor.

35 See the end of the next section for a more detailed analysis of financial flows in the model.

36 On other paths financial balance may get lost such that the bank can go bankrupt. These cases are not considered in the following paragraphs.

37 It is straightforward to show that the bank also keeps financial balance if total funds available to traders of type *B* and *D* are less than *N*.

38 Note that m_{2i}^{A1T} denotes the amount chosen at a certain information set at stage 4b) whereas in section 9.1 m_{2i}^{A1} denoted the *total* amount of money chosen by trader *i* at stage 4b).

39 Note that λ_i^{A2T} denotes the amount of the loan chosen at a certain information set at stage 4b) whereas in section 9.1 λ_i^{A2} denoted the *total* amount of the loan taken by trader *i* at stage 4b).

40 One may have concerns about comparing wealth expressed in a non-monetary model in units of the numeraire good with wealth expressed in money. But because the numeraire good of type *a* has a price of one also in the monetary model, wealth comparisons are economically meaningful.

41 For example, there is the fundamental question whether narrow banking designed to eliminate bank fragility due to liquidity transformation would destroy economies of scope in banking.

42 Hellwig (2001) suggests some caution in this respect by showing that the debt contracts in the Diamond model are sensitive with respect to the question whether agents are risk-neutral or risk-averse in the model. The risk attitude of the bank is less relevant (see Hellwig, 2000).

43 Rocheteau and Wright (2005) and Lagos and Wright (2004) are papers in the tradition of the search and matching literature which emphasize the relationship with more standard economic models to conduct monetary policy analyses.

Bibliography

Abele, H., 'Über geldwirtschaftliche Wachstumsmodelle', *Zeitschrift für Nationalökonomie*, 30 (1970) 125-158.

Abele, H., 'Einige Bemerkungen zu einer Theorie der Geldwirtschaft', in: G. Bombach (ed.), *Studien zur Geldtheorie und monetäre Ökonometrie, Schriften des Vereins für Socialpolitik* (Berlin: Duncker & Humblot, 1972).

Aiyagari, R. and Williamson, S., 'Money and Dynamic Credit Arrangements with Private Information', *Journal of Economic Theory*, 91 (2000) 248-279.

Akerlof, G., 'The Market for Lemons: Quality Uncertainty and the Market Mechanism', *Quarterly Journal of Economics*, 89 (1970) 488-500.

Alchian, A., 'Why Money?', *Journal of Money, Credit, and Banking*, 9(1) (1977) 133-140.

Alesina, A. and Summers, L., 'Central Bank Independence and Macroeconomic Performance', *Journal of Money, Credit, and Banking*, 25(2) (1993) 157-162.

Banerjee, A. and Maskin, E., 'A Walrasian Theory of Money and Barter', *Quarterly Journal of Economics*, 111 (1996) 955-1005.

Berentsen, A. and Rocheteau, G., 'Money and Information', *Review of Economic Studies*, 71(4) (2004) 1-30.

Bernanke, P. and Gertler, M., 'Agency Costs, Net Worth, and Business Fluctuations', *American Economic Review*, 79 (1989) 14-31.

Bernhardt, D., 'Money and Loans', *Review of Economic Studies*, 56 (1989) 89-100.

Betts, C. and Smith, B., 'Money, Banking, and the Determination of Real and Nominal Exchange Rates', *International Economic Review*, 38(3) (1997) 703-34.

Bhattacharya, S., Boot, A., and Thakor, A., 'The Economics of Bank Regulation', *Journal of Money, Credit, and Banking*, 30 (1998) 745-770.

Bhattacharya, S. and Thakor, A., 'Contemporary Banking Theory', *Journal of Financial Intermediation*, 3(1) (1993) 2-50.

Blanchard, O. and Fischer, S., *Lectures on Macroeconomics* (Cambridge, MA: MIT Press, 1989).

Brunner, K. and Meltzer, A., 'The Uses of Money: Money in the Theory of an Exchange Economy', *American Economic Review*, 61 (1971) 784-805.

Bryant, J., 'A Model of Reserves, Bank Runs, and Deposit Insurance', *Journal of Banking and Finance*, 4 (1980) 61-86.

Calomiris, C., 'Financial Factors in the Great Depression', *Journal of Economic Perspectives*, 7 (1993) 61-86.

Calomiris, C. and Gorton, G., 'The Origins of Banking Panics: Models, Facts, and Bank Regulation', in: R. G. Hubbard (ed.), *Financial Markets and Financial Crises* (Chicago: University of Chicago Press, 1991).

Cavalcanti, R. and Wallace, N., 'A Model of Private Bank Note Issue', *Review of Economic Dynamics*, 2(1) (1999a).

Cavalcanti, R. and Wallace, N., 'Inside and Outside Money as Alternative Media of Exchange', *Journal of Money, Credit, and Banking*, 31(3) (1999b) 444-457.

Chari, V. and Jagannathan, R., 'Banking Panics, Information, and Rational Expectations Equilibrium', *Journal of Finance*, 43 (1988) 749-761.

Clower, R., 'A Reconsideration of the Microfoundations of Monetary Theory', *Western Economic Journal*, 6(1) (1967) 1-9.

Corbae, D., Temzelides, T., and Wright, R., 'Directed Matching and Monetary Exchange', *Econometrica*, 71(3) (2003) 731-756.

Cuadras-Morató, X., 'Commodity Money in the Presence of Goods of Heterogeneous Quality', *Economic Theory*, 4 (1994) 579-591.

Deep, A. and Schaefer, G., 'Are Banks Liquidity Transformers?', *Harvard University, KSG Faculty Research Working Paper* RWP04-022, Cambridge, MA.

Diamond, D., 'Financial Intermediation and Delegated Monitoring', *Review of Economic Studies*, 51 (1984) 393-414.

Diamond, D. and Dybvig, P., 'Bank Runs, Deposit Insurance, and Liquidity', *Journal of Political Economy*, 91 (1983) 401-419.

Dow, S. and Smithin, J., 'The Structure of Financial Markets and the 'First Principles' of Monetary Ecnonomics', *Scottish Journal of Political Economy*, 46(1) (1999) 72-90.

Feenstra, R., 'Functional Equivalence between Liquidity Costs and the Utility of Money', *Journal of Monetary Economics*, 17(2) (1986) 271-291.

Freixas, X. and Rochet, J.-C., *Microeconomics of Banking* (Cambridge, Mass.: MIT Press, 1997).

Friedman, M., 'A Program for Monetary Stability' (New York: Fordham University Press, 1960).

Fudenberg, D. and Tirole, J., *Game Theory* (Cambridge, Mass.: MIT Press, 1991).

Gale, D., 'Money, Information, and Equilibrium in Large Economies', *Journal of Economic Theory*, 23 (1980) 28-65.

Goodfriend, M., 'Money, Credit, Banking, and Payments System Policy', *Federal Reserve Bank of Richmond Economic Review*, 77(1) (1991) 7-23.

Goodhart, C., *Money, Information, and Uncertainty*, 2nd edn. (Cambridge, Mass.: MIT Press, 1989).

Gorton, G., 'Banking Panics and Business Cycles', *Oxford Economic Papers*, 40 (1988) 751-781.

Gorton, G. and Pennacchi, G., 'Financial Intermediaries and Liquidity Creation', *Journal of Finance*, 45(1) (1990) 49-71.

Green, E. and Ping, L., 'Diamond and Dybvig's Classic Theory of Financial Intermediation: What's Missing?', *Federal Reserve Bank of Minneapolis Quarterly Review*, Winter (2000) 3-13.

Gurley, J. and Shaw, E., *Money in a Theory of Finance* (Washington, D.C.: The Brookings Institution, 1960).

Hahn, F., 'On Some Problems of Proving the Existence of Equilibrium in a Monetary Economy', in: F. Hahn and F. Brechling (ed.), *The Theory of Interest Rates*, (London: Macmillan, 1965).

Hellwig, M., 'The Challenge of Monetary Theory', *European Economic Review*, 37 (1993) 215-242.

Hellwig, M., 'Financial Intermediation with Risk Aversion', *Review of Economic Studies*, 67(4) (2000) 719-742.

Hellwig, M., 'Risk Aversion and Incentive Compatibility with Ex Post Information Asymmetry', *Economic Theory*, 18(2) (2001) 415-438.

Hicks, J., 'A Suggestion for Simplifying the Theory of Money', *Economica*, 2(5) (1935) 1-19.

Hicks, J., *A Market Theory of Money* (Oxford, U.K.: Clarendon Press, 1989).

Howitt, P., 'Beyond Search: Fiat Money in Organized Exchange', Manuscript (2000).

Huggett, M. and Krasa, S., 'Money and Storage in a Differential Information Economy', *Economic Theory*, 8 (1996) 191-210.

Jacklin, C., 'Demand Deposits, Trading Restrictions, and Risk-Sharing', in: *Contractual Arrangements for Intertemporal Trade*, E. Prescott and N. Wallace (eds.), Minnesota Studies in Macroeconomics, Vol. 1 (Minneapolis: University of Minneapolis Press, 1987).

Jacklin, C. and Bhattacharya, S., 'Distinguishing Panics and Information-Based Bank Runs: Welfare and Policy Implications', *Journal of Political Economy*, 96 (1988) 568-592.

Jevons, W., *Money and the Mechanism of Exchange*, 11th edn. (London: Kegan, Paul, Trench, Trubner, 1896).

Kashyap, A., Rajan, R., and Stein, J., 'Banks as Liquidity Providers. An Explanation for the Coexistence of Lending and Deposit-Taking', *Journal of Finance*, 57 (2002) 33-73.

Kindleberger, C., *A Financial History of Western Europe*, 2nd edn. (New York: Oxford University Press, 1993).

Kiyotaki, N. and Wright, R., 'On Money as a Medium of Exchange', *Journal of Political Economy*, 97(4) (1989) 927-954.

Kocherlakota, N., 'Money is Memory', Journal of Economic Theory, 81 (1998a) 232-251.

Kocherlakota, N., 'The Technological Role of Fiat Money', *Federal Reserve Bank of Minneapolis Quarterly Review*, 22(3) (1998b) 2-10.

Lagos, R. and Wright, R., 'A Unified Framework for Monetary Theory and Policy Analysis', *Federal Reserve Bank of Minneapolis*, Staff Report 346 2004 (2004).

Law, J., *Money and Trade Considered with a Proposal for Supplying the Nation with Money* (Edinburgh: Andrew Anderson, reprinted by Augustus M. Kelley, New York, 1966).

Leland, H. and Pyle, D., 'Informational Asymmetries, Financial Structure, and Financial Intermediation', *Journal of Finance*, 32 (1977) 371-387.

Lewis, M., 'Theory and Practice of the Banking Firm', in C. J. Green and D. T. Llewellyn (eds.), *Surveys of Monetary Economics*, Vol. 2, (Oxford, U.K.: Blackwell, 1991).

Li, Y., 'Commodity Money under Private Information', *Journal of Monetary Economics*, 36 (1995) 573-592.

Li, Y., 'The Efficiency of Monetary Exchange in Search Equilibrium', *Journal of Money, Credit, and Banking*, 29(1) (1997) 61-72.

Li, Y., 'Middlemen and Private Information', *Journal of Monetary Economics*, 42 (1998) 131-159.

Li, Y., 'A Search Model of Money and Circulating Private Debt with Applications to Monetary Policy', *International Economic Review*, 42(4) (2001) 925-946.

Menger, C., 'On the Origin of Money', *Economic Journal*, 2 (1892) 239-255.

Mill, J., 'Principles of Political Economy', Bk. III (New York: Ashley, 1929).

Millon, M. and Thakor, A., 'Moral Hazard and Information Sharing: A Model of Information Gathering Agencies', *Journal of Finance*, 40 (1985) 1403-1422.

Monroe, A., 'Monetary Theory Before Adam Smith' (Kitchener, Ont.: Batoche, 2001).

Mookherjee, D. and P'ng, I., 'Optimal Auditing, Insurance, and Redistribution', *Quarterly Journal of Economics*, 104 (1989) 399-415.

Niehans, J., *The Theory of Money* (Baltimore: John Hopkins University Press, 1978).

Osborne, M. and Rubinstein, A., *Bargaining and Markets* (San Diego: Academic Press, 1990).

Patinkin, D., *Money, Interest, and Prices* (Evanston, Illinois: Row, Peterson, and Company, 1956).

Rajan, R., 'The Past and the Future of Commercial Banking Viewed through an Incomplete Contract Lens', *Journal of Money, Credit, and Banking*, 30 (1998) 524-550.

Rocheteau, G. and Wright, R., 'Money in Search Equilibrium, in Competitive Equilibrium, and in Competitive Search Equilibrium', *Econometrica*, 73(1) (2005) 175-202.

Rogoff, K., 'The Optimal Commitment to an Intermediate Monetary Target', *Quarterly Journal of Economics*, 100(4) (1985) 1169-1189.

Schreft, S. and Smith, B., 'Money, Banking, and Capital Formation', *Journal of Economic Theory*, 73 (1997) 157-182.

Schreft, S. and Smith, B., 'The Effects of Open Market Operations in a Model of Intermediation and Growth', *Review of Economic Studies*, 65 (1998) 519-550.

Shubik, M., 'A Game Theoretic Approach to the Theory of Money and Financial Institutions', in: B. Friedman and F. Hahn (eds.), *Handbook of Monetary Economics* (Amsterdam et. al.: Elsevier Science Publishers, 1990).

Shubik, M., *The Theory of Money and Financial Institutions*, Vols. 1 and 2 (Cambridge and London: MIT Press, 1999).

Sidrauski, M., 'Rational Choice and Patterns of Growth in a Monetary Economy', *American Economic Review*, 57 (1967) 534-544.

Skaggs, N., 'Debt as the Basis of Currency: The Monetary Economics of Trust', American *Journal of Economics and Sociology*, 57(4) (2000) 453-467.

Stiglitz, J. and Greenwald, B., *Towards a New Paradigm in Monetary Economics* (Cambridge, UK: Cambridge University Press, 2003).

Stiglitz, J. and Weiss, A., 'Credit Rationing in Markets with Imperfect Information', *American Economic Review*, 71 (1981), 393-410.

Taub, B., 'Currency and Credit are Equivalent Mechanisms', *International Economic Review*, 35 (1994) 921-956.

von Thadden, E., 'Intermediated versus Direct Investment: Optimal Liquidity Provision and Dynamic Incentive Compatibility', *Journal of Financial Intermediation*, 7(2) (1998) 177-197.

von Thadden, E., 'Liquidity Creation Through Banks and Markets: Multiple Insurance and Limited Market Access', *European Economic Review*, 43(4-6) (1999) 991-1006.

Thornton, D., 'Money in a Theory of Exchange', *Federal Reserve Bank of St. Louis Economic Review*, January/February (2000) 35-60.

Townsend, R., 'Optimal Contracts and Competitive Markets with Costly State Verification', *Journal of Economic Theory*, 21(2) (1979) 265-293.

Townsend, R., 'Models of Money with Spatially Separated Agents', in: J. Kareken and N. Wallace (eds.), *Models of Monetary Economies* (Minneapolis: Federal Reserve Bank of Minneapolis, 1980).

Townsend, R., 'Currency and Credit in a Private Information Economy', *Journal of Political Economy*, 97(6) (1989) 1323-1344.

Trejos, A., 'Search, Bargaining, Money, and Prices under Private Information', *International Economic Review*, 40 (1999) 679-695.

Wallace, N., 'Whither Monetary Economics?', *International Economic Review*, 42(4) (2001) 847-869.

Walras, L., *Eléments d'Economie Politique Pure ou Théorie de la Richesse Sociale* (Paris: ed. Librairie Générale de Droit et de Jurisprudence, 1900).

Walsh, C., 'Optimal Contracts for Central Bankers', *American Economic Review*, 85(1) (1995) 150-167.

Wang, Y., 'Asymmetric Information and Demand for Money in an Overlapping Generations Economy', *Southern Economic Journal*, 66(2) (1999) 403-413.

White, L. (ed.), *Free Banking* (Aldershot: Edward Elgar, 1993).

White, L., *The Theory of Monetary Institutions* (Malden, Mass.: Blackwell, 1999).

Wicksell, K., 'Interest and Prices', English translation by R. Kahn for the Royal Economic Society (London: Macmillan, 1936).

Williamson, S., 'Laissez-Faire Banking and Circulating Media of Exchange', *Journal of Financial Intermediation*, 2(2) (1992) 134-167.

Williamson, S., 'Payments Systems with Random Matching and Private Information', *Journal of Money, Credit, and Banking*, 30(3) (1998) 551-569.

Williamson, S., 'Private Money', *Journal of Money, Credit, and Banking*, 31(3) (1999) 469-491.

Williamson, S. and Wright, R., 'Barter and Monetary Exchange under Private Information', *American Economic Review*, 84 (1994) 104-123.

Winkler, M., 'Intermediation under Trade Restrictions', *Quarterly Journal of Economics*, 104(2) (1989) 299-324.

Index